Strategy

STRATEGY

The Logic of War and Peace

Edward N. Luttwak

The Belknap Press of
Harvard University Press
*Cambridge, Massachusetts, and
London, England*

1987

Library of Congress Cataloging-in-Publication Data

Luttwak, Edward.
  Strategy : the logic of war and peace.

  Bibliography: p.
  Includes index.
  1. Strategy. I. Title.
U162.L874 1987   355'.02   86-26975
ISBN 0-674-83995-1 (alk. paper)

To my son, Joseph Emmanuel

Acknowledgments

I am grateful to Max King Morris and the Arthur Vining Davis Foundations for the grant given to the Center for Strategic and International Studies, Washington D.C., of which I was the beneficiary. I also received much help from individual members of the Center: its chairman, Amos A. Jordan, who assumed significant burdens to keep me working; Christa D. K. Dantzler, who suggested an original remedy when inspiration briefly fled; Walter Z. Laqueur, who offered his steady wisdom and encyclopedic knowledge in a continuing dialogue that has spanned the years; and David M. Abshire, at this time in public service but formerly the Center's chairman, who long encouraged this enterprise by words and deeds. A. Lawrence Chickering of the Institute for Contemporary Studies again subtracted time from his own writing to help mine. W. Seth Carus and Stephen P. Glick, once my students and now experts of caliber, gave me varied scholarly assistance from start to finish. As usual they were the first readers, and not the least critical, of my writing. When a dramatic impediment to any writing at all suddenly emerged, my sturdy friend Robert A. Mosbacher Jr. of Houston, Texas, acted immediately to alleviate a situation that official bodies should have confronted. Michael A. Aronson of Harvard University Press nurtured the book from the beginning, long before he joined Harvard. Over the best part of a decade of false starts, during which I completed other, less demanding books easily enough, he was the determined reader of several abandoned drafts, always insisting that a solution could be found. Not least of his contributions was to help persuade Joyce Backman of the Press to edit the text. Having known little editing before, I was unprepared for the peculiar difficulties that this book would present, and for the difference that an editor of the highest quality can make.

Contents

Preface

Perhaps it is because I was born in the disputed borderland of Transylvania, during the greatest and most sinister of wars, that strategy has always been my only occupation, and also my passion. That is a strong word for a subject both poorly defined and also suspect as an encouragement to strife. But to define strategy is the very purpose of this book, and any excuses become unnecessary once we realize that strategy pervades the upkeep of peace as much as the making of war.

No strategies are suggested here for the conduct of the United States on the world scene, or for the employment of its armed forces in war. My purpose, rather, is to uncover the universal logic that conditions all forms of war as well as the adversarial dealings of nations in peacetime. Whatever humans can do, however absurd or self-destructive, magnificent or sordid, has been done in both war and statecraft, and no logic at all can be detected in the deeds themselves. But the logic of strategy is manifest in the outcome of what is done or not done, and it is by examining those often unintended consequences that the nature and workings of the logic can be understood.

By now the critical reader will have had reason to pause before the inordinate ambition of this quest. Knowing that the events of war and peace are too irregular to be explained by science in its only proper meaning, namely by theories that can actually predict, one might suspect that only platitudes lie ahead or, worse, the pointless elaborations of pseudo-science. I can only plead that the verdict be deferred till the reading is done—but a word of explanation may be in order.

What became a long journey to a compelling destination began with no such ambitious purpose. In reading the literature of military history ancient and modern, in the professional study of contemporary military questions, and in sundry visits to the scenes of war, inevitably observed only through the dazzling refractions of false certainties, I like others before me could only conclude that each experience of conflict is unique, the product of an unrepeatable convergence of political aspirations, emotions, technical limits, tactical moves, operational schemes, and geographical settings. And yet, over the years, tantalizing continuities began to emerge, forming patterns more and more definite, some destined to be clarified by the literature of strategy-as-study, especially the *On War* of Clausewitz; and others not. What made the investigation compelling was that these patterns did not conform to commonsense expectations: they were not ordered by any familiar, straightforwardly causal logic.

As a vision of strategy emerged out of the shadows of words read, problems investigated, and events experienced, I found that its content was not the prosaic stuff of platitudes, but instead paradox, irony, and contradiction. Moreover, the logic of strategy seemed to unfold in two dimensions: the "horizontal" contentions of adversaries who seek to oppose, deflect, and reverse each other's actions, in peace as in war—and that is what makes strategy paradoxical; and the "vertical" interplay of the different levels of conflict, technical, tactical, operational, and higher—among which there is no natural harmony.

What follows, then, is the route map of an exploration. The quest begins in a series of encounters with the dynamic forces of the horizontal dimension; it continues as an ascent, level by level, through the vertical dimension of strategy; and it ends when the confluence of both dimensions is reached, at the level of grand strategy, the level of final results.

I

THE LOGIC
OF STRATEGY

Introduction

Si vis pacem, para bellum (If you want peace, prepare war) goes the Latin tag attributed to Roman wisdom, still much used today by speakers preaching the virtues of strong armament. Thus we are told that a prepared ability to fight dissuades attack that weakness could invite, thereby averting war. It is just as true that a prepared ability to fight can ensure peace in quite another way, by making war unnecessary as the weak are induced to give way to the strong without a fight; but that corollary would not be advertised nowadays, as it might have been before 1914.* Worn down by overuse into a cliché, the Roman admonition has lost the power to arouse our thoughts, but it is precisely its banality that is significant: the phrase is of course paradoxical in presenting blatant contradiction as if it were a straightforwardly logical proposition—and that is scarcely what we would expect of a mere banality.

Why is the contradictory argument accepted so unresistingly, indeed dismissed as obvious? To be sure, there are some who dis-

---

*"The war to end war" did not end it, but long before 1918 it started to impose new manners in public speech, at least within the Western democracies, whereby military power could no longer be celebrated except for purposes that may plausibly be presented as defensive. As usual, hypocrisy has served as the vanguard of operative belief, and the delegitimization of offensive war (war intended to change an unthreatened status quo) is now also extending to deliberate defensive war (war meant to prevent an anticipated negative change in the status quo). This more or less leaves only immediate self-defense as an acceptable motive for war. There is residual flexibility in defining the immediacy of the putative threat (the theme of rival interpretations of article 2 of the Charter of the United Nations), and the "self" of self-defense certainly extends to allies in collective-security groupings, but the practical consequence of this broad change in mentality has been to reduce the applicability of war as an instrument of statecraft for Western governments. The resulting imbalance vis-à-vis others less encumbered is obvious. For a brief discussion see Robert E. Osgood and Robert W. Tucker, *Force, Order and Justice* (1967).

agree, and the entire new academic venture of "peace studies" is dedicated to the proposition that peace should be studied as a phenomenon in itself and actively worked for in real life: *si vis pacem, para pacem,* its advocates might say. But even those who explicitly reject the paradoxical admonition do not denounce it as a self-evidently foolish contradiction that any breath of commonsense should sweep away. On the contrary, they see it as a piece of wrongheaded conventional wisdom, to which they oppose ideas that they themselves would describe as novel and unconventional.

And so the question remains: why is the blatant contradiction so easily accepted? Consider the absurdity of equivalent advice in any sphere of life but the strategic: if you want *A* strive for *B,* its opposite, as in "if you want to lose weight, eat more; if you want to become rich, earn less"—surely we would reject all such. It is only in the realm of strategy, which encompasses *the conduct and consequences of human relations in the context of actual or possible armed conflict,** that we have learned to accept paradoxical propositions as valid.

Of this the most obvious example is the entire notion of nuclear "deterrence," by now so thoroughly assimilated that to many it seems prosaic. To defend, we must stand ready to attack at all times. To derive their benefit, we must never use the nuclear weapons that we continue to build so assiduously. To be ready to attack is evidence of peaceful intent, but to prepare defenses is aggressive, or at least "provocative"—such are the conventional views on the subject. Controversy on the safety of nuclear deterrence is periodically rekindled, and there is certainly much debate on every detailed aspect of nuclear-weapons policy. But the obvious paradoxes that form the very substance of nuclear deterrence are deemed unremarkable.[1]

The large claim I advance here is that strategy does not merely entail this or that paradoxical proposition, contradictory and yet recognized as valid, but rather that *the entire realm of strategy is pervaded by a paradoxical logic of its own,* standing against the ordinary linear logic by which we live in all other spheres of life (except for warlike games, of course). In settings where conflict is

---

*Lacking careful definition, *strategy* has many. The word is used variously for strategy as the *doctrine* of this or that state or military institution, for strategy as actual *practice,* and for strategy as *theory, science,* and *analysis.* See Appendix 1 for more on definitions.

merely incidental to purposes of production and consumption, of commerce and culture, of social relations and consensual governance, with strife and competition more or less bound by law and custom, a noncontradictory linear logic applies, whose essence is captured by what we think of as commonsense.*

Within the sphere of strategy, on the other hand, where human relations are conditioned by armed conflict actual or possible, another and quite different logic is at work. It often violates ordinary linear logic *by inducing the coming together and even the reversal of opposites,* and it therefore, incidentally, tends to reward paradoxical conduct while confounding straightforwardly logical action, by yielding results ironical if not lethally self-damaging.

---

*The politics of repressive systems are another matter entirely; even if quite bloodless, they are still warlike. Because the major objectives of such systems are the upkeep and challenge of the apparatus of forcible control, by the ruling group and by dissidents among the unwillingly ruled respectively, all manifestations of political life (except for those purely ceremonial) take the form of military operations, with their own versions of attack and defense, of the ambush and raid. As in war, secrecy and deception are important, for rulers and dissidents alike, because they both shield the system and also form the basis of circumventing maneuver: the rulers' policemen seek to penetrate dissident circles by infiltration, and the dissidents try to protect the covertness that is their main strength. In the case of the Soviet Union, it is clear that the warlike innerparty politics through which the Kremlin leaders reach their preeminence is the training ground for their conduct of external relations. See my *Grand Strategy of the Soviet Union* (1984), chap. 1.

CHAPTER 1

THE CONSCIOUS USE OF
PARADOX IN WAR

Consider an ordinary tactical choice, of the sort frequently made in war. An advancing force can move toward its objective on one of two roads, one good and one bad, the first broad, direct, and well-paved, the second narrow, circuitous, and unpaved. Only in the conflictual realm of strategy would the choice arise at all, for it is only if combat is possible that a bad road can be good *precisely because it is bad* and may therefore be less strongly held or even left unguarded by the enemy. Equally, the good road is apt to be bad because it is the better road, whose use by the advancing force is more likely to be anticipated and opposed.

In this case, then, the paradoxical logic of strategy reaches the extreme of a full reversal: instead of A moving toward its opposite B, as war preparation is supposed to preserve the peace, A actually becomes B, and B becomes A. Nor is the example contrived. On the contrary, a paradoxical preference for inconvenient times and directions, preparations visibly and deliberately left incomplete, approaches seemingly too dangerous, for combat at night and in bad weather, is a common aspect of tactical ingenuity—and for a reason that derives from the essential nature of war. Although each separate element in the conduct of warfare can be very simple, a matter of moving from one place to another perhaps only yards away, of using weapons whose workings should have been drilled a thousand times, of issuing and understanding orders often of stark simplicity, the *totality* of these simple things can become enormously difficult when there is a live enemy opposite, who reacts to undo everything being attempted, with his own moves and his own strength.

First there are the merely mechanical complications that arise when action is confounded by the enemy's own action, as in the naval battles of the age of sail where each side tried to present broadside guns to impotent prow or hull; as in the air combat of front-firing fighters even today, when each pilot seeks to turn so as to reach behind the other; and as in land combat perpetually, whenever there are strong fronts, weak flanks, and weaker rears. But of far greater consequence is the elemental difficulty created by the enemy's use of his own force, his own deadly weapons. In the imminence of possible death, the easiest action that entails increased exposure will remain undone unless all sorts of complex intangibles (morale, cohesion, and leadership among them) can overcome the instinct of survival. And once the centrality of these intangible mysteries is duly recognized in what happens and fails to happen, no simplicity remains even in the most elementary of tactical actions conducted against a living, reacting enemy.

To have the advantage of an enemy who cannot react because he is surprised and unready, or at least who cannot react promptly and in full force, all sorts of paradoxical choices may be justified. Violating commonsense notions of what is best, as the shorter route is preferable to the longer, as daylight is preferable to the confusions of night, as full and ample preparation is preferable to hurried improvisation, the worst option may deliberately be chosen in the hope that the unfolding action will for that very reason be unexpected by the enemy, find him unready, and therefore diminish his ability to react. Surprise can now be recognized for what it is: not merely one factor of advantage in warfare among many others, *but rather the suspension, if only brief, if only partial, of the entire predicament of strategy,* even as the struggle continues. Without a reacting enemy, or rather according to the extent and degree that surprise is achieved, the conduct of war becomes mere administration.*

Although a widely influential thesis for the conduct of war has been erected on this one proposition,[1] advising paradoxical choices whenever possible in order to shape military action according to the "line of least expectation," the advice is routinely ignored, and with good reason.

---

*Although my purpose in this book is to describe the phenomena of strategy and is in no way prescriptive, it would obscure the very nature of the subject to leave the impression that warfare, which plays such a large part in it, is shaped by the interplay of clever schemes, as opposed to the moral factors that condition each side's ability to overcome the endless difficulties, unpredictable risks, and human suffering of war.

THE COSTS OF SURPRISE

By definition, each paradoxical choice made for the sake of surprise must have its costs, manifest in some loss of the strength that would otherwise be available. In war, the longer route or harsher course will tire men, wear out vehicles, and consume more supplies, and if the approach to combat is at all difficult or simply long, it will increase the proportion of stragglers who will not reach the fight in time to take part. Forces cannot be arrayed and moved so well, nor weapons aimed with like precision, at night as they can in clear daylight, and some, much, or even most of the strength in hand may therefore be ineffective or simply passive during the fight. Similarly, to act more rapidly than an enemy might expect, on the basis of his own calculations of how long preparations should take, usually requires improvisations correspondingly drastic, which will prevent the full use of the men and machines otherwise available for combat. More generally, all forms of maneuver—paradoxical action that seeks to circumvent the greatest strength of the enemy in some way—will have their costs, regardless of the medium and nature of combat.*

As for secrecy and deception, the two classic agencies of surprise that often set the stage for maneuver, they too exact some cost of their own. Secrecy is often recommended to those who practice war as if it were costless, but an enemy can rarely be denied all knowledge of an impeding action without some sacrifice of value-able preparations. Stringent security precautions will usually interfere with the early alert and thorough organization of those who will take some role in the fight; they will constrain the scope and realism of the exercises that can greatly improve performance in many forms of combat, and which are especially necessary if the action to come is inherently complicated, as in amphibious landings and commando operations. And of course every limit on the assembly and preliminary approach of the combat forces will leave them less well arrayed and less well positioned than they might have been.

With secrecy rarely absolute, the leakage of the truth can only be

---

*The word *maneuver* sometimes occurs as military jargon for mere movement. In common usage, movement need not be involved but the action must be paradoxical because commonsense (minimum-effort) action cannot be expected to circumvent: the enemy will presumably have arrayed his strengths precisely to oppose any obvious action. Surprise, by contrast, is not a precondition: it can make maneuver possible, but so can a speed advantage in execution.

countered by deception, so that the "signals" generated by such preparations as are allowed will be submerged by contrived "noise."[2] Deception can sometimes be achieved without any loss of strength by well-planted lies alone. But more often it will require diversionary action that misdirects the observant enemy precisely because it does not contribute fully to the intended purpose. Bombers sent to attack a secondary target, while simulating the massed formation headed to quite another place, will still inflict damage, if only at a less critical point; but ships sent out as a feint, whose only duty is to turn back as soon as the enemy has set course in their direction, may not otherwise contribute to the fight.

All these forms of deliberate self-weakening brought about by paradoxical choices can be justified by the sole benefit of surprise, if they weaken the enemy's reaction to an even greater extent. At the limit, surprise could in theory best be achieved by acting in a manner so completely paradoxical as to be utterly self-defeating: if, for example, almost the entire army is employed to mislead, leaving only a handful of men for the real fight, surprise should certainly be achieved, but the venture will most likely be defeated quite handily, even by an enemy completely deceived and quite unready. Obviously the paradoxical course of "least expectation" must stop short of self-defeating extremes, but beyond that the decision is a matter of calculations neither safe nor precise. Although the loss of strength potentially available is certain, success in achieving surprise can only be hoped for; and although the cost can usually be tightly calculated, the benefit must remain a matter of speculation until the deed is done.

FRICTION

In addition to the costs of surprise obtained by paradoxical departures from the enemy's line of commonsense expectation, there are also risks. To be sure, the entire purpose of achieving surprise is to diminish the deadly risk of exposure to the enemy's strength, *combat risk,* that is. But there is another kind of risk, perhaps not deadly in itself to the specific unit in question at that very time but possibly more dangerous to the larger force.

That second kind of risk, which tends to increase with any deviation from the simplicities of direct approach and frontal attack, is the *organizational risk* of failure in the implementation of what is intended: failure caused not by the enemy's malevolence but rather by breakdowns, errors, and delays in the supply, operation, planning, and command of military forces. When the attempt is made to reduce anticipated combat risks by any form of paradoxical action, notably secrecy, deception, and maneuver, the action will tend to become more complicated and more extended, thereby increasing the organizational risks in proportion.

The organizational aspect of warfare is the very one that looms largest to those charged with its conduct, in between intervals of combat that might be quite brief. Again, every single thing that must be done to supply, maintain, operate, and command the armed forces may be very simple once all the intangible mysteries that make combat possible are excluded. Yet together they are so complicated that the natural state of military forces of any size is chaos and immobility, from which only discipline and leadership can rescue any purposeful action.

Imagine a group of friends setting out for a trip to the beach, in several automobiles, carrying as many families. They were to meet at the best-placed house at 9:00 a.m. and immediately drive out to take advantage of the light traffic of the hour, so as to reach their destination by 11:00 a.m. One of the families was already in its car, all set to drive out to the rendezvous, when a child announced urgent need; the locked frontdoor was unlocked, the child left and came back, the car was restarted and the rendezvous reached with only brief delay by 9:15. A second family, which had a longer drive to the rendezvous, was somewhat more seriously delayed: an essential tackle box had been forgotten. Its absence was discovered almost within sight of the rendezvous, and by the time the long drive back was done, the tackle box found, and the meeting finally joined, it was nearer 10:00 than 9:00.

A third family caused even greater delay: its car simply would not start. After familiar remedies were tried as time passed, and after a longer wait for a towtruck whose stronger batteries could not help either, a neighbor graciously supplied his own car. Unloading and reloading were rapid, the driving impatiently fast, but by the time the third family arrived at the rendezvous it was well after 10:00. Still the journey could not start. Some children had been waiting for more than an hour, and now it was their turn to ask for a brief delay. By the time the driving actually began, the road to the beach was no longer uncrowded, and instead of the planned two hours the travel lasted for over three—including stops for one car's need for gasoline, another family's need for cold drinks, and the children's loud demand for lunch. In the end the beach was reached, but by then the planned arrival time of 11:00 had long passed.

At no point was our imaginary group impeded by the active will of an enemy; everything that happened was the consequence of unintended delays and petty accident, akin to the *friction* that impedes the workings of all moving machinery. (The term is of course from Clausewitz's *On War,* whose tonalities in the above will have been recognized by now: "Everything in war is very simple, but the simplest thing is difficult. The difficulties accumulate and end by producing a kind of friction that is inconceivable unless one has experienced war."[3]) Friction is the basic medium in which strategic action unfolds, and war's most constant companion.

In my mundane example, the initial delay at the journey's start was more than one hour, and the cumulative delay much longer. It is easy to imagine how the delay might grow with more families included. Eventually, if enough of them are added, the point can be reached where the journey could not start at all, so long as all must wait for the very last arrival. How many families must be included in the outing to prolong immobility till the day is done, one cannot say—but a few dozen should do the trick, and even that unwieldy assembly would not begin to compete in size with the several hundred men of a single army battalion, a modest warship crew, or the manpower of an air squadron or two.

A military force includes no children to delay it, and can repress lesser whims by discipline, but in all else it is likely to be far worse off than our ill-fated family group aiming for the beach. For one thing, its supply will have quite other dimensions, and any needs insufficiently anticipated cannot usually be made good by brief roadside pauses; a fleet at sea may be thoroughly supplied, but whatever is missing will have to wait the next replenishment; and for any air or ground unit away from well-stocked bases, the country around them might as well be a desert, now that food and hay no longer suffice to sustain war.

There was a mechanical breakdown in my example, but there will be many more in military forces whose weapons and vehicles, radars and radios, and all other things electronic and mechanical will only rarely be as reliable as most automobiles now are. Battle tanks, so well protected against the enemy's fire, are nevertheless surprisingly delicate in their inner machinery, and each one of the many electronic devices contained in a single combat aircraft is just as likely to malfunction as the ignition device of a family car.

No operating errors intervened to delay the beach party, in which all drivers performed without flaw. But in spite of the best of training, severe tests, and frequent exercises, no military force can hope for such perfection from all who must operate its varied equipment. Much unconscious skill is actually required to drive a car in traffic, but far more is needed to work a great many of the machines of war, and instead of the many years of daily practice that even youngish cardrivers can have, a good many military operators will only have months of infrequent experience, because they or their equipment are new on the job.

In my example, the plan was very simple with its one starting point, single route, and fixed destination, but it was badly flawed in failing to anticipate that a 9:00 a.m. starting time would not allow enough leeway to avoid the rush hour on the highway to the beach. Military plans soundly crafted will strive for such simplicity but rarely attain it, because the several elements of any given force must be coordinated to carry out several different actions. Although competent planners will attempt to allow for all the other sources of friction to the best of their ability, their own errors will add one more.

Finally there is the command of the action, or more fully the ongoing intelligence assessment, decision making, intercommunication, and supervision ("control") of command as a whole. In my example there was a plan of action but no command, intelligence, intercommunication, or supervision; had there been, the rest of the group might have rapidly discovered the third family's plight and stepped in to provide a replacement car more promptly. Military command structures and their intelligence and communications adjuncts are in place not only to exploit the fleeting opportunities of combat and contend with its sudden dangers, but also and just as much to overcome friction. In the process, however, one more venue is offered to the workings of friction: wrong, outdated, or misleading intelligence can induce errors of decision; communications networks may be highly advanced, reliable, and secure in every way, but messages may still be garbled or sent astray or not sent at all; and errors of supervision will be assured by the delicacy of the balance between the need to keep separate elements duly coordinated and the need to allow some freedom of initiative to each one.

Once all these sources of friction are taken into account in their totality, wherein the effect of some is multiplied and not merely added, the full significance of organizational risk becomes clear. Just as our imaginary group of families could easily miss a day at the beach altogether if its size grows to give sufficient scope for friction, any military action can fail internally even without encountering the enemy's deliberate counteraction,* simply as a result of the accumulation of breakdowns, errors, and delays, each insignificant in itself. It is in this context that any striving to obtain surprise must be seen: each paradoxical choice introduced for the sake of surprise, with its own deviation from the easiest and simplest course of action, will further increase friction and therefore the risk of organizational failure.

When combat risk materializes, it does so in the bloody shape of injury and death. When organizational risk materializes, the action fails in a manner that might be bloodless. It might then seem that organizational risk can be balanced against combat risk, in deciding how much complication is accepted for the sake of surprise. But this is only true of the single act of war, as in the case of a commando action carried out in peacetime. Otherwise, one risk compounds the other. Of course the warship that misses the battle by being misdirected through command friction, the tank battalion that runs out of fuel on its way to the front because of supply friction, the fighter aircraft that cannot intercept because maintenance friction prevents its takeoff, will all remain quite safe at the time. The direct approach and frontal attack are therefore easily condemned by advocates of paradoxical circumvention who focus on the single engagement, seeing very clearly the resulting lessening of combat risk while being only dimly aware of the resulting increase in organizational risk.

But once we examine not the single engagement but the wider

---

*A talented enemy, however, will try to direct his blows in the manner best calculated to compound inherent frictions, striking at supply lines if the force is already afflicted by shortages; against communications, if these are already unreliable; and so on. These are instances of the most ambitious kind of military operation: *relational maneuver*, the application of strength against specifically identified enemy weaknesses—a form of warfare, discussed later, which is itself highly vulnerable to friction.

conflict, it becomes clear that organizational risk is quite likely to compound combat risk. On the same occasion, the fleet in battle was weakened by the absence of the misdirected ship, and its other warships were more exposed to combat risk; likewise for the fellow battalions of the one that was stopped for lack of fuel, and the other fighters of the squadron. On the next occasion, those who missed the earlier fight will probably have to fight alongside forces weaker than they might have been, because of the added losses caused by their absence in the previous round—and this will increase their own combat risk as well.

THE PREVALENCE OF PARADOXICAL ACTION

Although the benefits of paradoxical schemes are thus offset not only by the combat potential lost but also by their added organizational risk, straightforward actions, entirely shaped by linear logic to make the fullest use of all available means by the most direct methods, are rarely encountered in the record of war—and still more rarely do they escape censure. At least some paradoxical elements will be present in the preparation and conduct of most competent military actions.

To be sure, military leaders whose forces are altogether superior to those of the enemy of the day may be quite justified in spurning surprise, for the sake of amply prepared action in full strength, conducted by the simplest methods at minimal organizational risk. This was the case, for example, during the first stages of colonial warfare in place after place, before the native warriors learned to disperse when faced by drilled troops with rapid-fire weapons; and it was the case again during the last months of World War II, when American, British, and Soviet armies of overwhelming firepower favored fully prepared offensives and frontal attacks against a German army in decline, just as the respective airforces abandoned all artifice in the massed daylight raids of the final months of bombing against Germany and Japan. That was still warfare, if unusual, *but the logic of strategy was no longer important within it,* because the enemy's reaction—indeed his very existence as a conscious, living entity—could simply be disregarded. If the enemy is so weak that his forces are best treated as a passive array of targets that might as well be inanimate, the normal linear logic of industrial production, with all its derived criteria of productive efficiency, is fully valid, and the paradoxical logic of strategy is irrelevant. (Clausewitz:

"The essential difference is that war is not an exercise of the will directed at inanimate matter, as is the case with the mechanical arts . . . In war, the will is directed at an animate object that reacts. It must be obvious that the intellectual codification used in the arts and sciences is inappropriate to such an activity."[4])

Although strategy comprehends both conflict and its avoidance, and of course the conduct of warfare at all levels from tactics to grand strategy, it can tell us nothing about the purely *administrative* aspects of any of these, wherein the doings and undoings of other conscious, reacting wills have no role. Just as there is nothing to be gained by deliberately choosing boots three sizes too small or willfully misusing weapons, because neither boots nor weapons will respond advantageously to such paradoxical action, so also there is no call to circumvent and surprise an enemy judged so very weak that his entire reaction can be safely ignored. Such fortunate conditions, however, are rare. Only an enemy grossly ill-informed, or driven by transcendental purposes, will deliberately choose to fight a vastly superior force, and if the case is that of the single force that finds itself overwhelmed, then combat is normally avoided, by retreat or surrender.

Somewhat more common, on the other hand, is the phenomenon of armed forces that act according to mistaken expectations of their own vast inherent superiority, and therefore rely overmuch on linear logic to optimize the administration of their own means, without a sufficient effort to surprise the enemy by suitably paradoxical conduct. Actually the prevalence of the paradoxical in the conduct of war should reflect the perceived balance of strength, and it often does. In a manner itself paradoxical, it is those who are materially weaker, and therefore have good reason to fear a straightforward clash of strength against strength in facing an unsurprised enemy, who can most benefit by self-weakening paradoxical conduct—if it obtains the advantage of surprise, which may yet offer victory.

If the unfavorable balance is not merely an accident of time and place in the setting of one engagement, but reflects instead the permanent circumstances of one state among other states, then the pursuit of the "line of least expectation" by paradoxical action may become characteristic of a national style of warfare. Of this Israel is said to provide the best contemporary example, although the clash of strength against strength has been avoided in its case as much to limit casualties as to offset actual inferiorities in numbers and means. In war after war, in many isolated acts of combat in between, the Israeli armed forces have chosen to accept both self-weakening and the added organizational risks of maneuver for the sake of surprise. Israeli forces much weaker materially than they need have been (because of secrecy, deception, improvisation, and overextension), and operating with so much self-imposed friction that their condition bordered on the chaotic, have regularly defeated enemies caught by surprise, whose strength was not fully present at the site or whose forces were materially or morally unready for combat.

The Israelis' steady preference for counterconventional, paradoxical action could not endure without eventually undoing its purpose. Over time, their antagonists began to revise their expectations. They learned from experience to mistrust estimates of Israeli moves that were based on commonsense calculations of the "best" course of action open to them. Finally, in the Lebanon war of June 1982, the Syrians were not at all surprised by the Israeli attempt to advance into their rear along the worst of mountain roads,[5] and they acted in good time to block the very narrow passage. It was the next Israeli move that the Syrians completely failed to predict, and then watched with disbelief, scarcely reacting as the hours passed: a perfectly straightforward frontal offensive by massed armored divisions into the Vale of Lebanon.[6] With the balance of forces greatly favorable to them for once, and with no time to lose because of the imminence of a cease-fire, the Israelis chose to sacrifice any hope of surprise by attacking frontally and in broad daylight—only to be pleasantly surprised by Syrian unpreparedness. Obviously by 1982, with their paradoxical style of war so fully exposed in previous encounters, for the Israelis the line of least expectation could only be the most direct frontal approach.

CHAPTER 2

THE LOGIC IN ACTION

That surprise cannot repeatedly be achieved by unvaried devices is obvious. But it is also an example, by no means very important in itself, of the workings of the paradoxical logic of strategy in its full dynamic form. So far that logic has mostly been considered from the viewpoint of only one participant, and in cases wherein the logic of strategy was in some degree understood and consciously exploited. Moreover, I have mostly mentioned single situations and single decisions, and therefore the logic of strategy has been viewed in a series of separate static glimpses. But there are of course at least two conscious, opposed wills in any strategical encounter of war or peace, and an action is only rarely accomplished instantaneously, as in a pistol duel; usually actions on both sides evolve reciprocally over time.

Once we focus instead on the paradoxical logic of strategy as an objective phenomenon, which conditions outcomes whether or not the participants try to exploit it or are even aware of its workings; and once time is duly introduced as a dynamic element, we can recognize the logic in its totality as the *coming together, even the reversal, of opposites.* And this is a process manifest not merely in the fate of counterconventional choices intended to achieve surprise, which eventually become quite predictable, *but rather in all that is strategical,* in all that is characterized by the struggle of adversary wills. In other words, if the passage of time is relevant and the paradoxical logic of strategy assumes a dynamic form, it *becomes* the coming together, even the reversal, of opposites. In the realm of strategy, therefore, a course of action cannot persist indefinitely. It will tend to evolve into its opposite, unless the logic of strategy is outweighed by some *exogenous change* in the circumstances of the participants. Unless such change occurs, the logic will induce a self-negating evolution, which may reach the extreme of a full reversal, undoing both war and peace, victory and defeat, and all they include.

Consider what happens to an army advancing victoriously in a typical setting of continental warfare. One battle or many have been fought, and one army prevails over the other, forcing it to retreat. Perhaps the defeated are scattering in panic or are about to be cornered and destroyed; the war may therefore be coming to an end by negotiation or capitulation—in which case there is still scope for a reversal of opposites, as we shall see, but not within the span of this one war. If, however, the defeated army still fights on, even in retreat, a pattern of reversal will begin to appear.

The victorious army is advancing away from its homeland and forward bases, whose training camps, industry, storage depots, and workshops sustained its recent success—and must now obtain what it needs by routes of reinforcement and supply that are becoming progressively longer. The defeated army by contrast is presumably falling back toward its bases, so that its own routes of reinforcement and supply are becoming shorter. The victorious army must make an increasing effort to sustain itself and may have to take men and equipment away from frontline combat to expand its supply units, or at least divert reinforcements for the purpose. The defeated army by contrast can now reduce its own transport effort and may skim combat-worthy manpower and equipment from supply units to strengthen the frontline forces.

The victorious army is entering territory until then in its enemy's keeping, which may contain an unfriendly population with armed partisans, perhaps, or regular troops deliberately left behind to fight as guerrillas. At best, the military government of the newly occupied population will demand some manpower and resources, perhaps offset by what can be requisitioned locally, but perhaps not. If there is armed resistance, with raids and sabotage against rail lines, road convoys, supply dumps, service units, and rear headquarters, the victorious army will have to take away combat units from frontline duties to provide guards, security patrols, and quick-reaction forces in rear areas judged unsafe. Or, if the victorious army is liberating friendly civilians who will offer no resistance or shelter to stay-behind parties, there is still a relative disadvantage in the advance: it is the defeated army that will have been the occupier, and it can now return guards, patrol units, and reaction forces to frontline duty.

The victorious army has momentum and the initiative in setting the pace and directions of advance, so that it may outrun and cut off the retreat of the defeated if its columns can move faster. But otherwise the army in retreat, unless harried without cease, can have the powerful advantage of the tactical defensive in each encounter. Its rear-guard units can choose favorable terrain for each fighting pause, so as to fire on the moving, exposed enemy from behind cover and even ambush unlucky enemy forces advancing too eagerly.

The effects of victory and defeat upon morale and leadership are considerably more uncertain. Combat morale defines not happiness but the will to fight in deadly peril, and victory may increase the former but diminish the latter: having just fought and won, the troops may both be very happy and also feel they have done enough for a while (Clausewitz described this phenomenon as the "relaxation of effort"). Conversely, defeat is often demoralizing, inducing passivity or even an active disloyalty, but it can also sting men to fight harder in the next battle, especially if they feel that their effort could have been greater in the previous encounter. Leadership too can be greatly enhanced by victory, and just as easily undone. With success already achieved once or several times, the impulse to exhort and drive men into the dangers of combat may be spent. In the defeated army in retreat, by contrast, leaders may have lost all authority; but if that is not so, the bitter memory of recent failure may drive them to demand more from their men and endow them with an intense energy to do so.

As far as the skills and procedures of war are concerned, there is no such even balance of possibilities. With victory, all of the army's habits, procedures, structural arrangements, tactics, and methods will indiscriminately be confirmed as valid or even brilliant—including those that could have stood some improvement or indeed were positively harmful, but with all their harm concealed by the undissected experience of success. Notoriously, defeat is by far the better teacher. Critical faculties are certainly more likely to be sharpened by failure; and if remedies are offered to improve performance, they are less likely to be resisted by inert conservatism because hierarchical defenders of the status quo will have been undermined by defeat. If industry and population are still being mobilized, and the victorious army is receiving powerful reinforcements, its rising strength is ensured even as it continues to advance—in other words, exogenous change can nullify the effects of the logic. But if that is not so, and the twin processes stand revealed, it will then be recognized that its very victory and successful advance will tend to weaken the victorious army, just as failure and retreat will tend to strengthen the recently defeated.

CULMINATION AND REVERSAL

In a dynamic context, the coming together of victory and defeat may extend beyond confluence, to the extreme of full reversal. In my example, if the victorious army can achieve total conquest or impose surrender in short order, its subtle weakening will have no substantive effect, no more than the tendencies that begin to strengthen the defeated. But otherwise, if the depth of territory and their own tenacity suffice to extend the conflict, the defeated will be able to benefit from the dynamic paradox, perhaps to the extent of becoming victorious in turn if the army till then successful simply persists in its advance, ruining itself by continuation after overshooting its "culminating point of victory" (again, Clausewitz's term). This does not mean of course that victory must inevitably lead to defeat if the war continues. But unless it benefits from an overpowering enhancement derived from its ultimate sources of military strength (from factors exogenous to the logic), the victorious army will have to pause and recuperate from its own successful advance if it is to overcome the unfavorable tendencies at work. By restoring its energies of morale and leadership through rest and replacements; by bringing forward its entire supply organization; by providing for the security of rear areas if threatened; and by revising those procedures, tactics, and methods that the enemy is learning to anticipate and undo, the victorious army can restore its capacity for further success, in effect pushing outward and into the future the culminating point of success.

The continental warfare of World War II manifested every variant of the coming together or reversal of victory and defeat, in a manner particularly dramatic because armor and airpower brought back deep maneuver on a Napoleonic scale, breaking the defensive primacy of the static trenchlines of 1914–1918. The German invasion of the Netherlands, Belgium, and France, which began on May 10, 1940, and ended on June 17 with the French request for an armistice, was achieved (if only just) within the span of a single culminating effort.[1] By then, the ten German Panzer divisions spearheading the advance had suffered so many breakdowns among tanks, half-tracked carriers, and trucks that their strength had to be sustained by captured equipment and the impressment of civilian vehicles. In the infantry divisions that formed the bulk of the advancing German armies, the troops had been marching on foot from the start, and most were exhausted. As for the German supply organization, which had to rely on the circulation of horsedrawn carts from rearward supply points to the combat units, it was so overextended that only the abundance of food and fodder in the prosperous lands just conquered prevented crippling shortages in the conquering army. Ammunition resupply was not a serious problem in a campaign of rapid maneuver and brief offensive thrusts, in which most combat encounters were little more than skirmishes. But the dashing Panzer divisions were only kept running because they confiscated gasoline as they advanced.[2]

When Hitler's armies attacked the Soviet Union almost exactly one year later on June 22, 1941, their one-bound reach had only been marginally increased by the addition of captured and confiscated French trucks and by a slight expansion in the mechanized forces. Among the 142 German divisions of the three army groups arrayed from the Baltic to the Black Sea on the eve of invasion, only 23 were Panzer, part-armored Light, or motorized. In the entire German army on all fronts, a total of 88 divisions were by then equipped with French vehicles; even so, 75 of the infantry divisions on the eastern front had to be stripped of trucks altogether to equip army-group supply columns, receiving instead 200 peasant carts each.[3] Such was the reality behind the facade of mechanized modernity that had played such a large part in the psychological impact of the blitzkrieg.

But the Soviet Union is a country far deeper than Belgium or France; its rail lines were much less readily usable because of a different track width and much sabotage; its few roads were so poorly surfaced that motor vehicles were rapidly worn out; and the tenacity of its resistance did not seem to diminish with successive, catastrophic defeats. Thus in mid-October 1941, when the German forces reached what in retrospect can be recognized as their culminating point of victory, Moscow was still some 60 miles beyond their most forward columns of advance.[4] With Hitler in command, however, there could be no pause for recuperation. The German forces on the central sector of the front, now with Moscow as their target, continued to advance through the month of November in twin thrusts from both north and south, to achieve one more great encirclement that would finish off the Soviet army, and the war.

With this, the German army overshot its culminating point of success, and was forced onto the downslope of the curve. Growing shortages of ammunition at the frontlines were silencing the artillery, and leaving even the infantry short, because distances from railheads to front were too great for the circulating horsecart columns and the few trucks. The railways were in any case unable to keep up with the supply needs because of an acute shortage of Russian-gauge rolling stock. In the process, ominously, winter clothing and cold-weather lubricants were left behind at remote marshaling yards, as immediate essentials of food, fuel, and ammunition received highest priority. In the mechanized forces, the number of functioning tanks, half-tracked carriers, and artillery tractors continued to decline, as wear and tear accumulated and field repair fell behind. By then, commandeered Russian peasant carts had become essential even for the Panzer divisions.

An active resistance of partisans and by-passed regulars had already begun in the rear, adding policeman's work to the duties of massacre and confiscation that already occupied Germans who could have been on the front. In part because of this, the flow of replacement manpower was steadily losing ground to rising casualties. Above all, German frontline soldiers were increasingly afflicted by the cold, physically exhausted, and demoralized by their very success. They had continued to advance mile after mile ever since June 22, capturing some three million Soviet troops by November and killing them by the tens of thousands in one engagement after another, but it seemed that just as many unconquered miles remained ahead and just as many Soviet troops still stood to resist them, with no end in sight.

But Hitler and his generals would not stop with Moscow so tantalizingly near. One more great effort was made, and the final German offensive of 1941, launched on December 1 at a time when the nearest German troops stood a mere 20 miles from Red Square, was carried out in subzero temperatures by forces whose last strength was rapidly ebbing.[5] Four days later, in the early morning of Friday, December 5, the Red Army launched its first large offensive of the war. Soviet troops in winter whites pushed the Germans

back over a distance twice as great as the depth of their last, ruinously successful, advance. After this Soviet offensive finally
checked the unbroken progress of German arms, two years more of
alternating war followed in which, as wave and counterwave, further spectacular German summer offensives only led to greater
retreats before Soviet attacks in growing strength. After losing
hugely by their own overextension, when epic victory in the Stalingrad salient was followed by excessive advance, setting the stage
for the German counterstroke of March 1943,[6] Stalin and his high
command learned to alternate each successful advance with a very
deliberate pause, to keep their armies safely short of the culminating point of victory.

As the Soviet Union fully mobilized its population and industry,
and obtained much American and British help (409,526 jeeps and
trucks *inter alia*[7]), it fielded increasingly superior forces, which
were employed with skill by a new breed of war-taught officers.
With the growing imbalance in the ultimate sources of military
strength, the alternation of German and Soviet offensives of 1942–
43 gave way to an unbroken sequence of Soviet victories, until the
final thrust into Berlin. But to the very end, even as German forces
in the east were reduced to an assemblage of wornout veteran remnants, raw recruits, rudely reassigned sailors and airmen never
retrained, young boys, old men, and the partially disabled, each
victorious Soviet offensive was carefully measured out to stop
short of excess, and it was "adventurism" rather than lack of
"drive" that Stalin's marshals were enjoined to avoid.[8]

The eleven-month war of the western front, from the Normandy
landings of June 6, 1944, to the German surrender, did not lack its
episodes of victory overshot on both sides, though only one side
could truly recover from the enfeeblement of overextension. And of
course the one-lane war of North Africa, fought back and forth
across the twelve hundred miles of desert between each side's
bases in Tripoli and Alexandria, was nothing but an entire series of
such episodes, until Montgomery's ponderous caution and crushing
material superiority yielded a slow but irreversible British advance
after the battle of El Alamein, from October 23, 1942. By then,
warfare in the romantic-adventuristic style by the British, and especially by Rommel's Germans, had given the fullest demonstration
of the principle, with victorious advance so grossly overshot that
offensive arrows sweeping across the map might amount to a mere
handful of vehicles running out of fuel—all set to be overrun by the

formerly defeated on the rebound, on their way to victories just as fragile.[9]

This was the pattern of the Korean war also, in which each side pursued its offensives to self-defeating extremes. The swift advance of the North Koreans that began on June 25, 1950, and that by August had conquered the entire peninsula except for the Taegu-Pusan enclave, had clearly passed its culminating point when MacArthur's counterstroke was launched on September 15 with the Inchon landings. Splendid victory was almost immediately overshot by an incautious offensive, setting the stage for defeat. Although the thinnest wedge of the American–South Korean advance that had cut through North Korea to reach the Yalu River and the Chinese border by October 26 was pulled back, MacArthur's "line" in November, stretching across the broad base of North Korea from sea to sea, existed only on the map. Instead of a solidly held front, with units shoulder to shoulder and strength in depth, American and South Korean divisional columns had merely advanced into several valleys widely separated by passable mountain country quite uncontrolled and even unpatrolled—and the troops in any case were morally spent by the conviction that the war had already been fought and won.

With wide passages open to them, the Chinese had the advantage of being able to advance deeply by infiltration before having to attack at all. When the overt Chinese offensive was launched on November 26, American and South Korean columns in retreat had to fight their way back through ambushes and roadblocks. By the end of January 1951 the Chinese had inflicted a vast defeat on MacArthur's forces and had advanced right through North Korea and into South, reaching some 40 miles beyond Seoul—much too far and too fast. Thus defeat and retreat were well-prepared when Ridgeway's counteroffensive thrusts of February, March, and April 1951 liberated Seoul for the second time in six months, along with most of South Korea.

Many more such examples could be adduced from the entire record of war prior to World War II, and some just as striking from the more recent past after the Korean war. But to elaborate further would merely obscure the generality of the phenomenon to be illustrated: the paradoxical logic of strategy, whose dynamic form is the coming together or reversal of opposites—*including* success and failure in prolonged, large-scale, continental warfare. The purely mechanical aspects of overextension, such as the obvious effects of sheer distance in wearing out men and equipment, are still only outward manifestations of a deeper phenomenon; they merely happen to loom large when the theater of war is itself large enough and war leaders are lacking in prudence. Actually we can recognize the same interaction between success and failure in *all* forms of warfare. This is so even if the mechanical aspects of overextension are entirely absent—so long as the duration of the action allows sufficient scope for the dynamic paradox to evolve.

Thus, for example, the six-year struggle between the British bomber forces and German air defenses during World War II was marked by drastic reversals of fortune until the last months of unresisted destruction, even though there were no abruptly extended distances to exceed a fixed transport capacity, no wearing out of unrepaired trucks and unrested horses, no exhausting infantry marches, and no other such physical processes at work. The reversals of success and failure in the air war over Germany were instead brought about by the reciprocal, if lagged, reaction of each side to the other's effort over time.

Convinced at the start of the war that the German fighter force, though trained for battlefield use,[10] could also assure Germany's air defense along with the antiaircraft guns of each locality, and indeed prevent any bombs at all from falling on German cities, the Luftwaffe's chiefs discovered otherwise in the summer of 1940, when the British Bomber Command started to bomb at night, with scant results at first but in virtual immunity.[11] Just when its leaders had become convinced that it would only require the training of sufficient aircrew and the production of enough bombers to inflict irreparable damage on the German war effort, thus ensuring victory without need of armies or navies, by the summer of 1942 the British Bomber Command encountered in full force the delayed effect of its own earlier success. Greatly improved German air defenses with more and better warning and tracking radars, new searchlight barriers, the first night-fighter squadrons, and more abundant antiaircraft guns, began to inflict losses that Bomber Command could not long sustain.[12]

Content with the growing success of its radar-based air defenses, and unwilling to take away more badly needed men, aircraft, and guns from the war fronts, the Luftwaffe was unprepared for the

British reaction, which resulted in a sharp increase in night bomb-ing during the spring of 1943.[13] The Germans could not cope with the sequence of British electronic countermeasures that were ham-pering the night fighters, and were utterly shocked when Bomber Command totally blinded German warning radars with the "Win-dow" countermeasure,[14] and used its sudden advantage in the un-precedented July 24–August 3, 1943, raids on Hamburg, which dev-astated that great city in mankind's first experience of the firestorm effect.[15] By then quite certain of the steady progression of its force, as more and better bombers were flying out on each successive raid, in November 1943 Bomber Command set out to destroy Berlin as Hamburg had been destroyed, only to collide with the German reaction to its earlier victory, in the form of effective Luftwaffe counter-countermeasures, novel tactics by day fighters as well as night fighters now more numerous than ever, and a greatly im-proved "running commentary" method of ground control.

The complete German system was so effective that only the di-version of Allied bombing to immobilize the French railways in preparation for D-Day masked the undoubted British defeat in the "battle of Berlin," even though it was by then the spring of 1944 and Germany was plainly losing the war. The damage inflicted on Berlin was unimpressive while British bomber losses exceeded the flow of replacements,[16] and the morale of the aircrews was break-ing: when they could, many crews dropped half their bombloads harmlessly into the sea, to gain height and speed before having to cope with the greatly strengthened German air defenses.

In these episodes, the effects of the paradoxical logic of strategy in its dynamic form are encountered at two very different levels: one narrowly technical and the other a matter of grand strategy at its broadest, dominated as always by political considerations.

MEASURES AND COUNTERMEASURES

The notion of an "action-reaction" sequence in the development of new war equipment and newer countermeasures, which induce in turn the development of counter-countermeasures and still newer equipment, is deceptively familiar. That the technical devices of war will be opposed whenever possible by other devices designed specifically against them is obvious enough. Slightly less obvious is the relationship (inevitably paradoxical) between the very success of new devices and the likelihood of their eventual failure: any sensible enemy will focus his most urgent efforts on countermeasures meant to neutralize whatever opposing device seems most dangerous at the time. Thus, ironically, less successful devices may retain their modest utility, even while those originally most successful have already been counteracted, perhaps to the extent of uselessness.[17] Eventually, of course, the less successful device is apt to be countered also, but in the meantime it may offer some span of utility—and this is all any device can offer in technological areas that happen to be evolving rapidly.

This was the case in the air electronic warfare of World War II, whose turbulent progress was propelled by dramatic scientific breakthroughs, by the furious pace of work in labs and factories, and by the intensity with which intelligence agencies worked to uncover enemy devices and techniques. In the ebb and flow of reciprocal development, the same device could be highly effective, totally useless, and positively dangerous within a matter of months, as in the case of the rearward-looking radars fitted on British bombers to warn of approaching fighters, which were first lifesavers, then jammed, and soon became a deadly danger to those who used them; a new device allowed German fighters to detect their beams and thus find the bombers at night.[18]

The effective lifespan of innovations was therefore the conditioning factor in determining the utility of their performance—a most confusing thought for scientists and engineers for whom, normally, utility and performance are one and the same thing—as indeed they are when performance acts on inanimate (or cooperative) objects. For example, a growing variety of electronic methods were invented to guide bombers to their targets at night, and the evolving state of technology also offered varied choices in the detailed configuration of the equipment associated with those methods. At each remove, both British and Germans, and later the American air forces, chose the most accurate and longest-range method, devoting development and production resources to obtain the relevant equipment in optimal form—only to see it countered while other methods only slightly inferior, and other equipment only marginally less optimal, could still be used effectively. It was eventually realized on all sides that the introduction of new methods and innovative equipment had to be managed very deliberately, and superior options were kept in reserve for campaigns of unusual importance.

Without such management, the life cycle of each new device employed in the air war would begin with an experimental phase in which few were available and the crews unskilled in their use, followed by a phase of rising success to a culminating level (which coincided with the preparation of enemy countermeasures), and followed in turn by an abrupt decline when countermeasures were also widely employed. Having acquired by bitter experience an insight into this manifestation of the logic of strategy, the leaders on all sides intervened to control the progression of technology, to make its span of success coincide more closely with operational priorities.

Although my purpose here is not to prescribe but only to understand the phenomena of strategy, the prescriptive implication is clear: when scarce development resources must be allocated between competing scientific concepts and engineering configurations, it is unwise to rely on scientific and engineering judgment alone. As such (they could be "strategists" also), scientists and engineers are unlikely to see merit in the diversion of resources to develop *diverse* second-best equipment alongside their optimal counterparts. But that is precisely what prudence demands. It will no doubt be argued that resistance to countermeasures is also an aspect of performance, one that would be given the highest priority if appropriate, so that any distinction between utility in conflict and performance in general cannot be valid—and neither can any resulting prescription. The argument is plausible, but it slights the full meaning of the conflictual predicament. It rests entirely on the assumption that the scientific and technological expertise relevant to the development of any given type of equipment will also correctly predict the countermeasures to come, against which resistance is to be designed in from the start, as part of overall performance.

This may well be true in some cases, especially for minor and prosaic innovations that will not disturb adversaries overmuch and are therefore apt to evoke a response equally prosaic within the established lines of technical development. But it is much less likely when the new equipment is notably successful in its impact on the overall balance of military strength. In the competitive arms building that may in occur in peacetime, and more so of course in war, the greater the success of any one technological innovation, and the more drastic the reaction evoked, the more likely it is that a wide variety of scientific principles will be explored in attempting to design countermeasures. Moreover, once the adversary creativity is unleashed, countermeasures may take the form of new tactics, methods, military structures, or even strategies—whose successful prediction is not at all a matter of scientific or engineering expertise.

Thus, in the same context of the aerial electronic warfare of World War II, the German response to the substantial British innovations that blinded German air defenses by the summer of 1943 was an entirely novel combination of searchlight signaling and ground control by "running commentary," amounting to a new *method* of air operations, in which fighters were no longer directed to intercept individual bombers but instead to pursue the hundreds of aircraft of the entire bomber "stream." So effective was this method, which was highly resilient to radar jamming, that the Germans were able to add greatly to their fighter strength by employing radarless day fighters for night interception as well. Concurrently, the Germans explored all kinds of new techniques to overcome British radar countermeasures, including infrared detection, quite outside the radar field of expertise. The British radar experts, who had shown such talent in designing radars and all countermeasures based on radar principles, and who were very successful in predicting German radar developments and countermeasures, naturally failed to anticipate the major German response to their own greatest success of the summer of 1943, which relied on radar principles not at all.

In this instance, as so often, utility in conflict and performance were not the same, since the latter included only a measure of resistance to *known and predictable* countermeasures and could not anticipate the full range of reactions that a major innovation can evoke in an observant and creative enemy still possessed of means and the will to resist. It is this constant presence that marks the realm of strategy and prohibits the pursuit of optimality. To design a bridge to cross a river, much is involved: soils must be tested to ascertain load-bearing properties, the dynamic forces the bridge will have to withstand must be calculated, and trusted theorems will have to be applied. But once that is done, the bridge can be built in safety. It is true that rivers sometimes flood their banks, or even abandon their accustomed channels to cut new ones, but no river of nature will deliberately set out to erode the structures of a bridge, nor will it deliberately set out to evade its span. Yet this is exactly what the objects of military technology will unfailingly do when significant innovation appears on the scene: hence the virtue of suboptimal but more rapid solutions that give less warning of the intent (lower-capacity but prefabricated bridges to surprise an animate river, as it were) and of suboptimal but inherently more resilient solutions (higher-cost, even lower-capacity pontoon bridges, with no structures to erode and fully mobile). This is why the scientist's natural pursuit of elegant solutions and the engineer's quest for optimality can often yield failure in the paradoxical realm of strategy.

CHAPTER 3

EFFICIENCY AND THE CULMINATING POINT OF SUCCESS

Having noted the obvious, in the likelihood of a counterreaction to any technical innovation, and the slightly less obvious relationship between the very success of innovation and the probability of its neutralization, we can approach the much less obvious but significant connection between the technical efficiency of new warlike devices and their vulnerability to countermeasures of all kinds.

In its familiar, sufficient, and only valid definition as the ratio of output to input, technical efficiency is a salient virtue in all material endeavors. Although it is invoked in loose language to comment on the worth of entire institutions that may have no measurable output at all, the criterion of efficiency can only be applied with mathematical precision in regard to machines, including the machines of war, by adding initial costs of acquisition and current operating costs, and comparing both with the ultimate output. Technical efficiency is not of course the only criterion to be applied in evaluating machines, for the ratio of current output to current input tells us nothing about the likely duration of their performance (reliability), and the costs of such upkeep as will be necessary over time. Subject to these, however, technical efficiency is the valid criterion of choice whether in selecting between different types of trucks or machine tools, rifles or tanks.

Some increases in technical efficiency can be obtained by the use of better materials or better design in detail within established forms, or even by minor adjustments in the inner workings of machines. It is by such processes that today's trucks can carry more tonnage than their predecessors of twenty years ago, of equal initial cost and greater fuel consumption, and that well-tuned truck engines can yield more horsepower than their poorly calibrated counterparts. More dramatic efficiency increases, however, will usually require the introduction of new machines of novel configuration. Sometimes this is made possible by the harnessing of different basic principles, as with today's word processors that are much more efficient than electric typewriters, as those in turn were more efficient than their mechanical forerunners. But, otherwise, dramatic increases in efficiency can arise only from the replacement of generic equipment built to do many things at varying standards of efficiency, by much more *specialized* machines or an integrated system of machines. Such are the machines that incorporate some novel ingenuity to produce one output altogether more efficiently, as canopeners open cans with much less effort than more versatile knives or as forklift trucks can position crates more efficiently than far more costly, if more versatile, mobile cranes.

It is precisely high efficiency derived from narrow specialization that has loomed large in the modern evolution of military technology. At each remove, novel specialized weapons have offered the attractive prospect of defeating far more elaborate and costly weapons, versatile in many ways but nevertheless vulnerable to the only "output" of specialized weapons. From the 1870s, for example, the combination of the newly invented self-propelled torpedo,[1] with fast steamboats to serve as its launching platforms, seemed to offer the possibility of defeating very efficiently the altogether more expensive battleships on which naval power then rested. Battleships, built as they were to fight other large warships, were armed with long-barreled guns of large caliber that could not be depressed low enough to defeat torpedo boats approaching under cover of night and revealed only at close range; even ocean-going torpedo boats would only present a small and unstable target, most difficult to hit. Moreover, the heavy armor of the battleship that made it so costly and formidable was then mainly applied to decks and superstructures, in order to resist the descending armor-piercing shells of other big-gun ships; hence the explosion of torpedo charges against unprotected sides below the waterline would be devastatingly effective. The conclusion to be reached seemed quite obvious: with the advent of the torpedo boat, the costly battleship had become fatally vulnerable, and if only inert conservatism were overcome, naval power could be acquired on a new and

more economical basis. That was the reasoning of the "young
school" of naval officers, the Jeune Ecole that influenced French
naval policy from the 1880s on, finding supporters even in the Royal
Navy as well as in the lesser navies that had better reason to wel-
come the demise of the battleship.[2]

The design of mobile cranes has not evolved to nullify the virtues
of forklift trucks, any more than knives have been modified to
dispute the primacy of canopeners in their one function. But then
neither inhabits the realm of strategy where each action is apt to
evoke over time a conscious and creative outmaneuvering reaction—which induces the paradoxical coming together of success
and failure in a manner all the more dynamic if the initial action is of
strong effect. And that applies as much to major technical innovations as to success and failure in the broader endeavors of war and
peace.

Precisely because of the extreme efficiency of narrow specialization, manifest in the potential ability of very small and cheap torpedo boats (the input) to destroy large and costly battleships (the
output), the new weapon greatly disturbed the equilibrium of naval
power, and the reaction was of correspondingly powerful effect. On
the rising curve of success, torpedoes were steadily improved in
their detailed workings to offer longer ranges and higher speeds,
while a new kind of very small yet ocean-going warship with the
fastest propulsion available was built to launch them. On this rising
curve of success, the new concept received prompt implementation
on a large scale. The French attempted to nullify their perpetual
inferiority to the Royal Navy's battleships by building no fewer than
370 *torpilleurs* from 1877 to 1903; and even the British built 117 "1st
class Torpedo Boats" by 1904.[3] The nascent German navy did not
neglect the innovation; nor did the navy of modernizing Japan—
which used its ocean-going torpedo boats with great success in the
surprise attack against the Russian fleet at Port Arthur in February
1904.

Thus the vision of ultraefficient naval power that the naval re-
formers of the 1870s had so vigorously promoted against the conservatism of "old school" admirals was fully realized long before
World War I. Yet torpedo boats scarcely played a role in that
conflict except as a threat to be guarded against, as we shall see.
Far from having made all larger and more costly warships obsolete,
it was the torpedo boat itself that was obsolescent, surviving only

as a minor weapon of marginal value. For by then the innovation had long passed its culminating point of success, and stood all the more neutralized *because of its very efficiency,* which had both evoked a strong reaction and precluded any remedial response: weapons highly efficient because narrowly specialized cannot accommodate *broad* counter-countermeasures.

By 1914 all modern battleships and battlecruisers, indeed all large modern warships, were prepared to neutralize the torpedo boat. Although the long-barreled guns of their main batteries could still not be depressed to fire at short ranges, the searchlights by then universally employed made it much more difficult for torpedo boats to approach closely undetected, even at night. And, just in case, numbers of quick-firing guns of small caliber had been added. Though armor protection was still at its thickest on decks and superstructures, new and highly effective protection was also provided below the waterline, not only by armor plate but by sealed bulges that could absorb the impact of torpedo detonations; at anchor, wire nets suspended alongside could shield warships by detonating torpedo charges at a safe distance from the hull. The ability of larger warships to carry extra armor, provide ample electrical power for searchlights, and accommodate quick-firing guns and heavy steel nets derived of course from the same characteristic that had made them appear so inefficient in the visualized duel with the torpedo boat. Their sheer size and power had merely affirmed their value as targets while seeming irrelevant to the duel—until all that costly versatility was harnessed finally to defeat the novel threat. Thus the broad prevails over the narrow to cut short its span of success.

Far from presaging a new ascendancy, the victory of the Japanese torpedo boats at Port Arthur was already an anachronism, a reflection of Russian naval unpreparedness. Against more modern navies, the new weapon's culminating point of success had already passed, and its sharp decline was evident by 1914. That the torpedo itself remained a useful naval weapon, and remains so still, is not in question. It found its place as one more specialized weapon for surface warships and especially for the new kind of warship originally built to hunt torpedo boats, the "torpedo-boat destroyer," or destroyer for short. The torpedo also became significant in aerial use and even more important as the key weapon of the submarine, with which it formed a much *less* efficient (more input for the same output) but far more effective combination in two world wars. And of course even the original torpedo-boat combination did have an important effect upon the naval balance, by forcing the large-ship navies to divert resources precisely to provide the defenses that eventually neutralized the new threat. As we shall see, such *reciprocal force-development effects* can sometimes be of greater value to one side or another in asymmetrical contests than the original combat ability offered by weapons of narrow ingenuity.

The fact remains that a nation embracing reformist innovation wholeheartedly, entrusting its naval strength to the originally ultra-efficient torpedo boat, would soon have found its strength wanting. The relationship between the initial efficiency of narrowly specialized weapons and their vulnerability to countermeasures is not accidental: it is a typical expression of the paradoxical logic of strategy in its dynamic form. The same phenomenon is evident—or will be—in regard to all other attempts to defeat the broad with the narrow, which achieve efficiencies all the more ephemeral the larger they are at the beginning of the cycle. And yet the sequence keeps repeating itself, propelled by the irresistible attraction of getting something for nothing, or at least of defeating costly weapons with cheaper ones.

Thus, for example, when antitank missiles were used to great effect by Egyptian infantry against Israeli battle tanks during the first few days of the surprise attack that inaugurated the 1973 October war, much was made of their revolutionary impact on land warfare. Loud voices were soon heard proclaiming the obsolescence of the expensive battle tank, and there were insistent demands for reform to overcome the conservatism of the "tank generals" and thereby save a great deal of money. How could million-dollar tanks be worth their keep, it was asked, when they could so easily be destroyed by antitank missiles that cost mere thousands? (And, incidentally, why should there be so much anxiety over the strength of the Soviet army when it is so largely dependent on its tank formations?) Very quickly a new Jeune Ecole emerged, which offered the attractive vision of a novel sort of high-technology infantry, cheaply armed with antitank missiles to offer military strength not merely highly efficient but also virtuous in being strictly of defensive effect. Actually the fundamental innovation that made the antitank missile possible was by no means new: hollow-charge chemical warheads were already in use during World

War II. Instead of depending on kinetic energy to penetrate armor by brute force, which requires high-velocity guns of great weight and cost, hollow-charge warheads function by projecting a high-speed stream of vaporized metal. Even the thickest armor can be penetrated, without need of long-barreled guns and their necessary recoil mechanisms and elevating assemblies, which only large and costly vehicles can carry into battle. Any means at all of conveying charge to target will do, whether by rockets light enough to be hand-lanched as in the original bazooka and the German Panzerschrek, or cheap low-velocity recoilless guns, or even by hand in the form of satchel charges simply thrown at tanks.

When the bazooka and its equivalents first appeared, some thought that the day of the tank was done. Any infantryman could now carry a weapon that could destroy tanks. If every squad of the two hundred and more of each infantry division were to contain just two or three, the infantry would be able to block its armored counterpart, so much more costly to equip and train, so much harder to supply in the field, and altogether more difficult to transport across great distances. Had it been a time of peace, the delusion might have prospered. But since war was at hand swiftly to punish fallacy, the bazooka and the rest of the hollow-charge rockets introduced during World War II were almost immediately recognized for what they were: excellent morale boosters for the infantry, until then apt to be shocked into flight by the mere approach of enemy tanks; weapons fairly effective in woods, forest, and jungle—scarcely tank country—but also in cities, unless the tanks sacrificed momentum to proceed at a walking pace with escorting infantry alongside; and then of course as weapons highly suitable for the aspiring hero, who would stand his ground amid the artillery explosions that commonly prepare the way for attacking armor and who would then aim his one ready shot at a tank whose machine guns had been firing at him long before the hundred-yard rocket could be launched. Of course, such duels were great rarities on the battlefield, for tanks fight in groups that protect one another as they advance. As we shall see, moreover, there are levels other than the tactical in the encounter, which favor the mobile armored force even more.

The advent of portable missiles to launch hollow charges decisively remedied the most obvious defect of their predecessors. Guided to the target, missiles can be propelled with accuracy at long range, so they need not be launched within machine-gun reach of their targets. But otherwise this weapon of narrowly specialized ingenuity is in no better position to make the tank obsolete than the bazooka was during World War II. In the fighting of the first few days of the October war of 1973, Egyptian infantry encountered Israeli tanks in rather small numbers, with no infantry in escort and without significant artillery fire in support (both being mostly re-serve forces, they were still unmobilized when the Egyptians launched their surprise attack).[4] Israeli tank crews, moreover, had received no particular training to prepare them for a fight with determined infantry that would stand its ground; and the tanks themselves were only really armed for combat with other tanks. As a result, it was not only antitank missiles that destroyed Israeli tanks but old-style unguided weapons as well, and in greater num-bers.

With its extreme efficiency against unprepared tanks, the anti-tank missile evoked a very strong reaction, setting in train with special rapidity the dynamic paradox that would turn success into failure. And because of its narrow abilities—the reason for its efficiency—the reaction was effective almost immediately and would become even more so over time. The same Israeli tank bat-talions that the antitank missile had seemingly made obsolete by October 9, 1973, or at least incapable of offensive action, were penetrating the Egyptian front one week later and advancing uncon-tested to encircle entire divisions just one week after that. Obvi-ously there had been no time for the development of any sort of technical countermeasure, and the response that turned success into failure was largely tactical.

With initial surprise overcome, and the reserve mechanized in-fantry and artillery forces mobilized to the front, the tank battalions no longer had to fight on their own—contrary to their prescribed method of war. Instead, they could advance behind a rolling bar-rage of artillery fire, not heavy enough to do much harm to Egyptian armor or entrenched infantry but very effective against antitank missiles, whose firers could not keep a target in their sights long enough amid the explosions, even if they braved the dangers of exposing themselves. The mechanized infantry, advancing along-side the tanks in their troop carriers, added to the suppressive effect with its own mortars and machine guns, which swept the ground ahead to force would-be firers to keep their heads down.[5] Even more effective were the mortar smoke bombs, which could keep a curtain of diminished visibility just ahead of the tanks, thus preventing missile operators from seeing their moving targets for long enough to guide their weapons to intercept. Finally, the tanks also had some means to protect themselves once the new threat was recognized; a portion of the armor-piercing rounds carried on board could be offloaded to make room for high-explosive shells effective against infantry, and tanks had their own machine guns as well as launchers for smoke grenades.

Thus the armored force, so costly because of its broad and versatile abilities, could outmaneuver the narrow efficiency that made the antitank missile so cheap, even before there was time to develop, produce, and distribute specific countermeasures. Some of the latter were already in use during the next encounter, the 1982 Lebanon war, when Israeli tanks went into action with "active armor" detonating plates to destroy hollow-charge warheads before they could explode, as well as more machine guns and better launchers for smoke grenades. By then far more accomplished antitank missiles had appeared on the scene, but they had little effect on the fighting except when launched from specially configured helicopters, to yield a combination no longer cheap by any means, less efficient therefore, but altogether more effective.[6]

STRATEGY VERSUS ECONOMICS

That ever-present adversary reaction that makes the strategic predicament what it is will not only disappoint most hopes of drastic efficiencies achieved by narrow specialization, but can also deny the more modest ambition of pursuing sound (linear-logical) economic practice. Specifically, although the armed forces are usually the largest of all social institutions, they cannot freely pursue economies of scale in acquiring equipment. The uninspiring uniformity that is the curse of modern industrial society is also the key to its blessings: displacing the myriad individual artifacts of the traditional craftsman, with their multitude of designs, many fewer standardized products are manufactured in far greater numbers at much smaller cost by efficient, specialized machines, tools, and jigs conjoined by laborsaving production lines. It is the *homogeneity* of the products (and of their components) that permits economical mass production, and the greater the homogeneity in all that is produced, the greater the economies. (It is only recently that the introduction of numerically controlled machinery is beginning to break the pattern.) For products that are themselves machines, moreover—including those too unusual to be mass-produced—homogeneity is the key to further economies of scale, in both maintenance and operation. The greater the homogeneity of a stock of machines, the smaller the number of diverse replacement parts and supplies that must be kept in inventory, achieving savings not merely in administration but also in substantive capital: the size of the replacement inventories required for uninterrupted operation can be more finely calculated when there is much use of fewer machines, rather than small use of many different ones. Similarly, the more homogeneous the machinery, the more economical is the training of their repairmen and operators, and the greater the likelihood that they will learn enough to do their work properly.

In diverse ways homogeneity is therefore the essential attribute that permits the efficiencies of economies of scale in acquisition, maintenance, and operation. As we have seen, not all that pertains to conflict belongs to the realm of strategy, and there is nothing to prevent armed forces from pursuing economies of scale by homogeneity in all that is purely *administrative,* where adversary wills have no role.[7] There is no obstacle to the efficient mass acquisition of boots or helmets, trucks or ammunition, so long as variant needs (sizes, capacities, calibers) are satisfied. But for military equipment that must function in direct interaction with the doings and undoings of a live enemy—within the strategic realm, in other words—homogeneity is no longer an unalloyed virtue and becomes a potential vulnerability.

If, for example, antiaircraft missiles are standardized on a single homogeneous type, in order to obtain economies of scale in production, in replacement-part stockage and training, the resulting savings could be very large as compared to an array of several different missile types. But in war a competent enemy will be able to identify the weapon's equally homogeneous performance boundaries and then proceed to evade interception by transcending those boundaries. Any given type of missile will have minimum and maximum altitude limits, and enemy aircraft can therefore underfly or overfly those limits. The missile can still exact a price because aircraft flying very low or very high cannot be all that effective, but such "virtual attrition" may not suffice to achieve the purposes of an antiaircraft defense (aircraft can attack targets by ultralow penetration or high-altitude bombing, even if less well than at some optimal medium altitude). The single homogeneous missile, moreover, will be vulnerable to a single, homogeneous set of countermeasures. Perhaps the economies of scale of standardizing on a single type can be so great that the one missile and its battery complex can be made resistant to any one countermeasure, for example by combining diverse forms of guidance that can automatically substitute for one another. But the target presented to the enemy's countermeasure effort will be unitary, enabling him to focus all his efforts—and even a redundant set of devices may contain a single weak point vulnerable to exploitation.

What is true of antiaircraft missiles is just as true of any other machine of war that must function in direct interaction with reacting enemy—that is, the vast majority of weapons. In each case, the application of linear-logical economic principles would result in standardization on a single type to obtain large savings in production, maintenance, and operation, just as with the trucks of a well-run commercial fleet or the machine tools of a competent engineering enterprise. Both trucks and machine tools exist in a competitive environment, and the truck fleet and the engineering company face the danger that their rivals will be able to undercut their prices by obtaining more efficient trucks or machine tools. But there are legal boundaries to what can be done in economic competition: competitors will not undermine the bridges the trucks must cross so that their standardized weight will exceed the bridge load limits, nor will they conspire with suppliers to restrict raw materials to grades incompatible with the specific tolerance limits of the standardized machine tools. In armed conflict, however, where there are no such legal boundaries, standardization must result in vulnerability for any weapon or device that interacts with the enemy, from fighter aircraft to missile submarines, from warning radars to field radios.

In the realm of conflict and strategy, therefore, economic principles stand in direct opposition to the demands of conflictual effectiveness, and though there is an obvious cost barrier to unlimited diversity, there is a vulnerability barrier to the unlimited pursuit of economies of scale by homogeneity. It is easy to see that a criterion of "equal marginal risk" could be applied to determine how much uneconomical diversity should be accepted in the purchase of equipment, but to establish such a criterion one must first recognize that commonsense economic thinking of seemingly universal applicability need not be valid in strategy.[8] Military institutions may be safeguarded against dangerous extremes of homogeneity, even without benefit of strategical insight, by the urge of different armed services to affirm their autonomy through the choice of their own distinctive weapons. But there is no such protection against the pursuit of economies of scale in the sizing of complex weapons, notably warships. The large warship offers exactly the same economies of acquisition and operation over smaller counterparts that have led to the concentration of the world's shipping capacity in huge tankers, bulk carriers, and container ships. As size increases, crews do not have to increase in proportion, and all sorts of other economies can be achieved in component elements, from bilge pumps to main engines. Large ships, too, are more stable in rough seas and have an important hydrodynamic advantage of speed.

Such advantages, however, as with the economies of scale of large airbases or tank-repair depots, are often obtained at the price of a proportionate concentration of value against which an enemy can focus his efforts. Should the world experience another submarine campaign against commercial shipping in the style of the two world wars, it may turn out that the advent of the supertanker confers a greater advantage on the attacker than even the transformation of submersile diesel-electric boats into today's nuclear-powered underwater warships. For commercial fleets that must survive in a peacetime competitive setting, the unlimited pursuit of economies of scale is essential (though nations that spend much to keep commerce-protecting naval forces might profitably divert some of those expenditures to subsidize small-ship inefficiency). But when we encounter a similar concentration of value in combat ships and auxiliaries several times larger than their predecessors of World War II, in major airbases and repair depots in places quite close to enemy territory,[9] we can recognize the displacement of strategy's paradoxical logic by economic priorities, perfectly valid but only in peacetime.

DESCENDING THE CURVE: FROM SUCCESS TO FAILURE

Except for passing mention of "reciprocal" effects in the development of weapons and of "virtual attrition," the fate of the reacting side in the dynamic interaction has been overlooked. But of course the coming together of opposites that leads from success to failure, and from failure to success, affects both sides in exactly the same manner, whether in the largest actions of war and peace or in the technical encounter between weapons and countermeasures. The side that is reacting successfully to some novel threat is itself approaching a culminating point, perhaps distant or perhaps near, but which in any case marks the start of its own decline.

On the one hand, with initial surprise overcome and with the passage of time to allow creativity and resources to be more amply harnessed, the reaction to the novel threat becomes increasingly effective. On the other hand, those resources and creative energies are being diverted from some self-directed, positive action that was underway before, in order to sustain the defensive reaction evoked by the novel threat. Eventually, if the culminating point of success is overshot, the means expended to mitigate the novel threat will be greater than the result is worth, in terms of the positive action thereby forgone. And in the meantime, of course, the adversary will have started to react in turn, to protect the threat first presented against the rising effect of countermeasures, with little scope for success (and expense) if that threat was narrowly efficient and with more opportunity for both if it was not, but in either case setting in train another cycle of the dynamic, paradoxical process of strategy.

Though the innocent enthusiast persuaded of the virtues of some ultimate weapon will be surprised by the variety of adversary reactions that will deny the success he deemed so certain, those who are themselves reacting successfully against the weapon may easily overlook the danger of overshooting the culminating point of success, by sacrificing too much offensive strength to protect what should be abandoned. This has yet to happen in the response to the antitank missile, but the costs of success have been high, adding to those already imposed by the hollow-charge threat in its unguided form, now present in a variety of hand-held rocket and recoilless weapons distinctly superior to their predecessors of World War II. Until then endangered only by their own kind, and by antitank guns themselves rather costly and scarce, by 1943 tank crews had learned to fear all places where soldiers equipped with hollow-charge weapons might await their coming; by the end of the war, with those weapons in widespread use, any passage through woods or narrow streets had become a dangerous experience.

Very soon after the first of the new weapons appeared, it was discovered that their threat could be mitigated by a close escort of infantry moving alongside, whose many eyes could probe the surroundings and whose small weapons could suppress and react in detail. But the cost of that effective precaution was very high because tank units in need of a foot escort could no longer surge ahead on their own even for tactical movements, and thus lost much of the dash and momentum that is the true strength of attacking armor.

The advent of the antitank missile greatly compounds the effect. Artillery fire once reserved for the most concentrated targets of the enemy array must now be diverted to its frontal edges, in order to suppress missile crews. And if mechanized infantry is to advance alongside the tanks to protect them, the men need combat vehicles much more elaborate and costly than the simple troop carriers that sufficed when the infantry's task was chiefly to mop up behind the advancing tanks. Finally, in the tank units themselves there must be a diversion of effort from offensive action to self-protection, by way of both material changes and more cautious tactics. Armored forces earn their keep by offensive strength, and everything done to protect them from the hollow-charge threat diminishes their net positive value, even if the culminating point—where more is lost than gained in the process—is not yet reached. That, however, may well be the condition of today's large-ship navies and of the American navy especially, whose aircraft-carrier groups are so preoccupied with self-protection against submarine and air attack that only a fraction of their original positive strength remains.

PROTECTING THE FLEET: OVERDOING SUCCESS

In true transnational fashion, the ability of Argentinian aircraft to sink large British ships with French missiles during the 1982 Falklands war provoked an American debate, which echoed the torpedo-boat controversy of a hundred years before. Once again the cheap weapon of narrow effect was promoted as decisively lethal to warships a thousand times more costly; once again demands were heard for a drastic change of policy to stop the waste of public monies on elaborate warships, on aircraft carriers especially, now supposedly made obsolete by their new vulnerability. This time, however, there was no need to await the development of countermeasures. In another echo from the past, the effectiveness of the missiles of 1982 was due to the peculiar unpreparedness of the

Royal Navy, whose lag in adopting widely used countermeasures was as severe as that of the tsarist navy in opposing the torpedo. Actually by 1982 the antiship missile had already long passed its culminating point of success, owing to the strong reaction evoked by its earlier appearances, dating back to the middle years of World War II[10] and by their prominence in Soviet use.

Hence United States navy chiefs had no difficulty in winning the debate. They explained that each aircraft carrier would go into action only with a panoply of escorting destroyers and cruisers, devoted almost entirely to their protection. Radar-confusing chaff and infrared flares projected outward by special rockets, as well as jamming, would divert missiles aimed at the carriers, while the missiles and guns of the escorting ships would shoot down undiverted missiles as well as any aircraft that ventured too near in order to launch them. That, they pointed out, was only the middle layer of the defense: 24 long-range fighter interceptors on each carrier, with 4 early-warning radar aircraft and 4 jamming aircraft to aid them, would assure the outer layer of the defense to which they were dedicated, having 4 tanker aircraft as well to keep them refueled at their distant stations. Finally, there was the inner layer of the defense, the radars, countermeasures, missiles, and guns of each ship, including special automatic guns reserved for that one purpose. So devastating was this answer to the missile enthusiasts of 1982 that the other side of the coin scarcely attracted notice. When all that is required to react (successfully) to the antiship missile is calculated, it becomes clear that, in addition to exceptionally costly escorting warships, much of the aircraft carrier's capacity is also absorbed by the need for self-protection against missile attack, with 36 aircraft out of 90 or so (and by far the most expensive) thus employed.[11]

As it happens, no Argentinian submarine was successful in sinking a British ship during the Falklands war. Had that been the case, thus provoking debate on the vulnerability of American warships to modern submarines as well, the leaders of the American navy would no doubt have described the abundance of antisubmarine measures that also protect the aircraft-carrier groups. These include a submarine in underwater escort, as well as 16 more of the 90 aircraft or so on each large carrier, and virtually all the weapons and sensors of destroyers and cruisers not already reserved for antiaircraft use. Once this further self-protection is added, the arithmetic reveals that out of an entire carrier group, with its several destroyers and one cruiser, its escort submarine and many supply ships, with perhaps almost 10,000 crew members on board, only 34 aircraft remain for positive use on behalf of national purposes, as well as a dozen guns of middling caliber, sundry missiles, and whatever landing forces are carried in additional ships. Isolated in clear contrast between sea and sky, unable to hide in the terrain as ground forces can, unable to move as rapidly as aircraft, surface warships are clearly increasingly endangered by the scientific advances that nowadays permit long-range observation and attack in many forms. To contend against adverse trends propelled by the entire progress of science, increasing expense and ingenuity as well as ship capacity have been consumed for self-protection. The net vulnerability of the best fleets has increased only slightly perhaps, but their condition increasingly resembles that of a widow in distress who attempts to support her family by taking in her own washing.

In historical retrospect, the sequence of the dynamic paradox in this example reveals first the supremacy of American surface and carrier forces, originally built to meet Japan's sea strength, which after 1945 were left facing a Soviet Union that was strong only on land. Then the Soviet reaction begins, in fear especially of heavy air attack from the carriers, against which land, coastal, air, and submarine forces are all developed with increasing success, eventually to ascend the curve toward a culminating defensive supremacy if the process should continue uncontested. But the American navy responds in turn, by building escort ships increasingly effective, by technical countermeasures, by converting more and more aircraft capacity to defensive use, and by an increasing propensity to stay away from dangerous seas (another sort of offensive loss). With a reaction so vigorous, the Soviet counterthreat to the aircraft carriers begins to slide down the curve toward failure, so that by the time the Falklands war intervenes to remind the world of naval combat, American carriers are very well protected, but only at vast national expense and with a great loss of offensive power.

Far more precise calculation than this text will allow would be needed to determine the culminating point of defensive success in protecting surface fleets, beyond which oceanic strength could better be secured by underwater and aerial forces.[12] Certainly no facile judgment is to be made in prose, any more than a naval institution deeply devoted to navigation on the surface can be expected to repudiate sturdy tradition in obedience to a strategic logic only dimly perceived. But such a culminating point does exist, and to exceed it means to fail even in apparent success, in a national if not in a more narrowly institutional perspective.

THE FAILURE OF SUCCESS

Far more commonplace is the overdoing of a successful defense in the vicissitudes of territorial warfare. The outpost, fortified zone, or garrisoned city that is deliberately left in front of the main defense lines, or which remains cut off in the course of a retreat, may serve the defense very well by providing warning, by blocking approach routes, and by absorbing disproportionate enemy attention. The attacker may find himself weakened in the theater balance as a whole as he fights at great cost for places that might have been bypassed, if their resistance had been correctly anticipated from the start.

It is usually the defense, however, that suffers the consequences of an oversuccessful resistance. If the forces cut off are defeated in short order, they may still have obtained an advantage for the defense. But if their resistance persists in prolonged, heroic endurance, attracting public notice, the locality that was perhaps once quite obscure or just another name on the map can be transformed into a weighty symbol, into which the reputation of military or political leaders may become inflexibly invested. If no help can be sent to the beleaguered, the defense will continue to obtain an advantage, moral as well as material, so long as resistance persists. But if there are ways of sending reinforcements by perilous routes under attack, by yet more precarious infiltration, or by air transport, then the continued success of the defense in holding the position can become ruinous in a larger perspective.

So it was most famously at Verdun in our century, where the failure of a German surprise attack in February 1916 gave the French a greatly needed defensive success—and also impaled their army on that victory, bleeding it white in ten months of battle (arguably the longest in history) to defend the Verdun forts. To keep up the resistance, day after day a great stream of men was sent forward under steady bombardment, with a great many falling before they ever reached the forts. By official figures notoriously understated, the French army suffered 162,308 killed and missing, another 214,932 wounded, during the ten months. The Germans had definite advantage from the continuing success of the defense of the forts, since their artillery could strike at French approach roads better than the French artillery could reciprocate; their lists, also understated, included only some 100,000 dead and missing. (A total of 344,959 Americans died in battle during *both* world wars, on all fronts and in all services.) More truthful estimates of later origin calculate a total of 420,000 dead, two-thirds of them French.[13] The massacre was still in its early stages when it became clear that the Verdun forts could more advantageously be abandoned than defended, because they amounted to an exposed salient wedged into German-held territory. But by then it was also too late for any such calculation: the forts had become a symbol beyond any strategical disposition, and the more Frenchmen lost in their defense—thus further affirming their military disutility—the more impossible it was to confess the futility of all those losses by an advantageous withdrawal. In such cases the successful defense persists at a cost that may emerge in future failure. And indeed after Verdun the French army was so weakened that the attempt to take the offensive provoked the crippling mutinies of 1917. The lingering effect of Verdun was still being felt in the fatal shrinkage of the French army that faced Hitler two decades later.

So it was again at Stalingrad, where the Germans consumed the strength of the Luftwaffe in the futile attempt to sustain the encircled Sixth Army during its eight weeks of resistance under siege that ended on February 2, 1943. Had there been no air supply, had the resistance therefore failed at an early stage, the Luftwaffe might have been saved for more useful duties, and many German troops might have broken through siege lines quite thin at first, to fight another day. Such encirclements and breakouts were almost a routine of the entire campaign, but the name of Stalingrad affixed to those square miles of ruins had become a symbol that Hitler would not surrender, until the decision was taken out of his hands by the capitulation of the generals on the scene.

Even the postwar years saw a dramatic case of a successful defense overshot, that of Dien Bien Phu by the French in Indochina. Dropped by air in November 1953 into a valley in the contested territory of northwest Vietnam, French troops of the first quality withstood the initial Vietminh attacks so well that the exotic three-part name instantly acquired heroic reverberations—a unique distinction in a confused, confusing, and most unpopular war. As the Vietminh gathered round in ever greater strength, the garrison held out for 112 days until May 7, 1954, claiming a steady reinforcement of the best men France had, brought in by aircraft that had to fly straight into the fire of antiaircraft guns. Originally meant as a strictly practical operation, whose modest aim was to oppose Vietminh infiltration into Laos, the Dien Bien Phu lodgment instead absorbed a ruinously disproportionate effort, which could not be interrupted because the place had become the symbol of French military capacity in the domestic opinion of France and the assembly of its politicians. When the besieged garrison was at last overrun, the entire French enterprise of Vietnam was repudiated by public and politicians alike—which might not have happened so soon, and so precipitously, if the French paratroops who first landed on November 20–21, 1953, had not succeeded so well in their combat of the first days.[14]

In strategy's dynamic paradox, a defense as much as an offensive can be too successful. It can evolve into a wider failure, whether in defending outposts, in protecting fleets that scientific advances are making insecure, or in preserving any other military instrument that emotions and institutional interest transform from servant to master.

CHAPTER 4

THE COMING TOGETHER OF OPPOSITES

We have seen the workings of
the dynamic paradox and the resulting ironies of reversal at the
technical and tactical levels of sundry encounters, and we have yet
to consider these phenomena at the middle levels of strategy. It will
be enlightening at this point to ascend briefly to the level of grand
strategy, where each particular matter interacts with the entire conflictual predicament.

The dealings of adversary national leaders may seem vastly different from those of the technicians and fighting men on each side.
It is certainly true that, to preserve or enhance their power and
authority within their own societies, national leaders must also
pursue inward political goals that may clash with those of the external contest. Hence political leaders are usually hampered in exploiting such insight into strategy as they may have. For example, they
cannot usually employ deliberately paradoxical action to circumvent external antagonists, because it is rarely possible to deviate
from the commonsense conventions of the time and place without a
loss of authority.* A conscious understanding of the phenomena of
strategy is, however, a great rarity in any case, and especially in the
rogues' gallery of the highest political leaders. Through sheer experience, many a plain sergeant has achieved an intuitive feel for the
workings of the strategical paradox at the tactical level, thereby
learning to take advantage of it in combat. And many of the celebrated military leaders of history owe their reputation to their insight into the same phenomena, which enabled them to achieve

---

*There are exceptions of course, exemplified by the personal role of national
leaders in that characteristically brutal phenomenon of our century, the starting of
war by surprise attack instead of by formal declaration.

results that may have seemed merely fortunate to those less well endowed.

But when it is not just one machine-gun nest that must be taken in one time and place—nor even a campaign to be conducted—when instead it is the full and variegated complexity of the entire conflictual predicament that must be confronted, only the greatest leaders will possess some understanding of the paradoxical logic of strategy, buried as it is under the peculiar complications of each subordinate level and obscured as it is by the overpowering emotions that conflict unleashes, its vibrant hopes and deadly fears. That the thing can be done at all should amaze. And yet the rare achievement can even be documented.

In the earlier discussion of the contest between the British Bomber Command and German air defenses, we saw how its technical and tactical aspects were encompassed by the predicament of each side at the level of grand strategy. The British venture into the bombardment of Germany, at first only against carefully selected military and industrial targets remote from cities, was precipitated by the initial success of the German forces in May 1940, in the invasions of Holland and Belgium. Thus among the paradoxical first fruits of an advance that had not yet reached the culminating point of success, Germany experienced its first air attacks, feeble at the start. When the Werhmacht most unexpectedly accomplished the total defeat of France in short order, driving the British army from the continent in June 1940, it deprived the British government of any other means of waging war except by air. And because German air defenses inflicted disastrous losses on aircraft attempting to bomb specific military and industrial targets in daylight, Bomber Command had to fly at night, when its aircraft could hit no target smaller than a fairly large city. Thus the paradoxical reward that the Germans obtained for the victory of their army, and the quality of their fighter forces and antiaircraft artillery for daylight interception, was the beginning of the destruction of German cities.

The rising curve of British success in that longest of all campaigns of World War II began from the lowest point of national failure. In August 1940, the Royal Navy was cowering in distant Scapa Flow in fear of German attack, the British army was hoping only to defend the beaches, and the Royal Air Force was so greatly battered by the Luftwaffe's attacks on its airfields that it actually welcomed the relief offered by the first German bombing of London, on

August 24, 1940.[1] On the following night, Bomber Command carried out its first attack on Berlin, even though it was not until July 1941 that the expedient of night bombing—which had to mean city bombing—became deliberate policy. As Britain's industrial and military mobilization was steadily accelerating, yielding more bombers and trained aircrew ready at the takeoff line for each successive raid; as the curve of success was rising with little effective German reaction, acceptable loss rates, and no culminating point in sight, Charles Portal, marshal of the Royal Air Force and chief of the Air Staff, offered a plan for a straightforward progression toward victory by bombardment alone: 43 selected cities and towns, containing a combined population of some fifteen million but also the largest part of German war industry, were to be bombed very heavily in six successive strikes, to leave them "beyond all hope of recovery."

In submitting his plan to Prime Minister Winston Churchill on September 25, 1941, Portal suggested that with 4,000 first-line aircraft, Bomber Command could "break" Germany in six months.[2] Characteristically, there was very detailed calculation in formulating the plan, much in the manner of an engineer designing a bridge over an unresisting river, but no calculation whatever of the enemy's likely reaction. Thus the quantum of bombing destruction required in the 43 cities was not set arbitrarily but rather carefully calculated on the basis of an "index of activity" based on statistics collected in the wake of the German bombing of British industrial towns. After an attack, factory production would suffer because of interruptions in the gas, water, and electricity supply; workers would absent themselves from fear, fatigue, or lack of food, breakdowns in public transport, and the general disruption of urban life. A given tonnage of bombs per unit of population would reduce the index of activity to a given residual percentage: in the case of Coventry, for example, calculation showed that the index fell to 63 percent on the day after the massed German bombing attack of November 14, 1940, in which one ton of bombs was dropped per every 800 of the population. Then a gradual recovery would begin, but if further attacks were made, the index would resume its ascent from a lower and lower base, until after the fourth or fifth attack it would be reduced to nil, and war production would completely cease in the affected town.

The plan, moreover, was admirably conservative in all its assumptions: no fewer than six attacks delivering one ton of bombs per 800 of the population would be made on each of the 43 towns; 18,750 tons were deemed necessary for their 15 million inhabitants. So generous was the allowance made for navigational errors, technical aborts, and intercepts that only a mere 25 percent of the aircraft were expected to reach the target, raising the initial tonnage required to 75,000 tons; and each sixteen-aircraft squadron was assumed to make only one hundred sorties per month (substantially less than actual rates) while the unit bombload was modestly set at three tons per aircraft. Two hundred and fifty squadrons would therefore be needed on line during the six months of the campaign, for a grand total of 4,000 bombers.

In a classic case of linear-logical thinking, the plan implicitly assumed that the Germans would neither dramatically increase the modest priority then given to air defense nor disperse their war industries, even as they were systematically destroyed. Portal and his subordinates were not fools and, no doubt if individually summoned to reflect on the matter, they would have repudiated any conception of war in which the enemy's entire creative energy and will of self-protection were ignored. But consider the circumstances and emotional urgencies of the time: in September 1941, when the plan was submitted to Churchill, the Germans were sweeping all before them in Russia, smashing defense lines and entire armies week by week, rounding up prisoners by the hundreds of thousands. Only evocations of Napoleon's fate stood against the hard facts that suggested an imminent Soviet collapse, and there was no sign of significant armed resistance to the German occupiers anywhere in Europe. In the United States, it is true, a modest rearmament was underway, but even the draft was being resisted and, more important, the country was firmly opposed to intervention—as it would continue to be until the Japanese government decided otherwise.

As for Britain, it was entirely unrealistic to hope that the British army would ever be able to effect a landing on the Continent with forces large enough to avoid prompt defeat, and Rommel's fighting in North Africa clearly suggested that only an unachievable material superiority could prevail over the German army's high morale, superior skills, and talented officers. If Hitler won his Russian war, as he had won his wars in Poland, Denmark, Norway, the Low Countries, France, Yugoslavia, and Greece, only the Royal Air

Force would stand in his path when he would turn back from the east to finish off beleaguered Britain—after first strengthening the Luftwaffe with all the vast resources that his conquests and the army's demobilization could provide. The previous year's defensive victory had been won, by a very thin margin, against German fighters and bombers prepared exclusively for short-range work in the battle of France and quite unready for a totally unexpected and very different battle of Britain.

No such luck could again be expected: once the Luftwaffe was actually organized for the task, by any sober calculation the Royal Air Force would be gradually destroyed in a futile struggle to prevent British cities from being bombed into ruins, before the inevitable invasion that would bring the new order of the Gestapo, SS, and concentration camp in its wake. Even if the Soviet Union somehow survived, which then seemed improbable, and a protracted war ensued saving Britain from invasion, it would still be only the Royal Air Force that could serve as a valid military instrument to bring the war to some acceptable conclusion. Hence Sir Charles Portal and his colleagues of the Royal Air Force—until recently very much the junior service—found themselves in a position of unexpected importance, inspiring perhaps but of such enormous responsibility as to be viewed with awe, if not terror. In that vortex of emotions, of pride, hope, and the deepest anxiety, it was a natural reflex to seek a way through the dark woods by a plan systematic and seemingly conclusive, in whose mechanics they could absorb themselves and whose most precise arithmetic offered relief from the dreadful uncertainties of the hour.

Prime Minister Churchill inhabited exactly the same circumstances, and as a man of strong and uninhibited feelings he must have been subject to that same emotional vortex in full force, compounded by a far greater personal responsibility. It was his refusal to accept Hitler's peace proposals of 1940 that had caused 93,000 British civilian men, women, and children to die in the blitz, and now left Britain in sinister isolation before the German victory in Russia that seemed certain. A parliamentary rejection of his leadership, his replacement by more reasonable men who could better deal with Hitler, a negotiated British admission into Europe's New Order, his exile to die in obscurity, are all black fantasies today—but they were sober possibilities in September 1941, as any glance at the contemporary evidence will reveal.[3]

For Churchill, too, a successful campaign by Bomber Command

was the only possible instrument of salvation, national, political, even personal. And yet, in a triumph of strategic insight that overcame emotional turbulence and cut across technical complexities, Winston Churchill's reply to Portal (1) decisively refuted the proposition that war could be won by bombardment alone ("all that we have learned since the war began shows that its effects, both physical and moral, are greatly exaggerated"); (2) anticipated the coming German defensive reaction to the modest amount of bombing already underway, specifically forecast the then unforeseen prominence of night fighters within it, and depicted the current campaign as heading for failure as Germany reacted ("it seems very likely that the ground defenses and night fighters will *overtake* the Air attack," as indeed they did after mid-1942); (3) predicted that the German reaction to successful area bombing would be to disperse and decentralize the war industries, instead of passively accepting their cumulative destruction ("all things are always on the move simultaneously [the source of the dynamic paradox], and it is quite possible that the Nazi war-making power in 1943 will be so widely spread throughout Europe as to be to a large extent independent of the actual buildings in the homeland"); (4) warned against the treachery of precise numbers in calculations that could not include the great unknown variable of the enemy's reaction ("I deprecate . . . expressing that confidence [in the plan] in terms of arithmetic"). Churchill concluded with these words: "One has to do the best one can, but he is an unwise man who thinks that there is any *certain* method of winning this war, or any other war, between equals in strength. The only plan is to persevere."[4]

Bomber Command was Britain's sole offensive instrument, and it did receive a very high priority for scarce high-quality manpower and industrial production. But it never attained a strength of 4,000 bombers on line (at its peak, in April 1945, it had 1,609 aircraft[5]) because Portal's implicit suggestion that the army and navy be reduced for its sake was firmly rejected. It is interesting to note that, after the entry of the United States into the war and the arrival of the Eighth Air Force on the scene, an inward-looking plan of systematic bombardment was actually implemented in 1943. This plan, moreover, not only violated the logic of strategy by discounting the enemy's defensive reaction, but also aspired to high efficiency by a specialized bombing effort, which ignored the enemy's industrial response.

Convinced that its bombers heavily armed with eleven machine guns apiece could protect themselves against German fighters by forming mutually protective formations that would need no fighter escort, the leaders of the Eighth Air Force intended to bomb in daylight, in order to hit specific industrial targets, as opposed to the random city bombing of Bomber Command. Its attacks, moreover, would obtain a high output for the bombing input by being focused against key links in German industry which also happened to be bottlenecks. The British Ministry of Economic Warfare had long advocated just this approach, and it had identified an ideal target in the Schweinfurt factories that reportedly produced two-thirds of all German ballbearings. Because each tank and truck, every engine for aircraft, ships, submarines, indeed virtually all machines with moving parts, required ballbearings, the ministry had long claimed that the destruction of the Schweinfurt factories would translate into a colossal decline of German war capacity across the board.[6]

Air Marshal Arthur Harris, chief of Bomber Command, ridiculed such schemes and scathingly referred to "panacea" targets; it was his belief that the target experts "went completely mad" over the ballbearings.[7] (One wag suggested that perhaps shoelace factories should be destroyed instead, to cause the Germans to surrender after they could no longer keep boots on their feet.) For the Eighth Air Force, however, which was rigidly committed to precision day-light bombing and whose strength could not quickly grow enough to make much impact by industry-wide bombing, the narrowly focused "bottleneck" approach was very attractive, and Schwein-furt the ideal target.

In the event, the Eighth Air Force first bombed the ballbearing factories in that city on August 17, 1943, and then again on October 14. Its concept of unescorted, self-defending bomber formations flying in daylight failed decisively. In spite of their eleven machine guns apiece, the bombers did poorly against German fighters, and their losses far exceeded any level that could be sustained: no fewer than 60 out of 376 American bombers were shot down in the first raid, and 77 out of 291 in the second.[8] As for the damage inflicted, it was not insignificant—but the impact on Germany's war capacity certainly was. Ballbearings in stock and some imports from Sweden and Switzerland supplied immediate needs, full production was soon restarted, and slide bearings were substituted for many uses, circumventing the potential bottleneck.[9] Thus the narrowly special-ized attack on Schweinfurt stimulated a broad organizational reaction that confounded its intent, just as the large ships of the past had been adapted to neutralize the torpedo boat, and modern armored forces evolved to cope with the antitank missile.

While the German response to precision bombing was decentralization and substitution, the wider response to bombing in general was nothing less than the conversion of the entire economy to a total war basis. This was a response that the Americans and British could not possibly have anticipated, because of the universal belief that the German economy was already fully organized for war and had been since before 1939. With compulsory universal labor enforced in Britain since 1940, and with all nonessential trades and services eliminated or severely restricted, it was never imagined that in Germany most women were still at home, that there were more than a million domestic servants, and that such trades as bookbinding were still thriving. Hitler, as the leader who quite deliberately started the war, was ill placed to demand sacrifice, and the state of the German economy reflected that fundamental political fact. It was only from 1943 that the German economy was truly mobilized for war, under the impulse of the Stalingrad defeat with its ominous consequences and worse forebodings. With energies more fully harnessed, the output of military equipment and supplies increased sharply, bringing about a totally unforeseen, unexpected, and inevitably paradoxical correlation between the tonnage of bombs dropped on Germany and the volume of German war production.

Within this process, the bombing was in itself a contributing factor. Though it did destroy factory buildings and workers, it also destroyed the urban framework of the leisurely days of peace; with the restaurants gone, canteens much more efficient in every way became the only alternative; with houses gone and their residents evacuated to the countryside, house servants were forced into industrial work. In some ways, therefore, the bombing actually assisted the German economy as it reacted to outmaneuver the huge but still narrow phenomenon of bombing.

The story is well known and has been recounted many times.[10] It is a classic case of seemingly definitive and systematically cumulative action not only confounded but also in part made self-defeating by the very nature of the strategic predicament. Churchill was of course exceptional in his intuitive understanding of the paradoxical logic of strategy, with its perversion of every logical action and its reversal of opposites. (The title of the concluding volume of his war memoirs is *Triumph and Tragedy*; it could have been "victory and defeat.") But there is no need of Churchills to cause grand strategy to exist. Just as the laws of physics governed the universe long before there were physicists to study them, so are those who command power on the international scene subject to the logic of strategy. Whether the decisions of national leaders are made in wisdom or in folly, in criminal ambition or in benevolence, whether they are praised or condemned, *their consequences* are governed by that logic so long as the conflictual predicament obtains, disappointing all expectations of continuity, all hopes of unceasing progression.

FROM WAR TO PEACE AND PEACE TO WAR

Thus war is the origin of peace, by the total victory of one side or another, by sheer exhaustion, or—much more often in history—because the conflict of aims that originally caused the war is resolved by the transformation of aims which war itself brings about: under the impact of its costs in blood, treasure, and agony, the worth of whatever was to be gained, or defended, is reconsidered against its true price, and then ambitions are diminished or renounced.

Having started the fight hoping that something of value was to be gained at acceptable cost, the attacker who meets with unexpectedly strong resistance might persist until even the full realization of his intended gain will offer no complete compensation for what he has already sacrificed in blood, treasure, tranquillity, and prestige. Having started to fight by another's choice, the defender will also have framed some initial purpose for his resistance—a purpose deemed worthy of sacrifice before its extent could be known. When the original hopes of attack or defense are disappointed, as so often happens, success may yet seem tantalizingly near, perhaps to be won with just one more effort, a few more casualties, a little more wealth expended after so many casualties suffered and after so much wealth consumed (the asymmetrical position of those who face the loss of everything in defeat is obvious and can be of great moment in strengthening resistance).

It may have been the prospect of gaining much for little that originally made war attractive. But if the costs of war are unexpectedly large, their very magnitude will be an incentive to persist during an intermediate stage: the greater the sacrifice, the greater the need to justify it by finally achieving the advertised gain. During that stage, the external conduct of belligerents is apt to be conditioned by the internal predicament of the original war party or war leader, whose fortunes will depend on how their past responsibility for the war is viewed—which in turn depends on the present view of the future outcome; the incentive to sustain the hope of victory is then very strong. But as the war continues, a shift in perspectives eventually takes place by which the results originally hoped for are finally compared not to the sacrifices already made but rather to the further sacrifices that seem likely if the war continues. The original war party or war leader may retain power, but in any case it is now that the aims of war can begin to be revised on one side or both, eventually bringing hostilities to an end when the aims of both sides finally become congruent.* That is how most wars, ancient and modern, have ended, with the characterizing phenomenon of war—the process of reciprocal destruction—itself being the agent of the subsequent peace.

War fully achieved, with forces fought out, every promising expedient duly tried and much destruction suffered and inflicted, therefore leads to a peace that can be stable—if the victor's demands are sufficiently modest to evoke no powerful resentment in the defeated, and if the immediate resistance of fresh belligerents fearful of the novel power of the victor is not aroused. If, by contrast, war is cut short by some external force before its aim-changing effect is achieved, a fragile peace will result. So it was in the past when war was still fought within the span of campaigning seasons and could be abruptly interrupted by early snows, only to resume in the spring, and so it is again today when rival superpowers intervene to impose abrupt cease-fires on their warring clients. This notably has been true of the Arab-Israeli wars since 1948—all prevented from having a peacemaking effect because the clash of aims subsisted in each case, in waiting to cause renewed war. The

---

*Even World War II, a most peculiar struggle between aggressors with very large but limited aims and victims who demanded unconditional surrender, came to an end only when the minimal Japanese demand for the continuity of the imperial institution was accepted. The Korean war, in every way a classic conflict (for which the term "limited war" was invented only because the extraordinary world war was temporarily accepted as ordinary), ended in classic fashion, with the reciprocal reduction of aims.

destruction of war is deplorable, but causes the peace to come; humanitarian sentiment may applaud its interruption, but then the likeliest outcome is renewed war, and not a peace perhaps achievable if destruction were left to run its course.

Even when fought with spears or clubs, war could always be totally destructive for the participants, to the point of causing the extinction of entire human communities. But until the advent of nuclear weapons, the scope of its possible destruction could be minimized before the fact by optimism and in any case remained quite uncertain. Hence the gains that war could offer might be seen in sharp, idealized relief against the dull background of its potential losses, which could easily appear as tolerable, even insignificant. By the normal workings of the paradoxical logic of strategy, nuclear weapons have remained unused ever since they evolved from the extreme destructive power of the very first fission devices (each worth a thousand-bomber raid), to the far greater destructive power of the thermonuclear weapons still with us today, of which middling specimens are equivalent to 100,000 bomberloads of World War II. No more than anything else in strategy can the utility of explosives increase in linear continuity. The ten-ton loadings of American bombers in 1945 were more useful than the two-ton loadings of 1940 German bombers over London, and hundred-ton or even thousand-ton loads could have been more useful still. But in that, too, reversal had to come eventually, instead of the steady progression that strategy will not allow, and now the destructive power of thermonuclear weapons overshoots by far the culminating point of military utility. They can therefore achieve the peace-inducing effect of war without need of its actual phenomena of destruction.

It is true that in the comparison between envisaged gains and sacrifices that shapes deliberate war-starting decisions, the scope of the possible damage suffered may still be clouded by uncertainty: even powers amply supplied with nuclear weapons may yet fight "conventionally" or employ only a few of the smallest weapons as gestures of token effect. But it is no longer possible to slight the destructive consequences of any nuclear attack, as the consequences of anticipated cavalry incursions, sieges, or even conventional bombing raids could always be minimized in the past by animal optimism, and by the perceptual assymetry between war gains vividly imagined and war losses dimly feared. It is the *definitive*, indeed measurable, character of nuclear destruction rather than the possible but uncertain magnitude of its scope that inhibits the resort to nuclear war. This quality of scientific predict-ability has altered the millennial terms of comparison between the worth of war aims and their cost. In the presence of nuclear weapons, the perceptual balance that was once achieved only in the midst of war, when its costs were experienced in the flesh, is now in effect before war begins.

Peace can be the origin of war in diverse ways, even though peace is only a negative abstraction that contains no characterizing phenomenon to lead to its own undoing, as war destruction even-tually destroys war or as the mere anticipation of nuclear destruc-tion largely destroys the possibility of nuclear war. Nevertheless, the conditions of peace (the absence of war) may sometimes create the preconditions of war merely because they relax the vigilance and dissuade the war readiness of the peaceful, while allowing the uninterrupted strengthening of those who crave the gains of war. Often in history, peace led to war because its conditions allowed demographic, cultural, economic, and social changes that disturbed the equilibrium of warmaking power and the equilibrium of collec-tive self-images upon which the peace had rested. Having no sub-stance of its own, the state of peace cannot disturb anything, but it does indifferently favor the diverse evolution of human capacities and mentalities, without regard to the symmetries and asymmetries that inhibit war. It was thus that the hitherto pacific Germans came to regard themselves as a warrior nation by 1870, in unfortunate coincidence with the French, who had yet to outgrow their martial self-image.

The transformation of mentalities that creates war-inducing ten-sions between the *status* of a country (perhaps the fossilized result of previous war) and its *self-image* must have profound causes, but its effects are very obvious: what was once deemed acceptable becomes an intolerable vexation; the degree of prestige once judged high enough becomes a felt humiliation; what once was an impos-sible dream is now seen as a realistic prospect. It was during the great post-Napoleonic peace that war-inhibiting ratios of military strength were displaced by the iron, coal, and steam engines of the industrial revolution, which yielded novel and war-inducing ratios of military strength between Prussia and the Hapsburg Empire by 1866, between Germany and France by 1870, between Imperial Russia and the Ottoman Empire by 1876, between Japan and China by 1894, and between the United States and Spain by 1898.

In war, the capacity to wage further war is abridged by war's own destruction, whether by the systematic bombardment of industry as in the last world war or by the excess of killings over the natural increase of fighting-age populations, as in the struggles of warring tribes from the first. In peacetime, by contrast, every form of human progress and demographic expansion also tends to increase warmaking capacities, and in a manner that will only be fortuitously symmetrical and therefore war-inhibiting. If peace did not induce war, there would be no war—for war cannot perpetuate itself and always accomplishes its own destruction.

THE DEFEAT OF VICTORY

If victory did not tend toward defeat, if growing power did not contain the cause of its own undoing, Hitler's swift expansion would never have culminated in a downfall, because all Europe would have been ruled by a single power long before his birth. And the same would have been true of Napoleon's conquest and collapse, and of all his lesser predecessors, going back across the centuries to the Roman Empire's own very long cycle of expansion and decline.

So great are the economies of scale of the larger power over the smaller in the accumulation of military strength, so significant even the mere geometric advantage of reducing the proportion of frontier length for the space, population, and wealth enclosed, other things being equal, that the larger should have prevailed over the smaller in Europe's abundant wars until only one state remained, enclosing all the space that could advantageously be reached from a single center of power. And this extended right across Europe and Asia Minor, deep into the North African desert, and far into Mesopotamia even in the technological circumstances of the Romans. What happened instead was the "balancing" of power, whereby the very strength of the larger power evoked the counterweighting fear and hostility of another large state till then indifferent, or induced smaller powers to coalesce in order to form a barrier of resistance to its further expansion. States whose means of action were growing, because of rising population and prosperity, or because a more centralized governance was harnessing more of both, could employ their rising strength to expand, but only up to a certain point.

This limit would be reached when the growing economies of scale were matched by the increasing resistance of a newly hostile state or coalition. A paralyzing equilibrium at that culminating point might then be accepted by the expanding state, or it might try to form an equilibrium-breaking alliance of its own, if it could find others interested in the venture. Or the barrier of resistance might be tested in war, and then the same logic of strategy would prevail whether the outcome were victory or defeat. If the expanding state wins its war, while still on the rising curve of success, its victory would evoke the fear and hostility of still other states that until then were shielded by the state or coalition lately defeated. Thus once again expansion would encounter a barrier of resistance. If the expanding state loses, its defeat would be moderated by newfound friends bent on resisting its victorious rival; or if it is a coalition that prevails, its very victory would weaken it, by reviving the contentions that were suppressed when cohesion was imperative to resist the expanding power. (A total victory would totally destroy a coalition, by the inevitable paradox.)

Beyond the direct participants in each contention, there are other powers large and small that are affected at each remove. The coalition formed to resist an expanding power in one region might itself be threatening to others elsewhere, which might then seek alliance with the larger power being contained, overturning the equilibrium within the arena because there is no equilibrium for them. The rules are very simple, but the game can be very complicated. By processes smoother when there are more states in direct proximity sharing more of a common culture, and by processes more abrupt and by clumsier combinations when there are fewer participants less closely conversant with one another, Europe's disunity was preserved from the days of the Roman downfall by the reversal of victory and defeat, of expansion and retreat. In still earlier days, we can see the same dynamics at work among the Greek city-states before the Macedonian primacy, insofar as our sources illuminate their vicissitudes, and later among the Hellenistic region-states that emerged from the division of Alexander's empire. And what we know of the dealings of the Gallic tribes with one another, of the Germanic tribes beyond the Rhine, and of the Italic states reveals the same paradoxical logic in action.

In our own day we see before us, in perfect clarity, the states of Europe in tentative and partial coalition to maintain a barrier of resistance against Soviet power, with the faint suggestion of a like resistance to American power as well—a resistance that would be much sharper (if still not warlike) if Europe were stronger, the Soviet Union weaker, and American support less urgently needed. But of course Europe holds no monopoly over the phenomena of strategy. Those who know of Japan before the Tokugawa centralization and during earlier periods also; those who have studied the ancient China of the warring states and the modern China of the warlords, as well as any of the intervals between consolidated dynasties; those who are familiar with the history of the Indian states before the British and before the Moguls, or with the doings of the tribes and rulers that neither encompassed; those who observe the abrupt alliances, sudden hostilities, and revolving coalitions of the contemporary Arab world; and indeed all who survey the dealings of rival states and warring tribes at any time and in any place may interpret events through the Italian Renaissance concept of the balance of power, and even apply its terminology, without fear of anachronism or distortion.[11]

Given the universality of the strategic predicament, it is the exceptions that demand explanation. Europe remained divided through the centuries and is still not united today, but China had long periods of unity in the past and is virtually united now. In Japan the rise and fall of warlords was finally brought to an end by a single government. Where before there were warring states there is now unity, as in Italy and Spain (and once in Germany), and of course the European experience itself begins with the Roman Empire, which could never have come into existence unless expansion could yield further expansion.

To note that the paradoxical logic of strategy reemerged as soon as a central power was weakened, if only by the personal failings of a ruler, diminishes the scope of what must be explained but not the need to explain. Actually the answer arises directly from the definition of strategy itself: in settings of consensual governance, as in those of production and consumption, where conflict and strife are bounded by law and custom, linear logic applies in full, and the paradoxical logic of strategy not at all. Continuity and stability are therefore possible, and without need of an ultimately exhausting effort to resist the dissolution of what is, and its replacement by its opposite. Hence the perpetual quest for *legitimacy* by the rulers and regimes that have no natural claim upon it, either from a dynastic authority still unchallenged, from some transcendental source, or from electoral reconfirmation. To have a formal and prolonged acceptance by set rules, as opposed to transient approval derived from a recent remission from destructive strife, or a ruler's personal popularity, or a good harvest, is of surpassing importance precisely because it alone can remove governance from the travails and reversals of the strategic predicament.

A few rulers of ascriptive legitimacy still exist here and there, and many more democracies; but the states ruled by repressive regimes of weak legitimacy or none at all are much more numerous still. In the latter, politics are warlike even if quite bloodless, and the paradoxical logic of strategy applies to full effect, requiring constant vigilance by the rulers and a steady effort to prevent the undoing of their power. There is thus a grand strategy of sorts even within the governance of single states.

So far we have observed the logic of strategy very largely in the setting of war. Yet it comprehends not merely warfare underway but human conduct in the context of possible war. Insofar as states act to prepare or to avoid war, or use a capacity for warmaking to extort concessions by intimidation without any actual use of force, the logic of strategy applies in full, just as much as in war itself and regardless of what instruments of statecraft are employed. Thus, except for their purely administrative aspect, diplomacy, propaganda, secret operations, and economic controls are all subject to the logic of strategy, as elements in the adversarial dealings of states with one another.

II

THE LEVELS
OF STRATEGY

Introduction

We have seen how the sequence of action, culmination, decline, and reversal of the paradoxical logic pervades the realm of strategy. It conditions both the competition and struggle of entire nations and the most detailed interaction of weapons and countermeasures in exactly the same way, for the same logic is manifest on the largest scale and also the smallest, in all forms of war and in adversarial peacetime diplomacy as well. The dynamic contention of opposed wills is the common source of this logic that never changes, but the factors it conditions vary according to the level of the encounter. The *technical* interplay of specific weapons and counterweapons is subordinated to the *tactical* combat of the forces that employ those particular weapons, and the strengths and weaknesses of those forces derive from all sorts of intangible and material factors that are very different from the scientific and engineering limitations of weapons. Completely self-contained acts of combat are possible (indeed this defines "commando" raids), but usually the tactical-level moves of particular units of the armed forces on each side are merely subordinated parts of larger actions involving many units, and this *operational* level governs the consequences of what is done and not done tactically. Again the factors conditioned by the logic are different: details of topography or disposition, for example, are now submerged, and it is the overall interaction of the respective schemes of warfare that matters.

Events at the operational level can be very large in scale, but never autonomous; they are governed in turn by the broader interaction of the armed forces as whole within the entire theater of warfare, just as battles are merely parts of campaigns. It is at this higher level of *theater strategy* that the consequences of single operations are felt in the overall conduct of offense and defense—those overriding military purposes that scarcely figure at the operational level, in which a bombing campaign might be launched by defenders while the aggressor is preoccupied with air defense, and in which an attack can serve to better defend a front while holding operations on some sectors often figure in offensive warfare.

The entire conduct of warfare and peacetime preparation for war are in turn subordinate expressions of national struggles that unfold at the highest level of *grand strategy,* where all that is military happens within the much broader context of domestic governance, international politics, economic activity, and their ancillaries. Because ultimate ends and basic means are both manifest only at the level of grand strategy, the resource limits of military action are defined at that level, and so is its true meaning: even a most successful conquest is only a provisional result that can be overturned by the diplomatic intervention of more powerful states or even repudiated by domestic political decision; by contrast, even a major military debacle can be redeemed by the political transformations it engenders, or undone by the newfound allies that weakness can attract in the usual workings of the balance of power.

The five levels form a definite hierarchy, but outcomes are not simply imposed in a one-way transmission from top to bottom because the levels interact with one another in a two-way process. Technical effects only matter insofar as they have tactical consequences, but tactical-level action depends in turn upon technical performance to some extent, just as many tactical events make up the operational level even as the latter determines their significance. Similarly, unfolding operations have their effect at the level of theater strategy, which defines their purpose, while military activity as a whole affects what happens at the level of grand strategy even as the scope of such activity is determined at that highest level.

Strategy, then, has two dimensions: the vertical dimension of the different levels that interact with one another; and the horizontal dimension of the dynamic logic that unfolds concurrently within each level. Our investigation began with the horizontal dimension, and references to this or that level were baldly introduced with no attempt at systematic explanation, so as to leave the scene clear for the first encounter with the paradoxical logic in action and its sometimes surprising results.

A neat set of definitions of the five levels, each carefully worded and laid out in suggestive tabular form, might now seem appropriate. But our subject is as varied as human life, often charged with powerful emotions, constrained by institutional habits and urges, clouded by the uncertain particulars of time and place of each encounter, so that definitional nets made by abstract phrasemaking can capture only the hollow forms of strategy and not its protean content. A great many definitions of tactics and of other levels of strategy are already in circulation, but it is enough to look at any one of them to visualize immediately a host of exceptions. And if these are embraced by the further definition of sundry subcategories, an entire glossary would eventually be needed to remind ourselves of what we mean by our own terminology, without advancing our understanding of the real content of strategy in any way.

Let us therefore proceed by plunging into the substance of strategic encounters, this time to dissect them into their component levels. As we focus on each level in turn before finally standing back to examine their dynamic totality, we will uncover the boundary lines of the *natural stratification* of conflictual phenomena. When we do venture upon definitions, then, we will not be erecting a verbal edifice of our own making but merely expressing observed realities.

Given this purpose, we may proceed within the boundaries of just one large case, the defense of Western Europe, which is examined level by level in what follows. We can begin by considering the claim, frequently heard nowadays, that the forces of the North Atlantic Treaty Organization* could successfully oppose a Soviet offensive in Europe by relying on "high-technology" nonnuclear defenses, so that the Alliance would no longer need the expensive armored and mechanized forces now fielded or—above all— nuclear weapons, except to dissuade the Soviet Union from using its own nuclear forces.

* Hereafter called "the Alliance."

CHAPTER 5

THE TECHNICAL LEVEL

The varied nonnuclear defense proposals for Europe now in circulation, which in practice focus on the defense of the four hundred miles or so of the "central front" marked by the West German border, are all based on some combination of two ideas. One is the notion, already familiar, of confronting invading tank and mechanized-infantry divisions with infantry in large numbers, abundantly armed with antitank missiles.[1] In some proposals, these would be regular troops and would wholly displace the present armored and mechanized divisions, which are certainly costly, and which some describe as "provocative" because they could undoubtedly be used to attack as well as defend. In other proposals, the antitank missile infantry would consist of reserve or militia units that would be added to the current regular forces, to provide a new first layer for the defense.

The other notion, not quite so simple, would harness recent advances in a variety of techniques to form complete "deep-attack" systems of satellite or airborne sensors, communications, control centers, and long-range missiles with separately aimed "submunitions," capable in sequence of identifying and locating mechanized vehicles and other moving targets hundreds of miles away, of relaying the information to computerized control centers where engagement decisions could immediately be made, and finally of attacking the targets en masse. Such systems could therefore attack tank and mechanized columns on the move, to delay, disorganize, and diminish them, long before they could reach the front to add their momentum and firepower to an offensive.

As we contemplate the two ideas, we might begin to imagine how the intended enemy would react, moving to negate or outmaneuver them with increasing effect, thus forcing them down from their culminating point of success while absorbing the increasing costs of

doing so. But my purpose is to uncover the general workings of
strategy rather than to examine the ultimate merit of these particular proposals, and we must therefore examine the still-picture view
of each level in sequence, rather than the moving film of dynamic
interactions within a single level. In approaching matters not entirely simple, we have the advantage of being able to start by retrac-
ing our steps through the familiar ground of the antitank missile
question, albeit in a novel way, before repeating the procedure for
the deep-attack proposal—which will eventually lead us into the
complexities of the nuclear balance.

THE WAR OF THE WEAPONS

Let us begin by examining the confrontation of weapons, each
assumed to be manned by competent crews, of which we need
know nothing else at this stage. On the one side, we see the tanks
and mechanized-infantry combat carriers that form the cutting edge
of Soviet divisions on the move, seeking to break through the Alliance front. On the other, we see the infantry with its antitank
missiles, perhaps stationed in open ground or perhaps protected in
concrete firing positions—but at this level of strategy we take no
account of that, just as we ignore how the Soviet tanks are moving,
whether exposed in full view or cleverly probing forward within
covered approaches. At this level, it is enough to see just one antitank missile and one Soviet tank or combat carrier, and they might
as well be facing each other on a featureless firing range.

We note that the antitank missile is a very cheap weapon as
compared to the tank or even the combat carrier, its cost perhaps 1
percent of the tank's or 10 percent at most of the combat carrier's;
and while it takes no more than two men to form a missile-launcher
crew, the tank will contain three or four men and so will the vehicle
crew of the combat carrier, not counting the infantrymen it takes to
the battlefield. By whatever computation we make of human service and life, that difference further improves the economy of the
antitank missile.

Next we see that the missile can assuredly be guided to its target,
and if we test a number of them we find that they strike home 90
percent of the time. The hollow-charge warhead will easily penetrate the thin armor of the combat carrier with high-velocity plasma
that will devastate everything and everybody inside. The tank

might have advanced ceramic armor and internal protection enhancements, but in our still-picture view we are already examining missiles equally advanced, with stand-off precision warheads of sufficient size to penetrate tank armor. The tank is of course firing with its machine guns and even the main cannon, or if it is a combat carrier then it too is firing, perhaps with a small mortar or automatic grenade launcher in addition to its machine guns. But the missile has a much greater range than those weapons, except for the cannon and mortar, and it has an excellent chance of destroying its target before the tank gunner or mortar man on board the carrier can find its range and hit accurately. At night matters stand the same, for each side is using night-vision devices, and actually the missile launchers of the Alliance should be fitted with more effective devices, offering a clearer picture at longer range with less ambient light; certainly the tank or combat carrier are much larger and more easily spotted.

In numbers, which can describe everything we can observe at this level of strategy, we see that 90 percent of all missiles will function correctly, 90 percent will in turn hit the target, 80 percent of them will penetrate the armor, of which 90 percent will cause immobilizing damage within—to yield a 58 percent cumulative probability of success.* We might then estimate that in straight duels fought over our featureless range by competent, emotionless crews, each tank can destroy one antitank missile before being destroyed in turn, and each combat carrier can destroy two, so that 1.58 missiles will be required to destroy tanks that cost one hundred times as much and 2.58 missiles to destroy combat carriers that cost more than fifteen times as much. We therefore see the technical confrontation of missile and armored vehicle categorically resolved in favor of the former, and with a very large margin of advantage.

As some do, we might stop here and present this technical result as the final and sufficient truth—as it might be if we were examining, say, an encounter between antiballistic missile defenses and Soviet long-range ballistic missiles within the great featureless range of space. Then indeed any exchange-ratio advantage greater than the possible disproportion in the resources that each side could apply to the effort would be a sufficient truth for some purposes at least, to determine for example the sheer feasibility of the venture.

---

*That is, immobilization; nonrepairable catastrophic damage is much less likely.

For us, however, to uncover the technical level of strategy in the encounter between the antitank missile and its foes is only a beginning, which yields a partial and highly provisional truth. The technical level has an importance of its own, to be sure, and now more than in the past when change was slow and differences in technical capacity were of much smaller effect. Such weapons as jet fighters, battle tanks, or submarines can nowadays outclass their slightly less modern predecessors in a manner not to be compared to whatever differences there were between any two competent swords of the same era—though even in classical antiquity technical superiority could sometimes be decisive, as when the Huns first appeared at the end of the fourth century with small compound bows, short enough to be used on horseback yet of unprecedented striking power.

This bounding of the technical level of strategy is not arbitrary. What we have uncovered (rather than defined) is the level within which the weapons of war and their interaction can be observed in a particular dimension of reality, a partial reality, to be sure, because all other material and intangible circumstances remain indeterminate—but reality nonetheless. The technical level as here defined certainly encompasses all the reality that is of professional interest to a great many people occupied in the military realm, specifically the scientists and engineers engaged in the development of weapons. On what aspects of performance are especially desired, and on how much performance is to be sought overall at the expense of numbers, scientists and engineers do receive instruction supposedly derived from higher-level considerations. Subject to that, however, their work proceeds entirely within the boundaries of the technical level, in pursuit of goals that are strictly technical—even though the weapons they develop will express their capacity at all the higher levels of strategy.

While the consequences of the technical reverberate throughout the realm of strategy, as indeed in all that is material of human life, only the abstract theories of science, mere immaterial words and numbers, set limits to its scope. In recent times, those limits have been expanding quite rapidly, but at any one moment they are impenetrable barriers for the technician as such. The theories or "laws" of science can be revoked at any time, but till then their power is absolute. Not so, by contrast, are the other guidelines that define the goals and limits of technical development, military or political.

SOLDIERS AND TECHNICIANS

Technicians will rarely be familiar with the detailed texture of the current military requirements they are instructed to meet. Also, such instructions will often obtain only a formal obedience: technicians are well aware of the transience of military requirements, as they see new doctrines and new "strategies" enunciated every few years while their own artifacts endure for decades. Technicians, moreover, are scarcely inclined to respect requirements formulated by authorites who are seen as lacking in knowledge about the full range of possibilities open to them. The militarization of technicians that has proceeded since ancient times, and the increasingly technical education of military men ever since the eighteenth century, has not closed the divide; each group is subject to a different authority, that of the corpus of applied science on one side and that of nontechnical military hierarchies on the other.

There is not merely a barrier of ignorance, then, but also one of divergent purposes. For the military bureaucracy, the maximal quality attainable in the single weapon must usually be sacrificed for the sake of numbers: to reduce the magnitude of the forces is to reduce the base of the hierarchy. For the technician, on the other hand, numbers have no value in themselves: maximal quality is the only goal of his ambition qua technician, expressed by the most complete single weapon with the highest possible performance.

Before and during World War I, it was the largest and best-protected battleships and the railway guns of longest range that excited technical ambition, the former in accordance with perceived naval needs, the latter not at all congruent with contemporary artillery requirements, which called for mobility. Before and during World War II, the paths of technical ambition proliferated to yield a galaxy of innovations, some of immediate military value (radar, for example, and the fission bomb) and others of negative value at the time (the German V-1, V-2, and V-3, the Maus super-tank). Today developmental ambition focuses on directed-energy weapons, on the larger supersonic fighters fully equipped electronically, nuclear-powered submarines now of cruiser size, and very large aircraft carriers. Naturally the effect is to reduce numbers, down to levels that do not correspond to the actualities of war in some cases—as with fighters whose annual output does not exceed the number that may be lost in a bad morning of large-scale air combat.

It is fashionable to deplore the tendency to pursue quality at the expense of quantity, at least in the United States, but the paradoxical logic of strategy, at any of its levels, is irrelevant to the question, and no insight we may have into that logic can guide the choice. The technical-level action that evokes a reaction may indifferently proceed from many simpler weapons or fewer and more ambitious weapons. It is, instead, linear commonsense logic that imposes limits on the pursuit of quality at the expense of numbers, because the marginal utility of quality increments must eventually diminish toward zero within the boundaries of scientific application at any one time: the very best rifle producible, constructed of the most advanced materials with the latest techniques, can be only slightly more effective than an ordinary modern rifle, which is based on the same scientific principles but costs much less. And so it is for bombers, missiles, submarines, or any other weapons we may compare. We know that we are not in the realm of strategy because, as unit quality increases, the increment of effectiveness obtained can only fall to zero and not go below it (unless reliability or some such is abusively removed from what is meant by quality). If strategy's dynamic paradox ruled the outcome, by contrast, quality increments would actually begin to reduce the effectiveness of single weapons after a certain point.

Tensions between military priorities and technical goals are constantly negotiated by technically minded military men, and militarily minded technicians, the marginal members of each group. But when the products of technical development are finally handed over to the armed forces, it is mainstream views, and prior institutional interests (often the remnants of previous technical developments), that will govern their employment. When the new is an incremental improvement over the old, military innovation follows directly, impeded only by incidental frictions likely to be resolved over time. But if the new is the result of invention, if the new weapon has no direct predecessor, then the armed forces must change by creating new units to adopt it, at the expense of some previously established units. Existing units are represented in the councils of decision to some degree, while the units yet to come obviously are not; and the overall expansion that relieves such conflict is always restrained by scarcity in one form or another (typically money in peacetime and manpower in wartime). This simplification of the familiar institutional barriers to innovation can be seen in hydraulic terms, wherein force expansion is the relief valve, and the outcome is manifest in the speed, or lack of it, with which the old gives way to the new.

But innovation may not only be slow or fast—it may also fail outright, either because of a social resistance that simply does not yield to technical change[2] or because of a complete misapplication. A famous case of aborted innovation, very rapid as it happens, was that of the *mitrailleuse*, a machine gun hurriedly adopted by the French army in 1869, in anticipation of war with Prussia. In a world of single-shot rifles, the mitrailleuse could fire 300 rounds per minute accurate to at least 500 yards; it was quite reliable and, against infantry unprepared for its rapid fire, it should have had decisive effects. A Belgian invention, the mitrailleuse was manufactured in great secrecy by French arsenals at the behest of Napoleon III, and considerable numbers were ready when war with Prussia began in 1870.

But secrecy had prevented field exercises and tactical debate. Because the gun was too heavy to be manhandled and was therefore placed on a light carriage, which made it look like a field piece; because the infantry was unequipped to supply its ammunition needs at a time when 100 rounds per man sufficed for weeks of campaigning and each battalion could count only on a few horse-wagons already burdened with tents, food, and impedimenta; and because Napoleon III was himself an artillery expert (of world caliber), it was the artillery that received the mitrailleuse. When war came, French gunners naturally employed the new weapon as if it were a field piece, that is, well behind the infantry lines where it was out of range of its target and was itself fully vulnerable to the enemy's counterbattery fire aimed at the French artillery lines.[3]

It was too much to expect that the gunners would depart from all their usual notions to place any weapon of theirs among the infantry—to do so would have seemed an egregious retrogression to seventeenth-century ways. Nor could the new weapons be handed over to the infantry without transferring much-valued artillery ammunition wagons as well. As it happened, in the battle of Gravelotte on August 18, 1870, the Prussian infantry advanced enough to come within range of mitrailleuses unreduced by counterbattery fire. Firing the 25-round plates of cartridges at the rate of 12 per minute, the new weapons executed a massacre, accounting for many of the 20,163 Prussian casualties of that day.[4] But otherwise the mitrailleuse scarcely figured in the outcome of the war. Had innovation not been thus aborted, it might have averted the disastrous French defeat.

POLITICAL MASTERS AND TECHNICIANS

While there are tensions between technicians and military men that only institutional innovation can resolve, chronic dissonance is merely normal between the technical and the political spheres. The political aims of the state are usually so distant and vague for the technician that they hardly enter into his calculations. In rare cases, authority abruptly intervenes from above, to issue orders positive or negative. An American president may choose to close an avenue of development technically quite promising because it offends his ethical sense or perhaps the aesthetics of his public image. Another may order technicians to develop new weapons beyond the contemporary boundary of scientific possibility, as if the progress of science could be directed and accelerated by political decision and funding. A Hitler or a Stalin could bring dictatorship to bear in the laboratory and workshop, to decree that ballistic rockets or fission bombs be rapidly built.

There are recorded cases of intrusion just as spectacular from the scientific side, most momentously on October 11, 1939, when the influential economist Alexander Sachs handed over to President Roosevelt a letter signed by the already eminent Albert Einstein and a memorandum signed by another refugee scientist, the then unknown Leo Szilard, whose idea it all was. Both documents invited the American government to investigate the possibility of initiating a uranium chain reaction within a warlike device. Szilard's venture had been made possible by the assistance of two other refugee scientists, Eugene Wigner and Edward Teller: each was destined for future fame, but their essential role just then was to drive Szilard to Einstein's Long Island beach cabin on successive occasions; Szilard did not have a driver's license. According to the account left by Sachs, Roosevelt seemed inattentive as he read the letter and memorandum, and it was only on the following day at breakfast that Sachs finally persuaded Roosevelt to take the matter seriously, by recounting an anecdote about Napoleon's refusal to finance Fulton's steamship project.[5]

It was by circumstances at least as fortuitous—within the terms of what is consequential in science and engineering—that Nazi Germany failed to develop its own fission bomb. Hitler's enthusiasm was readily kindled by the prospect of building rockets, fusiform and roaring, and his support of rocketry was unstinting and tenacious. Nuclear physics, however, was a field notoriously filled with non-Aryans (including Szilard, Teller, and Wigner as well as Einstein) and was further condemned by Nazi thinkers for its disruption of clear-cut certainties; nor did the nuclear chain reaction find a German advocate properly Aryan who was as persistent as Leo Szilard.*

Only the fundamental dissonance between the technical and the political could have caused matters of such colossal effect to be decided so frivolously. Of course the American fission-bomb project would have started sooner or later, even if there had been no Szilard to arouse attention. But the delay could have been decisive, if Hitler's tastes had been different and the highest priority were assigned: Germany certainly possessed the material means to make its own fission bomb had the project begun by 1939.

In the aftermath of World War II with its dramatic episodes of scientific warfare, and in the wake of Alamogordo, Hiroshima, and Nagasaki, the notion that political leaders should not disregard the possibilities offered by deliberate technical development became part of the conventional wisdom. While scientific offices proliferated within governments and armed forces, official scientific advisers were added to the household staffs of presidents, prime ministers, and secretary generals. That, however, did much less to reduce the dissonance than might have been expected. For it turned out that there were only two kinds of technical questions: routine issues, over which no political decision is needed at all, and the controversial ones, over which scientists themselves also tend to disagree, usually in terms that laymen cannot understand.[6] Politicians are still the captains of the ship of state, and soldiers operate its gundeck, but now there are technicians in charge of the engine room, whose doings propel the ship on uncharted routes toward an unknown destination.

---

*The postwar claim of the leading German nuclear physicists (Heisenberg and others) that they deliberately refrained from developing a bomb was fraudulent.

CHAPTER 6

THE TACTICAL LEVEL

Coming back now to the case study of the Alliance defense in Germany, we can examine the antitank missile and its direct opponents at the next level of strategy. The picture before our eyes becomes rather larger and much fuller in detail: larger because we can no longer simplify the encounter into a duel, but must instead consider entire units facing one another, containing as many missile teams and armored vehicles as might *directly* interact within one combat episode; fuller because we are no longer comparing missiles and armored vehicles facing one another on a featureless test range with automaton crews.

First we must consider terrain and vegetation. Germany's eastward terrain is contoured in some degree, with no high mountains but with hill and vale, or at least folds in the ground that can now be important. There are covered approaches that Soviet armored vehicles can exploit, to appear suddenly before the antitank missiles at short range and so rob them of their great advantage of reach over machine guns. In extreme cases, the emergence of the visible target might occur at such short range that the antitank missile cannot be used at all; as a counterpart to its long reach, it suffers from a minimal range limit, within which the missile just launched cannot be gathered in time onto the aiming line of sight. (Antitank rockets suffer from no such limitation.)

On the other hand, there is also vegetation in which the antitank infantry can find concealment, and of course it can do more than merely mask its presence: it may also obtain vitally important protection even from the slightest terrain cover, at least against direct-fire weapons. Moreover, if there is time before the fight (a significant variable that may depend on the very highest level of strategy), the terrain may not only be exploited in its natural form but also enhanced by barriers such as antitank ditches and fortification. A few hours of work with shovels and saws might suffice to transform an exposed hillside into a fortified zone, with concealed firing positions and overhead cover, to resist indirect-fire howitzers and mortars. Or continuous barriers to impede the path of the attackers, as well as fortified firing positions, might already be prepared in solid concrete instead of mere earth, making an excellent contribution to the defense (contrary to all post–Maginot Line prejudice).

But then if their layout is clumsy, if firing positions stand out from the natural surroundings as well-marked targets, fortifications might doom the defenders: at this level of strategy, such things can be decisive in themselves, within that short moment in which the tactical encounter may be accomplished. We therefore recognize that a wholly new factor has entered into the making of failure and success within the brief span of time that is relevant: skill—not merely in the mechanical working of the weapons, which was simply assumed at the technical level, but rather the more subtle *tactical* skill needed to make good use of the terrain and weapons at hand, within the particular context of each encounter.

Now what also matters greatly is the natural aptitude and tactical training of the men inside those armored vehicles and of the missile infantry opposing them: do they have the poacher's ready eye in spotting what is to their advantage in the terrain, given what they know of the enemy beyond? Can they swiftly calculate how the depth of their fields of fire in various positions and along various approaches matches the effective range of their weapons?

LEADERSHIP, MORALE, FORTUNE

Skill must be an individual attribute, but it is vehicle crews and missile teams who are doing the fighting—groups that is, however small, and what counts therefore is not personal skill but the skill effectively applied by groups as a whole, which depends on the competence of their leadership. Are the senior men in the missile-infantry teams also the ones best fitted to make the tactical decisions, or are they the products of an army that promotes docility more than ingenuity? Are the officers and sergeants in command of the armored vehicles and their crews real leaders or just followers of those still higher in the chain of command?

Nor does competent leadership suffice without troops willing to face danger. As soon as the tactical encounter actually begins, with the shocking blast of the artillery that routinely fires ahead of the advancing armor, the sinister hammering of the machine guns, the deadly boom of mortar bombs, when the earth seems to explode from within to fly into the air and tree branches sliced by bullets crash to the ground; as soon as an armored carrier here or a tank there is hit, and starts to burn or explodes; as soon as the missile infantrymen discover their neighbors next to them a second ago now dead, wounded, or buried in debris; as soon as the fighting proper begins, then we discover that much more than skilled leadership matters in the outcome.

Every instinct of nature should induce the attacking crews to pause in the safety of such shelter as the terrain offers, rather than continuing their advance into the unknown countryside before them, against an invisible enemy and his deadly missiles. And the same powerful instinct urges the infantrymen to flee instead of holding their ground against steel machines relentlessly descending upon them; the missile launchers will now seem desperately flimsy and their effect uncertain, as opposed to the mathematical certainty that in a few minutes the defenders will be crushed under the tracks of the advancing tanks, unless *all* are hit and stopped.

What overcomes instinct to make combat possible are just those intangible qualities that armies seek to cultivate by parade-ground drills (to make obedience automatic), by speeches, songs, and flags (to inspire pride), by uniforms and daily routines, by punishments and rewards: individual morale, group discipline, and unit cohesion. Of these decisively important but unmeasurable attributes, small-unit cohesion is usually the most important, because the willingness of men to fight for the sake of one another survives the terrible impact of battle far better than any other individual source of morale.

At the tactical level of strategy, therefore, the intangibles of skill, leadership, morale, discipline, and unit cohesion enter into our picture, usually to dominate the outcome. That is why military-balance estimates formed at the technical level alone are so systematically misleading: in presenting lists of weapons side by side, they offer comparisons of attractive precision that exclude the greater part of the whole.

There is another factor that powerfully influences outcomes

within each single tactical episode: fortune, that is, chance and probability—the chance that the troops on either side may be exhausted by lack of sleep, sickened by foul rations or unfed because of a supply breakdown, badly frightened by prior combat or some fatal accident of the sort not uncommon when lethal machines are hurriedly handled; and the probabilities of the weather. In central Europe, dense mist or thick ground fogs are common during much of the year. This can allow the tanks and combat carriers to appear suddenly before the defenders, giving them almost no time to fire off even one missile—if they are still in place after the profoundly demoralizing experience of hearing the roaring approach of unseen armored vehicles.

OFFENSE-DEFENSE ASYMMETRIES

All these things are therefore important at the tactical level, and have their counterparts in other forms of warfare, in the air and at sea as well as on land. But do features of terrain, vegetation, skill, leadership, morale, cohesion, and fortune affect the two sides differently? Does their addition to our picture modify the conclusion so categorically reached at the technical level? Do they change the provisional finding that infantry armed with antitank missiles can be highly effective against the all-mechanized Soviet army in the defense of central Europe? The answer is a definite yes in each case.

The Soviet armored force need only advance to execute its task, and most of the crews need do no more than operate their machines and fire their weapons through narrow-view sights and weapon slits, shielded from most of the terrorizing visions and sounds of battle by armor plate and roaring engines. To move in the right direction, and to do so by making good use of the terrain, leadership will be needed of course, but this can be provided by junior officers at the head of the column, men destined to risk more by riding half-exposed in open turrets.

The defending missile infantrymen cannot usefully participate in the fight by mere mechanical operation, with a diminished consciousness of the battle. They must stay active and alert to spot their targets at long range, in spite of intervening smoke incidental or contrived, in spite of fog and mist; they must then calmly acquire the targets in their sights and then decide the moment of launch, a delicate matter because, though the longest range is desirable, the greater the intervening distance the more likely it is that it will contain dead ground, in which the advancing tank might be hidden just long enough to evade the missile on its flight. After launch, the operator must keep the moving target in his sights during the long seconds of missile flight until impact. And throughout the entire procedure, from the spotting to the hitting, the missile troops must perform their exacting tasks while their senses are attacked by the effects of battle, with even the briefest distraction resulting in the loss of control over missiles in flight.

Then of course there is the great asymmetry in physical protection, unless there are elaborate fortifications. The armored force is vulnerable only to the missiles in our still-picture view, while the defenders by contrast are vulnerable to every weapon that can reach them: cannon, machine guns, mortars, grenade launchers, and, most important of all, the supporting artillery firing ahead of the advancing armor. Some are killed, others wounded, and many more will be incapacitated tactically, by being forced to seek cover instead of looking out to find and engage targets.

Actually not merely their senses but also their minds will conspire against the defenders. The advancing unit of Soviet armor is propelled forward by units coming up from behind; aside from a given direction of advance, its task is open-ended, with the choices and fate of commanders and crewmen only loosely affected by the strength of the *entire* defensive array, of which they may know little and certainly cannot calculate. But the defenders have ample opportunity to calculate: even in the best visibility that climate and terrain will allow, their maximum range of engagement cannot exceed 4,000 yards, and if Soviet armor is advancing at a mere 15 miles an hour, they will have only just over nine minutes' fighting time before enemy tanks and combat carriers will be upon them. If there is mist to reduce visibility in some degree, a fog to reduce it much more, the engagement range declines and with it the available fighting time. Theoretically, each missile-launcher team could engage a new target every thirty seconds or so, and such things are sometimes done on peacetime firing ranges. But in the actual sequence of combat, from spotting to hit, one shot per minute is a high maximum, of which 58 percent will succeed.

To know if the line can be held at all, or if flight is the only alternative to death or capture, the defenders must therefore esti-mate how many tanks and combat carriers are actually advancing upon them—and if it is more than five for each missile launcher that survives artillery bombardment, mortar bombs, and direct fire, then their lives or liberty will be lost in the next several minutes. Be-cause it is the Soviet army they are facing, and because chance has placed them where one of its columns aims to pass, the defenders must expect the worst: the tanks and combat carriers they actually see may be only a few, but many more must be coming up in short order. This abundance of armor is precisely the motive of the pro-posal we are considering, but for the antitank missile infantry on the line, strategic decision has created a tactical situation systemati-cally demoralizing, from which the only escape is not to stand and fight effectively, but rather to fire off a missile or two and then move smartly back.

For all these reasons, the initial finding at the technical level is now greatly changed. When we examine the encounter at the tacti-cal level, we see that the defenders can no longer hope to destroy tanks costing one hundred times as much with 1.58 missiles per tank; nor combat carriers costing at least fifteen times as much with 2.58 missiles per carrier, to yield excellent exchange ratios of 1:5.8 or better against combat carriers and 1:63 against the tanks. Instead we see many of the missile launchers lost to the precursor artillery shells, mortar bombs, and direct fire before they can engage the enemy at all; others incapable of acquiring even one target during the few minutes of combat because of intervening smoke; and still others losing targets already aligned in their sights because of the blast and shock of the explosions around them.

How many missile launchers will therefore be required in tactical reality to destroy a tank or combat carrier? Is it ten or twenty, as some Middle East war experience suggests? Or is it more, since central Europe does not have such splendid visibility? Because the cost differences are so great, the exchange ratios should remain favorable, but no longer by large margins. Our tactical-level finding, still provisional of course, is that the proposal is much less promis-ing than it first seemed, though it still merits further evaluation at the higher levels of strategy. But we now know that its success will depend to an unusually great extent on the qualities of the men involved. The intangibles of morale, discipline, and cohesion are almost always more important in combat than material factors, but especially so in this case, where we see such severe asymmetry between the stress that offense and defense must absorb.

So we discover that the merits of the proposals in circulation are critically dependent on what earlier had seemed to be mere administrative detail. Will the missile infantry be manned by cohesive militiamen, friends and neighbors beholden to one another but screened for aptitude and trained as seriously as part-time training will allow? Or will reservists who once served as conscript soldiers years ago be assigned from all over the country, to meet for the first time just as the fighting is about to begin? Or is the missile infantry to be an elite corps, selected young men, trained and commanded to ensure the highest moral qualities? And by what reasoning can wealthy nations consign the best of their men to fight with cheap weapons against enemies much poorer yet far more elaborately armed? Thus at the tactical level of strategy we encounter the human dimension of combat, as well as chance and probability, and we see the fighting unfold within a unique context of time and place. As climate and human circumstances vary, not even forces identically manned and armed, moving in identical ways on the very same ground, can twice refight exactly the same battle and get exactly the same result. By relying on the canceling out of chances, and by probability estimates based on the observation of many events (accuracies of weapons, patterns of climate), we can reach tactical-level conclusions of general validity, but only for particular forces with particular equipment and particular human characteristics.

Therefore the wisdoms of "tactics"—the detailed craft of war manifest precisely at this level—can neither travel very far nor last very long. There is no right or wrong that does not depend on the specific performance of weapons and the general nature of the antagonists: a given way of attacking an enemy outpost, flying an intercept, or engaging a ship might be suicidally bold or excessively timid, depending on the characteristics of the opposed forces; and manuals of tactics must be rewritten whenever significant new weapons appear, to make the formerly impossible into mere routine or to make what was once routine now impossibly dangerous. One may still read the texts of Aeneas, Vegetius, or Mauricius and find advice that endures nonetheless, but it would be idle to pretend that they contain much more than the obvious; and if we read the far less interesting manuals of the two modern world wars, we would find them just as outdated. Hence tactics are the proper concern of professionals alone, just as any normative "strategics" that would advocate this or that policy for one country or another can only be of contemporary validity (unlike strategy itself, which prescribes nothing and merely describes unchanging phenomena that exist whether we see them or not).

THE LIMITS OF THE TACTICAL

In our still-picture view of the engagement, there has been no scope for any shift in tactics on either side, no experience of success and failure that would evoke reactions on one side and then the other. It was merely assumed that both forces would execute simple tactics of frontal engagement, though with proper attention to the use of terrain. This of course might be valid in the initial collision between the first wave of advancing Soviet armor and the defensive belt of antitank infantry. But if the defense succeeds in repelling attack, a reaction will eventually be evoked, perhaps to suppress the defense by greater firepower or to circumvent it in some way. The defense can also react, by using the time it gains to dig alternate positions, by sending out hunting parties, or by letting enemy vehicles through before engaging them from behind. And then of course another round would begin.

The particular forces we have been viewing are not, however, independent agents pursuing their own goals. What is the entire fight for units at the tactical level, indeed their entire existence at the time, is merely a fragment of the larger scheme of things for the successive layers of command of the respective armies and national authorities. They devised the plans that caused the fight to take place as it did, in pursuit of their own larger goals. Now they strive to retain control over the fighting, to protect their purposes by developing reciprocal responses to its unfolding results—sometimes by trying to assist the units already engaged, sometimes by sacrificing them, and more often by introducing new forces that they can still control because they have not yet become absorbed in their own struggle for survival.

The interplay of action and reaction is thus no longer confined to the tactical level. We will need a quite different and much broader perspective to pursue the investigation, where the detailed particularities of context lose their importance and where the full array of rival forces is considered instead of only those immediately opposed. For this we must ascend to the next level of strategy, after noting that though we have viewed an episode of ground combat, every other form of warfare past and present, at sea, in the air, or even in space—including warfare loosely described as "strategic"*—must have its own tactical level.

---

*During the last fifty years or so, the habit has developed of applying the adjective "strategic" to long-range forces and weapons, as opposed to their shorter-range counterparts, and we hear of "strategic" and "tactical" bombers and missiles. We obtained this unfortunate terminology from the rhetoric of the early airpower advocates, by way of deliberate transposition: bomber aircraft claimed to be war-winning on their own were first promoted as strategic to convey their self-sufficiently decisive quality (as opposed to merely tactical roles in support of hitherto decisive troops); then the adjective became associated with the incidental attribute of long range, which *some* bombers would need in order to be of strategic effect in *some* geographic settings, and that in turn caused "tactical" to acquire the attribute of short range. The poor fit is obvious: if Belgium were to bomb New Zealand into submission, long-range aircraft would be needed, but tactical aircraft would suffice to achieve that same strategic purpose if adjacent Luxembourg were to be the victim; yet if Belgian aircraft were to hunt submarines off the New Zealand coast, a tactical mission, they would need to have a "strategic" range.

CHAPTER 7

THE OPERATIONAL LEVEL

It is a peculiarity of English-language military terminology that it has no word of its own for what stands between the tactical and the strategic, to describe that middle level of thought and action wherein generic *methods* of war contend and battles unfold in their totality. In the modern tradition of continental European military thought, by contrast, there is an adjectival term in common use directly translatable as "operational," and this level is indeed salient in German and Soviet professional military literature, whose primary concern is with *operational art,*[1] as opposed to tactics narrowly applicable to specific types of forces (infantry tactics, air-combat tactics, antisubmarine tactics).

Just as it is the weapons themselves that interact at the technical level of strategy, and the forces directly opposed that fight one another at the tactical level, at the operational level we encounter the struggle of the directing minds, as expressed in conceptual methods of action (blitzkrieg, defense in depth, "strategic" air bombardment, layered naval air defense), in the ongoing command of all the forces involved, and in the actual adventures and misadventures of those forces. The boundary of what is "operational" in methods, ongoing command, and action is self-evident in any real-life case, even if very difficult to demarcate in the abstract. Once again, there is no need for any arbitrary definition: we need only uncover the natural stratifications of strategy in any given episode to grasp what is operational and what comes below and above. But of course the demarcation between tactical, operational, and strategic requires the presence of a certain scale and variety of means if it is to have meaning.

At one extreme, for a primitive tribe whose entire force consists of identically armed warriors who always fight in a single formation, the tactical, operational, and strategic must coincide for all practical purposes. Such a tribe cannot suffer a tactical defeat that is not also strategic, nor can it develop a method of war that is more than a tactic. By contrast, say for the United States in World War II, quite different operational situations could coexist even within the same theaters of war, and very different operational methods were relevant in the amphibious campaigns of the Pacific, in the "strategic" bombing of German industry, in the eleven months of continental warfare that began with the Normandy landings, and in the struggle for naval supremacy in the Pacific waged chiefly by aircraft-carrier task forces.

Scale and variety are necessary conditions, but they are not sufficient: if the operational level is to have any substance of its own, the action must also consist of more than the sum of tactical parts—and that depends on the prevailing *style of war* in the given setting, more specifically on its place within the spectrum of attrition and maneuver.

ATTRITION AND MANEUVER IN WARFARE

Attrition is war waged by industrial methods. The enemy is treated as a mere array of targets, and success is to be obtained by the cumulative effect of superior firepower and material strength, eventually to destroy the full inventory of enemy targets, unless retreat or surrender terminates the process (as is usually the case). The greater the attrition content of a style of war, the more will routinized techniques of target acquisition, movement, and resupply suffice, along with a repetitive tactical repertoire, and the smaller is the need for the application of any operational method. So long as firepower-producing forces are brought within range of static targets (trenchlines, cities) or of enemy forces that must remain concentrated to achieve *their* purposes (not guerrillas therefore), so long as material superiority is indeed maintained and the firepower is of appropriate form and of sufficient quality, victory is mathematically assured. It is understood that the enemy's reciprocal attrition will have to be absorbed. There can be no victory in this style of war without an overall superiority in attritional capacity, and there can be no cheap victories, in either casualties or material loss, relative to the enemy's strength.

There is no such thing of course as attrition warfare in pure form, entirely devoid of cunning or artifice and reduced to an industrial process, but examples of warfare with a very high attritional content include the trench fighting of World War I, many of whose battles were dominated by highly symmetrical brute-force engagements between artillery forces; the Luftwaffe's attempt to defeat the Royal Air Force in 1940 by deliberately seeking air-combat engagements (in this case the German self-perception of material superiority was in error, because of the effects of distance, the quality of the Spitfire, and the excellence of British pilots); Montgomery's battle at El Alamein, and most of his later battles, in which the enemy was first barraged by vastly superior artillery and then frontally assaulted by infantry, before being overrun with armor; the German submarine campaign of 1941–1943, whose goal was to win the war by reducing the total tonnage of any and all oceanic shipping below the level needed to sustain the war effort; the Allied campaign in Italy (after the failure of the outmaneuvering attempt at Anzio), which degenerated into a frontal grinding action of very slow effect; the air bombardment of Germany and Japan, ostensibly aimed at industrial attrition but actually aimed at urban housing; Eisenhower's concept of a broad-front offensive after the breakout from Normandy, which Patton subverted insofar as he could; Ridgeway's Korean offensives of 1951–52, in which ground forces slowly advanced, in a solid front from coast to coast, against Chinese and North Korean forces systematically reduced by airpower and artillery; much of the American fighting in Vietnam, even though enemy forces stubbornly refused to assemble in conveniently targetable mass formations except at moments of their own choosing, so that attempts were constantly made to impose involuntary concentration by sweeps of concentric pattern ("search and destroy"); and, as a notional case so far, the targeting of urban populations and industry for nuclear attack, in order to dissuade opponents from aggression by threatening the destruction of stated percentages of each.

At the other end of the spectrum there is *relational maneuver,* action related to the specifics of the objective, where instead of seeking to destroy the enemy's physical substance, the goal is to incapacitate by *systemic* disruption—whether the "system" is the command structure of the enemy's forces, their mode of warfare and combat array (as when a linear front is pierced or a battle-fleet defense in depth is penetrated), or even an actual technical system (the deception of a radar, as opposed to its brute-force jamming or outright physical destruction).

Instead of seeking out the enemy's concentration of strength, since that is where the targets are to be found in bulk, the starting point of relational maneuver is the avoidance of the enemy's strengths, followed by the application of some selective superiority against presumed enemy weaknesses, physical or psychological, technical or organizational. While attrition is a quasi-physical process that guarantees results proportionate to the quality and volume of the effort expended, and conversely cannot yield success without material superiority, the results of relational maneuver depend on the accuracy with which enemy weaknesses are identified, the surprise achieved, and the speed and precision of the action. Some combination of surprise and speed is a precondition of success because the enemy who has time to react can shield those weaknesses against which the effort is unfolding.

Two consequences follow: first, relational maneuver offers the possibility of results disproportionately greater than the resources applied to the effort, and thus a chance of victory for the side materially weaker; second, relational maneuver can fail completely, if the selective strength narrowly applied against presumed weakness cannot perform its own task or encounters unexpected strength. In the language of the engineer, attrition fails "gracefully," just as it can succeed only cumulatively, because each error imposes only a proportionate penalty: if a given target is misidentified or missed, that target will have to be attacked again, but the larger action is not thereby endangered. Relational maneuver, by contrast, can fail "catastrophically," just as it can succeed with very little, because an error of assessment or execution can wreck the entire operation. In other words, attrition is warfare paid at full cost but of low risk, whereas relational maneuver can be of low cost but may entail high risk. True, if the risk materializes, no more can be lost than the relatively small effort that was made, of "low cost" as compared to the gain hoped for, but this can still be a great deal in absolute terms.

There is one more consequence: because it requires accuracy in identifying enemy weaknesses, as well as speed and precision in the action taken to exploit them, relational maneuver will not usually allow the free substitution of quantity for quality. Instead it will impose irreducible qualitative standards with numerical substitution possible only once those standards are exceeded, and limited in any case by the need for surprise and speed. Moreover, at the actual points of contact, where the selected strength is finally applied, combat is quite likely to result in extreme attrition at the tactical level, even if combat with the enemy's main strength is successfully avoided at the operational level.

Again, there is no warfare that consists purely of relational maneuver. As with attrition, what varies from case to case is the relational-maneuver content of the overall action, and that—here is the important point—defines the scope of operational-level methods. The more relational maneuver, the more important is the operational level. Examples of warfare with a high relational-maneuver content include the failed 1915 Gallipoli amphibious operation of World War I, which was intended to force Ottoman Turkey out of the war by a swift offensive against the then capital of Istanbul, in lieu of reducing Turkish armies in the field piece by piece from the Persian Gulf and Egypt; the blitzkrieg operations of the German army against Poland, Denmark, Norway, the Netherlands, Belgium, France, Yugoslavia, Greece, and the Soviet Union (until 1942), whereby linear defenses, organized to defend national borders against broad-front offensives, were instead pierced in narrow-front attacks by infantry and artillery, followed by the rapid penetration of motorized forces in depth, with wholesale disruption of supply lines, command centers, and planning expectations; the Anglo-American response to Germany's U-boat campaign, which exploited a lack of long-range air reconnaissance to find targets by grouping ships into convoys that moved inside a tiny fraction of ocean space; the 1940 British campaign in North Africa, which defeated an Italian army vastly superior numerically by a motorized penetration through its desert flank, to cut off the only line of communication along the Libyan coast; the 1941–42 Japanese campaign in Malaya, which defeated numerically and materially superior British forces by repeatedly outflanking their coastal-road communications through the jungle or amphibiously, each time forcing a further retreat down the peninsula; the deep-penetration offensive of Patton's Third Army in July-August 1944 that rolled up the German forces in northwestern France after Normandy; the failed attempt of September 1944 (Operation Market-Garden) to invade northern Germany through the Dutch backdoor by means of simultaneous parachute and glider landings, meant to seize successive bridges for a swift overland offensive by British armor-spearheaded columns all the way to the Rhine at Arnhem (which was undone by the slowness of British armor, among other things); Patton's December 1944 outflanking counteroffensive from the south against the German forces that had advanced westward through the Ardennes; the failed attempts to disrupt the German war economy by the concentrated bombing of industrial bottlenecks, instead of the generic bombing of urban-industrial areas; MacArthur's 1950 countermove into central Korea by way of the Inchon landings, whereby the invading North Korean forces were cut off rather than laboriously pushed back by frontal offensives; and some of the American action in Vietnam, as in the case of the highly successful but interrupted village-defense effort of the U.S. Marines, which energized local militia in bulk with a handful of marines; and, in a notional case, the targeting of political and military command centers for nuclear attack, as opposed to the population at large, in order to dissuade opponents from aggression by threatening their centralized control over society.

ATTRITION AND MANEUVER IN WAR PREPARATION

By now it will have become obvious that attrition and relational maneuver are present in peacetime military policy as much as in actual warfare. We may compare the two, for example, in the research and development of military equipment. Under an attritional approach, when the aim is to secure technical advantage by the generous use of resources, the conduct of research and development requires no particular tactical or operational focus: the goal is to obtain "best" systems, which maximize every aspect of performance, subject only to cost ceilings.

Accordingly, new equipment is developed *ex novo* to avoid prior design constraints. Large changes will often be needed in maintenance arrangements, supporting ancillaries, and possibly in training when the new weapons eventually arrive to replace what was there before. Only truly major gains in performance can justify the resulting costs, which are of course added to those of the development effort itself, so that large engineering or scientific advances must be achieved. That makes research and development expensive and also requires ample time for calculation, prototyping, trials, recalculation, further prototyping, and more trials. Finally, because the period of gestation is so long, it is only by coincidence that the particular characteristics of new weapons will match the *specific* configuration of enemy vulnerabilities or the *specific* tactical requirements of the forces to which they are issued. Perhaps that was the original intention, or perhaps technical goals alone guided the entire effort—but in either case by the time the new equipment arrives, former enemy weaknesses may well have become strengths while the operational methods of the users may have changed as well.[2]

Under a relational-maneuver approach, by contrast, the aim of research and development is precisely to obtain technical abilities that exploit specific enemy vulnerabilities and are congruent with tactics and methods shaped by the same purpose. To do so in timely fashion, that is, while the presumed weaknesses persist, new equipment cannot usually be developed *ex novo* and must instead be obtained by the modification or recombination of components already in hand. This obviously imposes design constraints that hinder the full exploitation of all the possibilities offered by scientific and technical progress. Moreover, because improved designs are introduced at relatively short intervals, compatibility with equipment previously issued is essential to avoid ruinous integration costs, and that imposes further design constraints. Finally, truly major technical advances ("breakthroughs") are less likely.

What is true of research and development applies as well to all other aspects of military policy. Attrition implies the independent pursuit of the best in general, whether in the training of armed forces, the construction of bases and facilities, or the acquisition of equipment; in relational maneuver, however, "best" solutions are sacrificed in order to emphasize the abilities that exploit the vulnerabilities and limitations of specific enemies. With neither ever present in pure form, their relative weight in the overall conduct of military policy will usually reflect national self-images in the appropriate international context.

NATIONAL STYLES IN POLICY AND WAR

Nations who see themselves as materially strong or merely rich in resources, in comparison with the threats they deem salient—a perception that may or may not reflect current realities—will generally feel free to pursue an attritional approach. Those who view themselves, rightly or wrongly, as materially weak will accept the subordination of their own notions of what is best and will instead adjust their priorities to the vulnerabilities they see in others.

In military policy, as in the conduct of war, there are thus definite national styles, marked by a particular position on the attrition-maneuver spectrum. But clearly these styles are less than pervasive, and the exceptions created by men or circumstances may be important (as Patton and his Third Army were in 1944) or even briefly dominant (as MacArthur was in Korea). National styles do not arise from the permanent condition of nations, and certainly not from fixed ethnic characteristics. Because they reflect self-images of *relative* material strength or weakness, they depend on the specific enemy with which the comparison is made, and they can change over time as circumstances change, perhaps abruptly. Britain, for example, followed a relational-maneuver approach in opposing continental great powers for more than two centuries until 1914, by avoiding their strength in foot regiments while weakening them by naval blockade, and by gaining allies through diplomacy and gold. Diplomacy played a large role in Britain's colonial wars as well, but when it came to actual fighting, attrition was clearly dominant: recalcitrant potentates and unsubdued tribes were not elaborately outmaneuvered but instead confronted by close-order musketry. And Israel between the wars of 1967 and 1973 provides an example of rapid change in national style. The post-1967 self-image of material superiority led to the progressive abandonment of relational maneuver, so that when the October 1973 war began, frontal attack and linear defense were dominant—until the shock of defeat during the first few days of battle brought about an even faster reversion to relational maneuver in full form.[3]

National styles are therefore stable enough to be worth defining, but neither all-pervasive nor permanent; and when change comes, they become less homogeneous during the period of transition, as in the case, at this writing, of the American armed forces: whereas the army has reacted to its material weakness vis-à-vis the Soviet army by adopting a relational-maneuver operational method for the central front in Germany, attrition continues to dominate the methods of the more complacent marine corps, as well as those of the air force and navy, whose relative strength is indeed greater.

It should be obvious by now that attrition and relational maneuver are not confined to the operational level. They are evident at each level of strategy, both below and above. Their introduction at this particular level of strategy is nevertheless justified because the importance of the operational level depends on the extent to which relational maneuver is present. If the action being considered is essentially characterized by attrition, as with much of the trench warfare of World War I, a larger-scale operational view of the fighting will show only the same tactical episodes repeated again and again, on one segment of the front after another. So we learn nothing that we would not know just as well by examining any one of the separate episodes from a tactical viewpoint.

The same holds true in all forms of warfare: the first stages of the battle of Britain, Germany's attrition campaign against the Royal Air Force, consisted of daily bombing attacks against British airfields and aircraft factories, leading to the repetitive air combat of German escort fighters against the Hurricanes and Spitfires of Fighter Command that tried to intercept them. The outcome was not determined by anything more than the arithmetic sum of the results of those encounters, with no operational (as opposed to strategic) goal on either side and no operational-level methods of war.[4]

When by contrast the relational-maneuver content is high, the operational level becomes correspondingly important both in the contemporary execution and in retrospective analysis. Of this the best illustration is perhaps the armored blitzkrieg, the classic form of offensive warfare of our time, which is worth examining in some detail both because of its continuing importance and because no other method of war is so clearly dependent on relational maneuver.

BLITZKRIEG: THE REWARDS AND RISKS OF MANEUVER

If we examine a deep-penetration armored offensive in a tactical-level picture, or rather a whole series of them, we will see only meaningless and indeed misleading fragments of its totality. We might observe a long column of tanks, infantry carriers, and trucks moving in single file deep within enemy territory, advancing almost unresisted. We must be watching a triumphant victory march if there is war at all, since we see no fighting to speak of, except for the odd skirmish when tanks at the head of the advancing column crash through checkpoints of the military police or collide with road convoys innocently driving toward the front. We can be quite certain, it seems, that the invaders will soon reach their goal, even the capital city, and win the war.

When we redirect our close-view telescope, we discover how the column managed to pass through the defensive frontline, that solid barrier of troops and weapons that runs all along the border: we notice a break in the line, made just a short time ago by an infantry assault supported by both artillery and air strikes. But the breach is no more than a narrow passage. On either side of it, strong forces of the defensive front remain, distracted it is true by feints and minor attacks from the troops thinly distributed to face them all along the front, harassed perhaps by desultory air attacks, but essentially intact. The narrow passage now looks very vulnerable indeed; it seems that the defensive forces on each side need only move over a little to link up again and close the gap. We might therefore calculate that the long deep-penetration column is heading straight for self-destruction. It is already very far from the frontal territory securely held, behind which its supply depots remain. We see trucks traveling down the one route opened by the pencil-thin advance, bringing fuel and ammunition to resupply the column, but those strong defensive forces we saw before will surely bring that traffic to an end as soon as they converge to close the breach in the front. Then the tanks, carriers, and the rest will start to run out of fuel. Once the column stops, its extreme vulnerability will stand revealed: the long thin line of vehicles is all flank and no front, open to attack in every one of its parts. It appears that the spectacularly imprudent attackers are themselves accomplishing a complete victory for the defense. To encircle such a large force should normally be very difficult, but this time we seem to be witnessing a case of deliberate self-encirclement: it is as if the attackers have chosen to provide their own transportation to prisoner-of-war camps by driving so deep inside the territory of the defense.

But if now we replace our narrow tactical view with a broader operational perspective, the picture is entirely transformed. First, we discover that the deep-penetration column we earlier saw in isolation is only one of several. Each, it is true, originates in a breach of the front that remains quite narrow, but the columns are converging and now it is no longer clear who is encircling whom, because the penetrations are segmenting the territory of the defense as so many slices in a cake. Then we see how the defense is reacting and we encounter the crucial and determining fact: those forces of the defense still so strong on either side of each breach are not converging toward one another to close the gaps. Instead they have been ordered to withdraw as rapidly as they can, in order to reconstitute an entirely new front, deep behind the old frontier line. Clearly the intention is to cope with those advancing columns by confronting them with solid strength where now there are only supply depots, training camps, transport columns virtually unarmed, military-police units, field hospitals—and all the higher military headquarters.

When our view extends inside those headquarters, of corps, armies, and army groups, we see vast confusion, and some excusable panic: enemy tanks are fast approaching, and the new frontline to be reconstituted ahead of them still exists only on the planning map. Actually the withdrawing forces of the defense are losing the race. They, after all, had been totally intent on their assigned mission, which was to ensure a determined resistance against frontal attack. Accordingly, the infantry was distributed by companies and battalions, no doubt in proper trenchlines all along the front, with the guns and howitzers of the artillery scattered by batteries, also entrenched. And the tanks of the defense, perhaps more and better tanks than those of the enemy, were not grouped by the hundreds in multidivisional columns but instead distributed in small groups, all set to support the infantry in each segment of the front.

When the unexpected withdrawal orders reach them, commanders and staffs are shocked by the idea that they should retreat before an enemy that is not advancing in their sector, and abandon the front on which so much work has been done. They do their best, but the trucks that had brought up the infantry in relays during the mobilization of months ago are now scattered in transport pools all over the country, reassigned to supply units. There are certainly not enough trucks to move all the troops in one wave. The artillery has tractors for some of its pieces, but many of them had been brought up by rail. Besides, except for the tanks, it is difficult to withdraw forces that are even now firing and being fired upon by the enemy. His forces, it is true, seem rather weak, for clearly the main effort is being made elsewhere by those deep-penetration columns, but still to disengage troops actually in combat is very hard.

Nevertheless we see that forces of the defense here and there are beginning to withdraw. They are on their way to new positions quite far to the rear, whose separate segments are to connect in order to form the new frontline. But as they move, they encounter delays and frustration. The rear services had started to move before the frontline combat forces, and now their heavy trucks are blocking the roads. Farther behind the front the congestion becomes even worse: civilians too are evacuating, in cars, carts, buses, and on foot. After fighting their way through the traffic, if they can, the forces in retreat quite unexpectedly have to fight in earnest. It turns out that enemy combat teams had peeled off the deep-penetration columns to move sideways across country, and now they await all comers in ambush positions. The forces in question are actually very small, but those who encounter them cannot know that. In any case, there are heavy losses from the first minutes of the encounter, when the enemy can open fire unresisted against troops sitting inside trucks, artillery towed by its tractors, and tanks caught by surprise. If the defensive forces in retreat are determined, they will fight their way through, but much time is lost, casualties are suffered, and after-fight exhaustion adds to the demoralization of retreat.

One more shock awaits those forces that do reach their assigned positions. They find nothing ready for them, no trenches or gun positions, no food or field kitchens, no wire communications for their headquarters, and above all no ammunition dumps to replace those left behind at the front for lack of transport. Aside from the sheer lack of time, there is another cause of unpreparedness: the enemy's deep-penetration advance slicing through the rear zone has overrun a good many transport and service units, destroying many of their trucks and scattering the rest. Depots and logistic centers have also been overrun, and service units in any case cannot reach their assigned positions on the new line, since enemy combat forces are between them and their destinations.

The newly arrived forces nevertheless begin to settle in; the troops work hard to dig trenches and excavate gun positions, mustering what ammunition they have. Enemy aircraft make occasional raids, which interrupt the work, kill or wound some men, and demoralize more. Food is a problem, which prompts unit commanders to resort to an ancient expedient: they send off foraging parties into nearby villages to take what they can. And yet the situation seems to be improving: the line drawn on headquarter maps is becoming an actual front as more and more forces arrive to take up their assigned positions. There are still long segments that remain uncovered, others are manned only by small units and incomplete formations, but a new defensive line is definitely emerging.

It is too late, however. The advanced forces of the deep-penetration columns have already reached well beyond the new front and are now overrunning rear-service units, bases, and depots, as well as working headquarters, whose clerks, cooks, staff officers, and radio men are forced to engage in hopeless combat with tanks and mechanized infantry. There are no more good options, and the high command of the defense must strive to recover control by redeploying the combat forces. Some are still stranded at the old frontline; others are still in transit or caught in traffic jams. Only the troops that had been forming the new front can act quickly, and so they are now ordered to retreat once again. Perhaps they have the energy and determination to obey, but even those in best condition will not be able to outrace the enemy rolling steadily ahead.

Thus the entire wrenching process may have to be repeated yet again, until very little combat power remains among the mass of disorganized forces, scattered all over the map, disconnected from their support units, cut off from resupply, and increasingly demoralized. Mass surrenders begin, as soon as any enemy troops are actually encountered; capitulation, or retreat on a continental scale if the defenders control that much land, are the only options that remain for the high command. It is only now that the tactical parts once again become consistent with the operational whole, to yield a quite unexpected outcome. Until the forces of the defense are actually seen in chaotic disarray, the tactical view continued to mislead because nothing had intervened to remedy the extreme tactical-level vulnerability of the long deep-penetration columns. The decisive impact of their concerted structural and psychological effects is only manifest at the operational level.

In hindsight, we know that the decisive mistake was to order the first withdrawal, instead of making sideways attacks against the narrow breakthrough passages. But the headquarters of the defense never had this kind of clear operational view. At the beginning, and for some time afterwards, they did not know that the enemy had broken through the front with any intention other than to push forward his own entire front. Reports of course came in to describe the breaking of the front here and there. But reports of attacks large and small were coming in at the same time from all over the front, so that the emerging picture formed on headquarter maps was actually quite reassuring: the enemy, it appeared, had launched a general offensive. In most places, his attacks had failed, and successful unit commanders were eagerly reporting their defensive victories, with the usual overstatement of the magnitude of the enemy forces they had repelled. In a few places, obviously, the enemy had prevailed, but only on very narrow segments of the front. What was therefore expected were further enemy attacks everywhere else along the front, to replicate the isolated instances of success. Alternatively, the enemy would reluctantly have to pull back its successful forces because their flanks were so dangerously exposed.

At this stage, then, a straightforward, linear mindset conditions the perceptions of commanders at defense headquarters. Their own operational method is to protect the frontline by properly distributed forces; they automatically assume that the enemy also means to fight in a linear way, to push back the entire front by a broad offense. The enemy's maneuver "relates" to the limitations of their operational outlook by supporting their preconceptions: although the best attacking forces are grouped in a few places to stage narrow-front thrusts, or else are arrayed behind them in the deep armored columns waiting to start their own advance, there are also *some* forces all along the front, under orders to stage whatever small attacks they can or at least open fire as if they were about to attack.

The linear operational method has no doubt been drilled into the minds of the defenders through years of planning, exercises, and staff college courses; it has a powerful hold. So when the first reports come in of enemy tanks racing ahead of their own front, the most plausible explanation is that the enemy has decided to stage some raids; the defenders then wait for the expected word that the raiding forces are withdrawing to the security—and resupply—of their own side of the front. As more reports arrive, which suggest that the penetrations are not mere raids and that behind the tanks there are entire formations of mechanized infantry and artillery, doubts must begin to form in the minds of the defenders. But they can still be resisted quite easily: the reports, after all, will not come from the senior formation commanders on the front, who are concentrating their attention on the enemy forces opposite. Instead they mostly originate from airforce pilots, who are quite liable to confuse a friendly transport column with enemy forces, or else from military-police checkpoints, shocked remnants of road convoys and service units, civilian police, village mayors, and such. There is a war on and nerves are taut, so a great many false reports are coming in, of enemy parachutists supposedly landing everywhere and indeed of enemy tanks not merely deep behind the front but altogether too deep to be there at all.

At this point, information becomes war's most powerful weapon. The deep-penetration columns are advancing as rapidly as they can, toward the war-winning objectives marked on their maps; they report their progress as they go on, but the senior officers at headquarters in the rear have no great need to issue further orders. Their own commanders, riding at the head of each column, decide on the spot whether to attack resisting forces astride their path or merely by-pass them to continue the rapid advance. The progress reports are collated as they come in, to show the ever-deeper penetrations on the map; this is crucial to prevent the air force from raiding friendly forces and to focus its efforts against defending units that could otherwise strive to block the columns or even attack them on their exposed flanks. Actually the higher headquarters of the offense need little information and communications are mostly one-way, from the front to the rear, with very few orders going the other way, from rear commands to the columns.

The situation of the defense is entirely different: when its commanders finally come to understand that there will be no broad-front offensive after all, timely and accurate information about the movements of the deep-penetration columns becomes crucial. If defense headquarters could get a good operational-level picture of the unfolding battle, the right course of action—namely to close the frontal gaps or at least set up roadblocks *behind* the advancing armor to block its resupply—would immediately become clear. By now, however, the channels of communication of defense headquarters are saturated by the mass of reports coming in, some accurate when originally sent but now outdated, others greatly overstated, and others the product of fearful fantasies. As the information is sorted out, to determine where the enemy is and how fast he is moving, how wide or narrow his penetrations are and where they might be most vulnerable, commanders and their staffs are simply swamped by the sheer volume of incoming messages— and while they are at work to discover how matters stand, matters are not standing at all, as the enemy continues to advance. Even satellite observation, modern aerial photography, and more advanced communications would not change matters greatly, as the evidence of recent wars has shown.[5] As soon as *movement* begins, so does the fog of war.

What is happening is therefore an information race, which preconditions the redeployment race to come. On one side, the advancing deep-penetration columns are generating all kinds of reports; on the other, defense headquarters strive to process the information quickly enough to yield a valid if not totally current ("real-time") picture of events. If the defense wins the race, if the ability to assimilate and analyze information is not overwhelmed, there is still a chance of outright victory: any available forces can be sent to attack the columns, if properly located, and they will then find them rather vulnerable, as indeed they are at the tactical level. But if the information battle is lost, if the situation as seen at the operational level remains too confused to aim counterattacks in timely fashion, then a general withdrawal offers the only hope of salvation, by the restoration of a front too strong to be immediately pierced by the deep-penetration columns.

This would leave the enemy in control of much territory, but resistance could at least continue effectively *if* the frontal combat forces can disengage, regroup in columns, move faster than the enemy, and quickly redeploy with any fresh forces available to create a new front, and *if* there is in fact a great deal of territory to yield. For only a very deep withdrawal can be successful, by exceeding the one-bound penetration range of the enemy, beyond which his armored columns must stop to allow the supply organization to catch up and to absorb replacements, refit vehicles, and rest men.[6] In other words, the outcome no longer depends on the interaction of forces at the operational level but rather on the geographic depth of the *theater of war,* and to consider the question any further we would have to ascend to a higher level of strategy.

THE CASE STUDY RESUMED

After this lengthy illustration of relational maneuver, we are ready to reconsider the antitank infantry proposal for European defense, this time at the operational level. We now know that the technically excellent and tactically adequate (but no more than that) antitank missile defense must also be effective at the operational level if it is to be effective at all. And we also know that the encounter of armor and antiarmor can no longer be examined in isolation, but only in conjunction with all the forces on both sides that would actually interact on the battlefield: artillery, the line-holding infantry of the defense and the dismounted infantry of the attackers, such airpower as affects the battlefield itself, the helicopter forces that one side or the other can employ, perhaps in commando style, and also any barriers and fortifications that might exist. Moreover, if it is the less radical proposal that we are considering, which would add a frontal layer of antitank missile infantry to the armored and mechanized formations instead of replacing them, then of course they too must be considered and they would indeed remain the most important element of the defense.

As we seek to estimate the effect of antitank missile infantry among the many-sided interactions of the operational level, we now recognize that the fight between the armor unit and the missile unit that we watched at the tactical level is quite inconclusive by itself, as inconclusive as any one air duel in a struggle for air superiority or any one hide-and-seek struggle between a submarine and the aircraft, destroyers, and submarines of a task force. For as we widen our view, we see that behind the first unit of Soviet tanks and mechanized infantry there are many more, forming a deep column waiting to fight their way through the front. What we learned at the tactical level continues to be true, but the meaning of this truth is transformed: the Soviet armor that the missiles are destroying is there, in a sense, precisely to be destroyed, as it destroys launcher teams in turn and exhausts their stock of missiles. The tanks and combat carriers are not merely firing ammunition, they themselves *are* ammunition, which the penetration column is expending to clear the way for its own advance. Of course the Soviet army would rather lose less than more in breaking through the line, but so long as the passage through the front is achieved, the tactical result, that "exchange rate," is unimportant at the operational level—if there is indeed only one defensive line. The success or failure of the ensuing deep-penetration offensive will not depend on whether the advancing forces as a whole have lost 5 or 10 percent of their numbers as the price of entry into the vulnerable rear areas.

The operational method of each side is now the critical factor. I have not surveyed operational methods in any detail, except for one or two illustrative cases, because my purposes are analytical. Operational methods relate to the operational level of strategy as tactics relate to the tactical level, that is, as prescriptions whose validity strictly depends on who is fighting whom and in what circumstances. Still, having discussed at length one such method, the blitzkrieg, I should reiterate that so long as the attritional content is less than total, there are air, naval, and even "strategic" nuclear operational methods, just as there are tactics for each.

In air warfare, for example, interception and airfield attack are two distinct operational methods in the struggle for control of the air, each of which may be implemented with a variety of different tactics. Equally, the use of airpower against ground forces may take the operational form of battlefield interdiction, whereby the targets are units not yet engaged in battle, or of close air support. And as already noted, there are varied methods of bombardment—area, precision, and "deep interdiction"—whose main target is overland communications and whose main purpose is to prevent the arrival of enemy forces and supplies in the combat zones. Similarly, to cite a naval example, the protection of shipping against submarines may be accomplished by different operational methods, which include the use of minefields, picket ships, and submarines in ambush to keep the enemy from reaching the sea lanes of interest; area defense, by the active hunting of submarines in transit with long-range aircraft and mixed task forces of destroyers, aircraft carriers, and submarines; and finally convoy protection by immediate escort. In each case the dividing line between tactics and operational methods is obvious.

Reverting to the case study and the critical role of the operational methods of each side, we already know that the attackers are trying to achieve the blitzkrieg effect[7]: the disruption of the lifelines of supply and the entire supporting structure of the defense, the forced evacuation of forward airbases and nuclear storage sites, and above all *the unbalancing of command decisions,* to misdirect any counterattacks and impose disorganizing retreat.

As for the defense and its choice of operational methods, we already know that one-line frontal attrition by missile troops alone cannot be successful against a deep-column attack, unless that "line" were actually a broad band of missile teams in impossibly large numbers. It is not that attrition is an inferior form of warfare but rather than its material demands are directly proportionate to the task, and in this case the task of each defensive unit attacked is huge, because of the numerical asymmetry between defensive forces distributed all along the front and offensive forces highly concentrated against narrow segments of that front. Of course attrition is a matter of arithmetic and it *could* succeed, but only with a much more costly defensive array than the missile-infantry force alone. First, antitank barriers such as minefields, sharp-sided ditches, and concrete obstacles would be needed to ration the enemy's rate of approach, so as to keep the number of incoming Soviet vehicles below the engagement capacity of the missile troops; their numbers and the effect of the barriers substitute for one another and can therefore be traded off. Second, in another trade-off, fortified firing positions would be needed, to ensure high exchange rates between missile teams and vehicles destroyed. Naturally, the economy of such a fortified frontal defense would depend on the length of frontage that must be covered, not an operational-level question at all but rather one that would take us into the level of theater strategy. In any case, without barriers and fortifications more costly than the missile launchers themselves, replacement of the armored and mechanized forces of the Alliance, deemed "provocative" as well as costly, and the still greater aim of making nuclear counterattack unnecessary, cannot be realized in practice—no matter how impressive the tactical results of the missile infantry might seem in their own terms. Thus the technically superior and tactically adequate missile infantry is found to be ineffectual at the operational level.

When we next consider the less radical version of the European defense proposal, which calls for the addition of a frontal layer of antitank troops to the existing armored and mechanized forces, we see that even one-line attrition would have a certain value. In part, its merits can be assessed by the mere summation of tactical effects: the delay imposed on the offense, very valuable indeed to gain mobilization time if the enemy has achieved surprise, and less so otherwise; and the attrition that can be exacted, for if there is mobile warfare still to come a reduction in the enemy's numbers by any given percentage is no longer irrelevant to the outcome. But the value of the new frontal layer of missile infantry can be more than the sum of those tactical parts, if an operational method of defense is developed to combine the action of the mobile forces with the new missile defense. By revealing the enemy's major thrusts where breakthroughs do occur, and by continuing to shield other segments of the front where they do not, a setting is created in which the mobile forces of the defense can be much more effective than before—precisely at the operational level—because they can move in a sideway direction to counterattack the flanks of the invasion columns, while their own outer flanks are sheltered in the lee of intact segments of the front.

This presumes of course either a timely mobilization or else a delay imposed by the frontal defense sufficient to allow the mobile forces of the Alliance to muster out of their barracks and move up to the front for counterattack. In either case, the result would be a great improvement over the current situation. Now, if there is sufficient warning to mobilize and deploy the ground forces of the Alliance, they would be fully engaged in defending the front instead of being free to counterattack; and if the enemy attacks by surprise, the armor and mechanized forces moving belatedly toward the front would have to engage advancing Soviet forces head on in most cases, forgoing the advantage of taking the enemy on the flank.

In the case of the less radical proposal, therefore, the technically superior and tactically adequate frontal defense by missile infantry is operationally valid, and what counts is just how valid it is in comparision with its forgone opportunity of adding mobile armored and mechanized strength. This will depend in turn on how the force is manned, whether by scarce regulars taken from the mobile forces or by reserve and militia troops now scarcely employed at all. Hence those same institutional specifics that at first seemed inconsequential, and which were then discovered to be important at the tactical level, turn out to be decisive at the operational level, albeit for quite different reasons.

Because they are static, there are only two operational methods for the employment of the missile troops: frontal defense on their own and in combination with counterattacking mobile forces. Obviously there are other ways of employing the missile troops, in settings more favorable than those of frontal defense, where they have to absorb the undiminished momentum of the offensive. One possibility, already mentioned, would be an elastic defense, which would seriously oppose the enemy's advance only after a long retreat had exhausted its first-bound range; another would be a defense in depth much closer to the front, either in the form of multiple lines to impose successive delays or in the form of islands of resistance, to keep interfering with enemy movements, deplete his strength, and shield major military facilities or cities. But neither possibility is relevant to the operational level, for the interaction of the forces in combat is no longer at issue; it remains quite unchanged, whether on a new line far to the rear or in the multiple lines and resisting islands of a defense in depth. Instead it is the territorial layout of Alliance defense that is being reconsidered, raising questions that wholly transcend the scope of the operational level. For the sake of a possibly better defense for all members of the Alliance, which might be cheaper and require nuclear counterattack less urgently or perhaps not at all, the national territory of just one ally would be exposed to invasion and destructive warfare. The purpose of the Alliance would then have to be recast, to diminish the overriding priority of preclusive territorial defense, in favor of a notion of collective security that would not call for the protection of all territory of all members all of the time. This clearly is a matter of political decision, within each allied country and between them, which no wisdoms of strategy can dictate.

To be sure, the phenomena of strategy shape the *strategic* consequences of political decisions, but they have other consequences as well, which national leaders may find more important. If decisions on strategic matters are motivated by cultural, historical, economic, or electoral considerations, who can say on the basis of strategic reasoning that it should not be so? An understanding of strategy may or may not serve purposes set by political decision, but it certainly holds no authority over the definition of those purposes. Of course even the strategic consequences themselves can only be appraised in political terms: to find that x will lead to victory and y to defeat need not mean that x must therefore be the preferred political choice—for other considerations may motivate a preference for defeat over victory, and no insight of strategy can claim a higher rationality to dictate otherwise. We will have reason to bear in mind this distinction as we move up to higher levels of strategy.

A FIRST VISION OF STRATEGY WHOLE

To facilitate this ascent through the levels of strategy, I have continued to hold the horizontal dimension—the ebb and flow of action and reaction within each level—in static equipoise. This is not mere abridgment of reality but an actual distortion, because vertical interactions between the levels influence, and are influenced by, the paradoxical logic of strategy that unfolds within each horizontal dimension, to cause the sequence of success, culmination, and decline. If a new weapon appears, the reaction manifest at the technical level in the form of an enemy counterweapon may evoke a tactical reaction, which could in turn induce an operational-level response. Or else that first reaction may itself be tactical, and the response may be technical, to which a further reaction may be manifest at the operational level. Obviously there are a great many combinations of vertical and horizontal interaction, but perhaps the most common sequence is for technical changes to induce tactical consequences, which in turn evoke an operational reaction; of this the use of armor in deep column to pierce through fronts that the machine gun made immune to infantry attack is itself an example.

Even with our vertical progress from level to level far from complete, we can no longer visualize strategy only in its horizontal dimension, as an agitated sea in which the waves and counterwaves of the paradoxical logic tend to nullify one another, in a perpetual striving for an impossible equilibrium. Nor can we see strategy as a multilevel edifice, offering a different truth on every floor. We must instead contend with the complexity of combining both images in our minds: the floors are no longer solid but in agitated motion, sometimes to the point of breaking into one another, just as in the dynamic reality of conflict the interactions of the vertical levels themselves combine and collide with the entire horizontal dimension of strategy.

CHAPTER 8

THEATER STRATEGY I:
MILITARY OPTIONS
AND POLITICAL CHOICES

$\mathbf{T}$he logic of strategy at the theater level governs the relationship between military strength and territory, and we can understand much of it in visual terms, seeing deployments and movements in a bird's eye view, or perhaps one should say in a satellite overview. Of course strategy has a spatial aspect at the lower levels also, but at the tactical level it is the detailed nature of the terrain that matters, and at the operational level geography merely provides the shifting backdrop of combat encounters that could be much the same in other settings as well.

At the theater level, however, it is some specific territory that is the very object of contention. It may be as large as a subcontinent or as small as an island, but unless that theater of war is marked off by political boundaries, it must be sufficiently separated from other theaters by important geographic barriers or sheer distance to be defensible or vulnerable on its own. Whether it amounts to a province, an entire country, or even a vast regional grouping of countries, a theater of war must form a self-contained military whole rather than just one part of a larger whole.*

While conditioning the interaction of adversary forces in spatial terms, the logic of strategy at the theater level totally ignores the political, economic, and moral character of the territory in question, treating cherished national lands rich in resources or production exactly on the same footing as alien deserts—except insofar as

---

* As Clausewitz notes in *On War* (book 5, chap. 2), the defining characteristic of a theater is that, in a larger war, operations outside its boundaries should have no *direct* effect within it, and only the indirect effect of generally weakening or strengthening the adversaries.

specifically military features are concerned. It is not surprising then that, in the making of policy, the logic of strategy at the theater level is itself often ignored, even if it is fully understood.

In the case of Korea, for example, the concentration of powerful North Korean forces with many tanks and much artillery near the border, the known ability of North Korean infantry to infiltrate in depth, and the bellicosity of the North Korean regime all make it highly probable that a war would begin with a surprise offensive of extreme intensity. Such an assault, however, could not be long sustained, and it could not progress very far into South Korean territory, since the mass of North Korean artillery is immobile and would be outranged and the foot infantry would soon run out of energy and supplies. In these circumstances, the logic of strategy at the theater level has the effect of greatly weakening a South Korean defense that would defend all and strengthening a defense that would defend less. If the first 50 kilometers of South Korean territory from the border were defended only opportunistically at the start of a war, with advantageous delay and ambush fights followed by deliberate withdrawals, the North Koreans would virtually defeat themselves by advancing that far. Once fully mobilized, the South Korean army would have the numbers and the means to counterattack in superior strength all the way to the border and across it, while airpower could inflict heavy losses on North Korean forces as they advance and retreat, indeed as soon as they move beyond the supporting cover of their predominantly immobile air defenses.

Such a scheme of "elastic defense" is definitely favored by the logic of theater strategy, but of course it ignores the nature of the territory that would be fought over—twice—as well as occupied by the North Koreans in between: it is not a desert but rather a densely populated farmland that extends to the northern edge of Seoul, where some eight million Koreans live and which contains the seat of all national institutions and a substantial part of the country's industry. And Korea is of course a divided country, whose two governments each claim sovereignty over the whole. The loss of those first 50 kilometers might induce a collapse of public confidence in the South Korean government and demoralize the armed forces, possibly to the point of nullifying their material strength. As a result, not surprisingly, South Korea's theater-defense policy ignores the logic of strategy at the theater level and seeks to provide a preclusive ("forward") defense of the whole territory. The logic may be ignored, but of course its consequences are manifest all the same, in some combination of insecurity or defensive costs greater than they would be otherwise. For South Korea, there is some insecurity and much cost: large forces are kept in a high state of readiness at all times, and elaborate barriers and frontal fortifications have been built.

As we have seen, nothing within the logic of theater strategy can justify another order of priorities, or indeed any priorities at all, no more than a known relationship between unemployment and inflation can mandate political choices as between the two: in some countries, high inflation is tolerated but not high unemployment; in others, it is the other way around. The economic *logic* that defines the relationship between the two does not prescribe the choice of economic *policy*. Similarly, in the Korean case the *logic* of theater strategy defines a relationship between the elasticity of the defense and its costs and risks, but theater *policy* strictly demands an inelastic defense.

EUROPE'S CENTRAL THEATER

In the satellite overview that theater strategy allows, we see the lands of West Germany extending from the Baltic Coast and Denmark all the way south to Austria and Switzerland, with the North Sea, the Netherlands, Belgium, Luxembourg, and France marking their western limits. Along the bell-shaped eastern edge, some 625 miles of the border march with East Germany and Czechoslovakia, and it then follows the eastward turn of Austria's frontier. Upon mobilization, as units of the Belgian, British, Canadian, Dutch, German, and American armies move out of barracks and bases to deploy into their assigned positions, the "central front" that was only an abstraction until now acquires a physical form. It is not a solid line of course with units stationed shoulder to shoulder, but rather consists of separate clusters of men, vehicles, and weapons positioned within a band of territory: roughly one third of the tank, mechanized, and light-armor units (the "covering forces") have advanced to a few miles from the border, and the rest lie in larger clusters several miles behind them. Even though the front does not therefore follow each twist and turn of the borders, it would still extend to 600 miles or so; the eastward border with neutral Austria must be protected as well, given the ease with which any Soviet invasion could pass through that poorly armed country.

We can now finally dispose of the missile-infantry proposal examined at each level of strategy so far. As soon as we contemplate the length of territory the Alliance must protect, we immediately understand why only the most elaborate barriers and fortifications could possibly justify a one-line frontal defense of missile troops. For we discover by simple arithmetic that in those segments of the front where the two sides would actually meet in battle, the cheap, abundant antitank missiles can actually be outnumbered by expensive Soviet tanks and armored infantry carriers. If we visualize an offensive just starting, we see a first wave of seven Soviet "armies" approaching the West German border, with almost 10,000 tanks among them, many more other combat vehicles, as well as much artillery and all manner of support units.[1] Those Soviet forces rolling foward are not distributed in a thin, long line running north-south, parallel to the border. Instead they would be formed into four or five long columns, moving westward against the front, not in single file of course but in a phalanx, as much as several miles wide where the terrain allows. Even so, we see that the Soviet forces are attacking a mere fraction of the entire 600-mile line: the columns are colliding with narrow segments of the front, as narrow as the width of a two-lane road in some places and nowhere broader than ten miles or so. Thus even if a huge force of missile troops were raised, with tens of thousands of antitank launchers, the armored vehicles rolling forward could still easily outnumber them where combat actually takes place.

The arithmetic of attrition must therefore guarantee defeat unless it is overcome by elaborate barriers and fortifications. It cannot be otherwise when the number of missile launchers must be distributed over 600 miles of frontage, whereas Soviet armored vehicles can attack in concentrated force where they choose to do so.[2] The missile troops could be concentrated too, indeed could outconcentrate the Soviet columns, if they were mobile enough. But that cannot be done merely by supplying trucks to transport them up and down the front, along such roads as there are in border areas that the division of Germany has made peripheral. Nor can it be done by keeping the bulk of the troops in wait at rearward cross-roads, ready to reinforce segments of the front that come under attack. Incapable of cross-country movement and thus road-bound, motorized missile troops in transit would be highly vulnerable to air attack and quite unable to move forward against the artillery fire that would reach over ten miles behind the front. Perhaps the reinforcement needed to counterconcentrate could be provided in more timely fashion by helicopters, with missile troops aboard or themselves armed with launchers, but this is certainly not a cheap alternative. In addition, those most fragile of aircraft would be exposed to the many antiaircraft weapons that accompany Soviet divisions and also to the curtains of descending artillery fire.

If trucks are much too vulnerable as well as road-bound, and if helicopters are vulnerable as well as too costly, then well-armored ground vehicles, fit to go across country, remain the one feasible choice to allow mobility under fire and therefore counterconcentration. Armored and tracked, such vehicles could certainly bring the missile troops where they would be needed. They would also replicate the present carriers of the mechanized infantry, which includes antitank missiles among its weapons. And if there are to be armored vehicles, why not arm some of them with built-in weapons usable without dismounting? And if there are to be built-in weapons, why rely on bulky and costly missiles with slow rates of fire, when guns remain superior for antiarmor combat at the closer ranges? The tank is thus rehabilitated and we have come full circle, with the conventional solution not merely sustained by institutional inertia but rather reaffirmed by the needs of battle.

Should confidence in the radical proposal persist, the issue is settled once we widen our geographic view. As we look across the expanse of East Germany, Czechoslovakia, Hungary, Poland, and beyond them into the western regions of the Soviet Union, we see that behind that first wave of seven Soviet armies another and larger wave is approaching, with yet more formations assembling within the Soviet Union to come up in turn. (For further information on the makeup of the Soviet army, see Appendices 2 and 3.) Even if the reinforcing divisions are not so fully manned, so freshly trained, or so completely equipped with the very latest weapons like those of the first echelon, the impact of such a great mass of advancing armor would surely overrun the frontal array of exhausted and depleted missile troops, if they have somehow resisted till then.

But as we finally dismiss the radical proposal, we make a disturbing discovery. Once it is mobilized, the Soviet army can overwhelm not only a hypothetical missile-troop defense but also the array of armored and mechanized forces that would now defend the central front. This is why the Alliance continues to rely on the supplement of nuclear counterattack. If warnings of impeding invasion are detected, believed in spite of contrived deception and self-deception, and also promptly acted upon by the five national governments concerned, the NATO forces held ready in peacetime should be able to resist the first echelon of the offensive—even though the benefits of the initiative for the Soviet side should yield a concentration advantage at first, as well as the opportunity to stage a great many dislocating commando assaults and diversionary penetrations by special units. That first phase of acute danger, when units driving out of peacetime garrisons to race into their planned positions would be afflicted by road congestion, air attacks, sabotaged bridges, commando ambushes, and contrived diversions, would be followed by another in the first hours of battle, when the major vectors of Soviet movement must be successfully guessed and countermovements concerted between different national armies. Nor could the Allied airforces help much as yet, for they would be just starting on their own battles, to defend airbases and attack those of the enemy.

Only by the most epic efforts and effective command could the defense prevail against the offensive mass of seven Soviet armies. Now greatly in need of rest and reconstitution, the Allied forces would very soon have to fight against the next and larger Soviet echelon, with scant reinforcements of their own. The Allied airforces should by now be of greater assistance, and battle losses might be matched in part by the gain in battle experience, but a defensive victory cannot be prudently expected.

OFFENSE-DEFENSE FORCE RATIOS

No mention has been made so far of the supposedly inherent numerical advantage of any defense, the oft-quoted ratio of three to one that the offense supposedly needs to win. *At the tactical level*, it is true, a company of defensive troops who need not advance to accomplish their task can dig in to hold a line and can therefore kill and wound the exposed attackers more easily than the latter can kill or wound them; in the circumstances, a ratio of three to one is as good a rule of thumb as any, when frontal attack must meet an entrenched defense. *At the operational level,* however, we see that the offensive side need not attack that particular line at all but can instead move to by-pass it on one side or both, in a simple case of relational maneuver. If the entrenched troops remain where they are, the defense fails absolutely and may be destroyed in the process if the offense chooses to pause for an enfilading or rear attack. On the other hand, if the defense reacts against the enemy's outflanking move, it can only do so by thinning out the line in order to extend it far enough or else by moving in turn to intercept the attackers, in a state of equal mobility and equal exposure. In the first case, the ratio advantage is preserved, but the balance of strength where combat occurs is altered in the enemy's favor; in the second, the balance of strength where the forces meet is preserved, but the ratio advantage is surrendered. In either case it no longer requires three companies or battalions to defeat just one.

In the conditions of World War I on the western front, the tactical ratio advantage was redeemed in full *at the level of theater strategy* because the continuity of trench lines from the Belgian coast to the Swiss border precluded any simple by-passing; and the ratio advantage was preserved against the operational-level reaction of concentrated column attacks against narrow segments of the front because, with field telephones to call for help and railways as well as trucks to bring it, the defensive counterconcentration proceeded faster than the advance of foot soldiers against artillery, barbed wire, and machine guns. Indeed, the intellectuals who dominated the postwar French general staff[3] could prove mathematically the counterconcentration superiority of defense over offense, inexorably derived from the *speed* advantage of sideways railway and truck movements along the front over the rate of foot-infantry advance against its fire. It only remained to compensate for the initial start that the offense might have, which all the best efforts of intelligence might not totally eliminate. That, however, could assuredly be done, for an uninterrupted defensive line would preserve the tactical advantage of entrenched troops who could not be by-passed, thus allowing one unit to hold five or ten at least temporarily until reinforcements arrived, just as one could indefinitely hold three. By this reasoning, so long as German mothers did not breed more than three times as many sons, the French would be able to resist any offensive, unless weakened by futile offensives of their own. Victory was assured therefore, but one more element was added to reduce its price: concrete-lined trenches and hard-built weapon sites already prepared in peacetime, instead of unsanitary mud trenches and dugouts improvised under fire; and elaborate forts to shield the artillery, much needed for counterbattery work to prevent the enemy's artillery from crushing the line infantry, as well as to attack the enemy's own advancing foot soldiers.

Such was the compelling linear logic that yielded the idea of the Maginot Line, which indeed achieved its culminating success in 1940, when the German offensive by-passed it by way of Belgium in order to evade the formidable strength of its barriers, solidly entrenched infantry, and fortified artillery. By the usual paradox of strategy, the Maginot Line failed to protect France because it was oversuccessful: no defensive line can possibly achieve more than to dissuade the enemy from even trying to attack it. In retrospect, one may conclude that a less formidable defensive array, a half-successful solution, might have served France better, by offering the possibility at least that the Germans would attack the line and become entangled in positional warfare. As it was, the Maginot Line, deemed impassable at the tactical level, evoked a relational theater-strategy response in the form of the oblique German thrust across the unfortified Belgian Ardennes all the way to the Channel coast.

Without the Maginot Line to skew the balance, the mathematics of counterconcentration based on the speed advantage of railways and trucks over soldiers on foot were utterly overthrown by the operational-level response of the blitzkrieg, whose deep-penetration columns moved at motor speed to outrace the sideways gathering of defensive strength. Their armor spearheads, largely immune to artillery interdiction and unopposed by obstacles, simply nullified the tactical-ratio advantage of line forces of plain infantry, and would in any case have outnumbered even line forces bristling with antitank guns. We can only wonder at the deep-seated emotional preferences that have completely reversed the twin lessons of 1940, to condemn the fully successful Maginot Line and uphold the spurious universal validity of three-to-one ratios valid only at the tactical level.

BATTLEFIELD NUCLEAR WEAPONS

Unshielded by fancied inherent advantages, the present plans of the Western Alliance for defending the central front must trust in the deus ex machina of "battlefield" nuclear weapons, which are to be lowered onto the stage if there is no other way of averting the front's penetration and collapse. Nuclear weapons are mostly kept for suasion* and nonuse, and we will consider them as such at a higher level of strategy. For now, however, let us see what they mean at the level of theater strategy.

Battlefield nuclear weapons with explosive yields and radiation effects quite modest by intercontinental nuclear standards,[4] in the form of shorter-range rockets, artillery shells, and demolition charges as well as aircraft bombs of broader scope, provide a technical-level response to the magnitude of the Soviet army by offering a ready means of carrying out devastating counterattacks. Under the current policy of the Alliance, in the course of frontal battles nonnuclear attacks would be met by nonnuclear defense for as long as possible; but if Soviet formations continue to arrive and the defense can no longer hold them back, then battlefield nuclear weapons will be called up.

When first fielded in 1952–53,[5] American nuclear weapons for battlefield use quickly rose on the curve of effectiveness: they were easily integrated within the frontal defense plans of those days, when small force clusters in shallow disposition almost formed a true line. But this technical reaction to Soviet theater-level strength reached its culminating point of success quite soon, for by the later 1950s the Soviet army had its battlefield nuclear weapons also. Hence if the Alliance command tried to shield crumbling sectors of the front by attacking Soviet invasion columns with nuclear weapons, the Soviet command could reply by breaking open other sectors of the front with its own battlefield nuclear weapons. Leaving aside for the moment any consideration of what additional nuclear weapons might be used by either side, against targets other than ground formations in combat, we can simply assume a symmetrical response if battlefield nuclear weapons were to be employed by the Alliance.

Action and reaction do not nullify each other in this case, however: once nuclear weapons are employed, the Soviet army can no longer conquer lands by invasion but would only preside over their devastation. Hence if the Alliance can persuasively threaten to use its battlefield nuclear weapons in case of need, it should be able to dissuade a Soviet attack that would aim at conquest, since its only outcomes must be either nonnuclear defeat or nuclear war. As

---

*The term is meant to describe both persuasion and dissuasion, in all their forms. The subject is discussed in Part III.

always with suasion, it is the adversary alone who controls the process: it is *his* leaders who must believe in the threat and calculate its punishment as greater than what they hope to achieve. And this makes security obtained by suasion inherently less reliable than defensive denial would be. Still, nuclear weapons present a threat less easily minimized than that of cavalry regiments or even armored divisions, since their technical results are far more certain and indeed accurately predictable.

In this case, however, the effectiveness of suasion would be circumscribed by motive: if the Soviet leaders were to attack the Alliance out of desperation rather than in the hope of conquest, they might not be dissuaded at all by the prospect of causing a belt of nuclear destruction down the middle of Central Europe. Illegitimate power is forever insecure, and one envisaged sequence is that a general revolt in Eastern Europe spreading into the Soviet non-Russian borderlands—a revolt caused precisely by the subversive example of Western European freedom and prosperity—might induce the Soviet leaders to choose aggression to dim that light, to deprive unrest of its impulse by presenting a worse prospect than continued oppression.

Another possibility, at least in theory, is that the Soviet Union might attack for defensive reasons, to preempt an Alliance offensive that its leaders believed to be imminent. The notion of a Western aggression concerted in secret by the Dutch parliament, the West German chancellor, the grand duke of Luxembourg, the Belgian cabinet, as well as the White House and Whitehall, might seem entirely fantastic to Westerners. But the Kremlin leaders preside over a government that has a seemingly infinite capacity for suspicion, as a great many hapless dissidents seriously interrogated to uncover nonexistent conspiracies can attest; and no date in history is more clearly remembered in the Soviet Union than June 22, 1941, when invasion came as a dreadful surprise, hugely devastating. If self-defense were the motive of aggression, however ill conceived, Alliance battlefield nuclear weapons would retain their physical capacity to nullify an impeding Soviet nonnuclear victory, but not the ability to dissuade attack altogether.

So far, only the suasion that the prospect of *battlefield* nuclear war might or might not accomplish in the minds of Soviet leaders has been considered. It would distract us from our present purpose to study in depth the progression of threats that follows from the initial attempt at nuclear suasion, beginning with the long-standing

Soviet effort to persuade the European allies that it would react to battlefield nuclear strikes with nuclear attacks of its own against more sensitive targets, notably airbases or even European cities (to overcome by suasion the paralyzing effect of battlefield nuclear war); and continuing with the American counterthreat of nuclear attacks against equivalent targets in the Soviet Union, including cities (to inhibit by suasion any extension of nuclear war beyond the zones of frontal combat). As always in the realm of strategy, move evokes countermove, even if there is no substantive action or reaction in suasion, but only the perception or misperception of threats and of latent capacities to inflict harm. To pursue the sequence, upon which reciprocal counterforce threats to the nuclear forces themselves are superimposed, would take us out of the theater level and into the next level, of grand strategy. For now let us remain where we are, by noting that the Alliance threat of battlefield nuclear strikes, which is meant to dissuade Soviet hopes of achieving a nonnuclear victory, must have an inward effect on the Western allies as well, especially on the government of West Germany.

It is from German territory that most of the shorter-range weapons would be launched, and it is West Germany's frontal zones that would suffer nuclear attack in the event of a symmetrical Soviet reaction. Nor can the government in Bonn be indifferent to the fate of the German lands ruled from East Berlin in the event of war: East Germany would then become enemy territory, containing the principal targets of battlefield nuclear strikes—but this would not be alien territory for fellow Germans.

Because it is so damaging to those who threaten as well as to the threatened, the Alliance counterthreat could therefore be self-inhibiting. Obviously, however, such reasoning has not prevailed because member states and *especially* West Germany continue to reaffirm the threat of battlefield nuclear attack in the event of an impending Soviet nonnuclear victory.[6] They prefer to accept the ensuing risks rather than to raise stronger nonnuclear forces capable of defeating nonnuclear invasion on their own, without appeal to the higher court of nuclear war.

A NONNUCLEAR DEFENSE IN EUROPE?

The risks of the Alliance's present reliance on nuclear weapons are obvious, but the consequences of increasing its nonnuclear strength could be paradoxically adverse. It may be that the refusal

of the European allies in general, and of successive West German
governments in particular, to increase their nonnuclear forces by
any wide margin is motivated only by a shortsighted desire to econ-
omize in military expenditures. But it could also be fully justified by
sound (that is, paradoxical) strategic reasoning.

To be sure, if the nonnuclear forces of the Alliance had enough
strength to defend the central front against a Soviet nonnuclear
invasion, there would be no need to employ battlefield nuclear
weapons. In the event of war, therefore, that most valuable precedent of nuclear nonuse that has endured since 1945 could be preserved, and the world would be spared the ultimate danger of a
step-by-step progression from battlefield to intercontinental nuclear
war. But if nuclear use is absent in a war, nonnuclear combat must
always occur. Thus the paradoxical consequence of avoiding the
nuclear form of destruction—very alarming as it would be for people all over the world, but possibly of small dimensions if only the
modern lower-yield weapons are employed—might be even more
destruction, nonnuclear but still enormously damaging for the affected populations of Europe in general and of West Germany in
particular.

Further, if the leaders of the Soviet Union start a war, they must
do so with the intention of breaking the central front and invading in
some depth. If the nonnuclear forces of the Alliance become strong
enough to defend the front and repel invasion, the Soviet leaders
might well react by using their own battlefield nuclear weapons.
After all, whatever hopes or fears might induce them to start the
fighting would be replaced by the still greater fear of the consequences of defeat for their regime, indeed for the survival of the
Soviet Union as a political entity. Thus the paradoxical consequence of avoiding nuclear use, by increasing nonnuclear strength,
might be to provoke the Soviet Union's own use of nuclear
weapons.

Finally, the present nonnuclear forces of doubtful adequacy confront the Soviet Union with the prospect that, in the event of an
invasion, the central front would be penetrated rather quickly, causing a chaotic situation in which battlefield nuclear weapons might
be employed in a panic reaction, regardless of Soviet efforts to
dissuade national leaders from authorizing their use, by threats of
still more catastrophic attacks of their own. The paradoxical consequence of stronger nonnuclear forces might be to permit the stabili-

zation of the front in the early phase of a war, during which the Soviet Union could both move forward the forces it needs to break the front and also exercise its full powers of persuasion on the governments of Europe, to induce them to renounce any and all nuclear use on the battlefield by the threat of far more destructive nuclear attacks. Then, too, the more time a nonnuclear defense of the central front allows for deliberation, public debate, and media coverage, the less likely it is that an American president will retain the freedom of action to agree to nuclear use on the battlefield at the request of European authorities, or to reaffirm the American promise that nuclear attacks on European cities would evoke American attacks on Soviet cities. By strategy's usual paradox, nonnuclear strength might therefore yield weakness.

CHAPTER 9

THEATER STRATEGY II: DEFENSIVE FORMATS AND THE GUERRILLA OPTION

On the offensive side, the great choice in theater strategy is between the broad advance that only the very strong may employ—for otherwise the army advancing everywhere must be everywhere outnumbered—and the narrow advance that offers the opportunity of victory even to the weak, by focusing strength at the expense of a more complete weakness everywhere else. In its operational-level simplicity, in the ease with which a parallel advance can be coordinated, and above all with its absence of exposed flanks, the broad-front advance is safe if costly in losses, as we have seen. But risk and profit inexorably increase together the more narrow the advance, culminating in the pencil-thin penetrations of the prototypical German blitzkrieg, part adventure and part confidence trick. By the usual reversal, it is only those who already have a margin for imprudence in their superiority of means who can afford the cautious broad advance, while those already at risk must be bold to have any chance of success at all. The paradox aside, by now in any case familiar, there is no great complexity here, or at least none that transcends purely military considerations.

On the defensive, however, each format governs not only the deployment of military forces but also the fate of the territory exposed to danger, and linear logic—which would equate defense with protection—quite normally clashes with the paradoxical logic of strategy, compelling complex choices between diverging political and military priorities. This is so especially in the case of an elastic defense, which would defend no specific tract of the territory in order to better defend all of it, by releasing its forces from protective duties. The resulting freedom of action to evade the enemy's main thrusts, to move at will and concentrate in full, gives the defenders every advantage of the offense, while they still retain their inherent advantage of fighting in a known and presumably friendly environment. Often regarded as ideal from a purely military viewpoint, this is the least desirable of formats for those who govern, regardless of whether it is wealth, welfare, or control that they seek to maximize. Similarly, in the opposite case of a preclusive forward defense that would seek to deny any enemy intrusions whatsoever, the political best and military worst again coincide.

Both extremes are of course rarities. In practice only approximations are encountered: even when Stalin's high command decided to elude the renewed German blitzkrieg of 1942 by a defense sufficiently elastic, it would not abandon Stalingrad; and even the present commitment of the North Atlantic Alliance to a forward defense of West Germany does not mandate the protection of every inch of its territory, even if an elastic defense is rejected in principle.* In reality, therefore, policy usually compromises between linear political priorities and their paradoxical military counterparts, with more scope allowed to the former when the sense of security is greater (justified or not), and more to the latter when the fear of imminent disaster is greater.

There is obviously an entire spectrum of choices between the extremes of an elastic defense, which does not resist at all but rather saves its full strength for counterattacks, and a fully preclusive frontal defense: policy can freely impose its preference by defining the boundary between what is to be protected at all costs and what may be abandoned at least temporarily. But there is another format that diverges from this spectrum, a "defense in depth," in which a frontal zone more or less deep is neither preclusively protected nor abandoned to free-ranging maneuver. Instead that zone is selectively defended by self-contained groupings of forces forming many islands of resistance laid out in depth, to form a grid rather than a line.

---

*The one-bound reach of Soviet armored and mechanized forces, with their inherent supply capacity, is so deep that a defense sufficiently elastic to absorb their momentum would scarcely defend West German territory at all, but rather sacrifice it to defend the rest of western Europe. Moreover, the Soviet Union would certainly seek to dissuade any attempt to *recover* German territory by nuclear threats, which need not be unpersuasive even if the war had remained nonnuclear till then.

Shielded by favorable terrain or artificial barriers, psychologically and organizationally prepared to fight on their own, and certainly supplied to do so, such islands of resistance ("hedgehogs" was the preferred term in World War II) serve to hold important passages along major avenues of advance and valuable infrastructures such as airfields and major depots, at least for a while. But their main function must be to offer protected bases from which disruptive incursions and lesser counterattacks can be launched, ideally in coordination with the counterattacks of the main forces kept back to secure the territory behind the frontal belt given over to the defense in depth.

If the islands of resistance are to be strong enough, and if they are to be laid out in sufficient depth, there cannot be many of them; they certainly cannot form a continuous front. Hence the enemy could still advance without pausing if he so chooses, by-passing them all to reach his objectives beyond the defense-in-depth belt. But that opportunity is also a snare: just as in the past an advancing column could not simply by-pass an unsubdued fortress holding forces ready to sally forth without the risk of severe losses, so even today an armor-mechanized penetration cannot simply ignore forces with offensive strength free to attack its vulnerable flanks. Yet to pause in order to reduce each island of resistance in turn must interrupt the critical tempo of the advance, whereas to assign containment forces at each remove would result in a growing dispersion of strength (even as it naturally wanes in the course of the advance).

The dilemma thus created for the attackers by the defense in depth can be compounded in detail if the defenders also have the means and moral capacity to launch smaller raids on the supply columns, service units, and lesser detachments that the enemy advance itself brings within their reach. To the extent that the terrain confines the offensive to narrow avenues of advance that can actually be blocked, it is not a dilemma that faces the attackers, who must instead overcome the resistance of each successive defended island along their chosen path. But of course strategy allows no unlimited linear progression in this matter either: the more the terrain across the entire theater of war confines movement, the more valid the format becomes—until the culminating point is passed in truly constrictive terrain of the Himalayan type, in which a firm defense by a *linked* chain of strong positions, each blocking the exit of one of the few narrow approaches, becomes preferable to any defense in depth.*

For the North Atlantic Alliance and its central front in Germany, there is no danger of overshooting the limits of advantage that a defense in depth could offer: some sectors contain mountains but not of Himalayan or Alpine caliber, and they offer no opportunity for the absolute blockage of any major avenue of penetration. Still, even in the North German plain and the so-called Fulda Gap, there are significant terrain obstacles, both wooded ridges and urban areas that extend far enough into the rear to accommodate a grid of islands for a deep defense. A defense-in-depth theater strategy would certainly be a relational-maneuver response to the present Soviet threat, for it would largely circumvent the armored "mailed-fist" momentum of the Soviet army: deprived of the solid obstacle of the central front to break through, the invasion columns would instead have to fight their way across the entire defended belt and even disperse their units to *control* territory, thereby becoming vulnerable to the elusive forces of the defense.

Many schemes have been circulated for the defense in depth of the Alliance central front which variously advocate the retention of the present armored and mechanized forces, though kept back to maneuver freely instead of being locked into frontal positions;[1] and combinations of the same forces with missile light infantry in small units to be moved about by helicopters;[2] or with local militias that would fight in guerrilla fashion, along with regular light infantry;[3] or with small units of regular infantry distributed in garrisons to defend the stone-built villages that dot the German countryside.[4] In some schemes, antitank barriers would be added, to slow down Soviet armored columns; in others, with or without barriers, fortified positions would be provided for some of the troops, to enable them to delay passage through roads and terrain corridors in a deep zone behind the front. In all the schemes, the purpose is to delay indefinitely the fast and deep penetrations that Soviet armored columns would seek to achieve by fighting one hard frontal battle. Instead the Soviet columns are to be entangled within the deep defense, until they are cut off and defeated piecemeal or counterattacked in strength.[5]

The defense-in-depth alternatives suggested for the central front

* An option available to neither China nor India: both want to control Himalayan territory rather than defend from behind it.

differ in detail, but they share one thing in common: they are all examples of original military thought, which arguably diverge not only from ossified plans but also from political realities. Moreover, all the schemes appear to suffer from the classic delusion of the "final move," for in reacting to the deep-penetration theater strategy imputed to the Soviet army they fail to allow for the likely reaction they are apt to evoke, in the form of a new Soviet theater strategy. In other words, they ignore strategy's fundamental phenomenon. Before addressing such criticisms, the considerable merits of these schemes in purely military terms are worth recalling.

At the tactical level, as we have seen, troops fighting from within fortifications against attackers who must move in the open benefit from favorable "exchange ratios," as their fire acts with full effect while the attackers' fire does not. Small, agile units that raid Soviet columns opportunistically, and which would disperse as soon as they are counterattacked, should also experience favorable ratios. Moreover, so long as those who cover them with their weapons can endure under fire, barriers such as antitank ditches, solid obstacles, and minefields can improve the tactical effectiveness of blocking positions, by reducing the enemy's rate of advance, ideally down to the target-engagement capacity of the defensive weapons in place. At the operational level, the combined effect of barriers and road-blocking fortifications would reduce the relative mobility of the invaders, making it more likely that sufficiently strong counter-attacking forces could be positioned advantageously to engage the flanks of Soviet columns. At the theater level, all these schemes would circumvent the Soviet army's greatest strength, its ability to break through solid fronts, while exploiting its weakest point, its lack of small-unit flexibility.[6]

Defense-in-depth schemes have nevertheless been rejected by successive West German governments and therefore by the Alliance as a whole. This is sufficient evidence that they diverge from established policy—but policy can change at any time, and the charge of political unrealism is of a more fundamental order. At the technical level of strategy, or the tactical or operational, the goals pursued are self-evident and beyond debate: higher scores, better exchange ratios, and victory in battle are certainly more desirable than their opposites. At the theater level, however, the very meaning of success and failure is a matter of political decision. Defense-in-depth schemes may defeat a Soviet invasion without, however, *defending* West Germany in the meanwhile, and whether the concurrent ruin of both the Soviet army and much German territory is a success or a failure is an open question. The amount of territory that would be given over to prolonged warfare varies with each specific scheme, but none can offer a preclusive defense of the entire national territory, as the current "forward" defense is now meant to do.

Those who advocate schemes of defense in depth argue that the danger of exposing some part of West German territory to non-nuclear destruction should be preferred to the ultimate danger of exposing all of it, including cities, to nuclear devastation. The choice is complicated by the different risk levels associated with the two dangers: it can certainly be argued that battlefield-nuclear dissuasion is apt to be more reliable than its nonnuclear counterpart. But actually the terms of the choice itself are questionable, because the current policy contains a third option. The West German government can prohibit, at any time, the use of nuclear weapons based on its territory. Hence if dissuasion fails, a Soviet invasion begins and the front cannot hold; the West German government then refuses to authorize nuclear counterattacks and asks for an armistice instead. Soviet terms are likely to be harsh, but even that may still be preferred to the actual use of nuclear weapons—or to the widespread destruction that prolonged nonnuclear warfare would inflict on Germany's crowded lands. Defense in depth is far more attractive as an alternative to the official policy than to its possible unofficial wartime variant.

GUERRILLA WAR AS A THEATER STRATEGY

The dissonance with societal realities is even more evident in schemes that accord a large role to volunteer militia forces, though it occurs in the light-infantry schemes as well. To pave the way for advantageous counterattacks by the regular armored and mechanized forces, both the militia and light-infantry schemes envisage many small ambushes and raids against the supply columns, detachments, and exposed flanks of the Soviet invasion columns—in other words, a guerrilla resistance. This is merely a pure version of defense in depth, whereby nothing at all is defended preclusively while the control of everything is persistently contested.* Indeed, what makes such schemes attractive is the operational-level advantage that guerrilla fighters enjoy over conventional armies. They have no technical-level advantage, but rather the opposite; and they do not often have a tactical advantage when combat takes place. But they certainly have an operational advantage: insofar as they fight elusively, without trying to defend terrain points against determined attack, the militia or light infantry would remain free to do as much or as little fighting as they choose, when they choose. What the schemes therefore envisage is that the Soviet invasion forces would be harassed at every turn, with their road columns frequently ambushed, their smaller detachments surprised and destroyed, and their supply dumps sabotaged. They would be unable to come to grips with the guerrilla-style defenders, who would disperse before superior strength, thereby destroying without being destroyed in turn.

Guerrilla warfare is a relational-maneuver response to superior military strength of conventional form, and one of the weaknesses it relates to is the self-restraint of the enemy. Jewish, Kikuyu, Chinese communist, Greek, and Arab guerrillas fighting British troops in Palestine, Kenya, Malaya, Cyprus, and Aden, even Vietnamese and Algerians fighting French troops in Indochina and Algeria, and certainly the Vietcong fighting Americans, could rely on their enemy's self-restraint in dealing with the civilian population at large. There were exceptions of course, with harsh behavior by some troops here and there and even the occasional act of deadly violence, but no systematic retaliation was countenanced by the

---

*Guerrilla (from the Spanish "little war"), better characterized by the German *bandenkrieg* ("war of bands"), in contrast to large-formation regular warfare, is of course a theater strategy in itself, actually theater-scale enlargement of agile, light-infantry tactics. In the context of an internal struggle for the control of government, on the other hand, guerrilla war is only the military component of a grand strategy, *revolutionary war*, whose political component is subversion—the displacement of an administration by means of propaganda and terrorism. The relative admixture of propaganda and terrorism is a valid indicator of the nature of the political struggle: when much terrorism is employed, a consensual form of government cannot be the aim of the insurgents. Walter Laqueur's *Guerrilla* (1976) remains perhaps the most useful compendium. The classic anatomy of revolutionary war is contained in the opening of Roger Trinquier's *La guerre moderne* (1961).

military authorities (whose goal after all was to win over "hearts and minds") let alone by the governments at home, acting under the scrutiny of parliaments and press.

If, by contrast, such inhibitions are absent or weak, the freedom of action of guerrillas can be greatly restricted by the threat of violent reprisals against the civilian population, which contains their families and friends. When each guerrilla assassination results in the execution of innocent civilians held hostage just for that purpose; when each successful ambush is followed by the annihilation of the nearest village; and when each raid on a headquarters or depot is followed by massacres, not many guerrillas will feel free to assassinate, ambush, and raid whenever opportunity offers. Their emotional ties to the civilian population from which they derive is a potential weakness, which ruthless occupation forces can exploit in their own relational-maneuver response.

The reprisal policy of the German forces during World War II was very effective in minimizing the results that guerrillas could achieve, in most places, most of the time. Of course the mere diversion of German manpower to oppose them must be the largest part of any estimate, but with that duly included, it is now generally agreed that the military impact of the Norwegian, Danish, Dutch, Belgian, French, Italian, and Greek resistance was unimpressive.[7] The Polish resistance was more an effort to organize a secret army for an eventual war of liberation than an ongoing guerrilla campaign, and when it did emerge to fight, it did so in perfectly conventional form, by attempting to secure Warsaw in August 1944, with attacks on Germans avoided until then to spare the population from the inevitable reprisals.[8] Only Tito's communists and the Soviet partisans were truly effective as guerrillas during the war, precisely because they were willing to compete with the Germans in ruthlessness, at very great cost to the civilian population.[9]

When guerrillas are fighting within the setting of an internal struggle for power (a revolutionary war, that is), of the sort that has been widespread since the end of World War II, reprisals will usually be counterproductive.* But there is an equivalent substitute: local self-defense militias, armed by the government to resist guerrilla intrusions within its sphere of control.

*The exceptions include internal struggles between central authorities and separatists, ethnic or regional, who enjoy strong local support.

Point Defense

It may seem strange that to harm civilians at large and to arm them can be equivalent, but this is so in the paradoxical realm of strategy, where both measures can achieve the same purpose. In the first instance, the *symmetrical* theater-level response to guerrillas is to emulate their dispersion. Instead of an area defense, provided by large formations ready to sally out to engage enemy forces—an ineffectual procedure against elusive opponents—many small units are detached from the battle formations, to provide a "point defense" of as many vulnerable targets as possible, along with police and any militia at hand. In this way, guards on bridges, dams, and power stations, as well as town and village garrisons, road checkpoints, sentries, and patrols, compete with the diffused strength of the guerrillas, and do so advantageously in most cases because regular troops are apt to be better disciplined, better trained, and better armed. Naturally, if a conventional war is underway at the same time, the opportunity cost of point defense in the rear areas is the loss of combat strength at the front, and that is one of the causes of the paradoxical convergence between uninterrupted advance and defeat.[10] In the context of revolutionary war, on the other hand, point defense is the most important function of the armed forces, to safeguard the workings of society and state until the motives of the insurgency are removed by reforms, counterpropaganda, or decolonization.

In either case, however, the obvious operational-level guerrilla response is to adopt a more concentrated form of warfare. Having initially resorted to guerrilla warfare because of their inability to match the strength of large government formations, when the point defense is organized to oppose their small bands the insurgents discover that guards, garrisons, checkpoints, and patrols are all individually vulnerable to larger bands, gathered to attack specific objectives. As the process develops, a distinction often emerges between guerrillas who remain in small localized bands and "main forces" that operate in wider areas, perhaps countrywide. At this stage the guerrillas could defeat the point defense in detail, by employing their main forces for successive attacks against small regular units. But as the guerrillas try to do so, they must become rather less elusive in their larger groupings, both for physical reasons (hundreds cannot hide in nature as fully as a few) and also because the ingathering of main forces must remove some of the individual guerrillas from their immediate habitat—and as strangers they are less likely to be shielded by the locals. This enables the government to engage the guerrillas in a concentration/countercon- centration contest, on terms that vary according to the available means of supply, communication, and mobility. If there is no great difference between the two sides and the contest evolves on equal terms, the spiral may continue to ascend until both are fielding large formations, and *guerra* fully displaces *guerrilla*.

This is unlikely, however, because the insurgents will rarely be able to gather all their localized small bands into the main forces, and will not usually want to do so anyway, because the advantage in supply, communications, and mobility generally remains with the government.[11] Hence main forces and battles are likely to coexist with elusive small bands and their opportunistic attacks on any targets of value left undefended. The result is that those who are fighting insurgents are confronted with the concurrent need both for large formations—to fight the main forces—and for point defenses. This places them in exactly the same predicament as that of an army still engaged in conventional war at the front, which has con- quered actively hostile populations and seeks to minimize the diver- sion of its forces to provide point defenses in the rear. For an occupation army, the solution is to dissuade guerrilla action by reprisals, deadly or not (property destruction can be just as effec- tive), rather than preclude it by distributing small units throughout resisting areas. In fighting domestic insurgents, on the other hand, the equivalent solution is to induce the inhabitants of insecure areas to form self-defense militias for point defense, thus enabling regular detachments on garrison and guard duty to revert to their forma- tions for large-scale actions against the insurgent main forces.

German Guerrillas?

Reverting to our case study of the Alliance, as we contemplate a Soviet invasion of Germany confronted by guerrilla attacks, it is obvious that the tempo of the fighting would make it impossible to recruit, train, and arm Soviet-sponsored collaborationist militias, even if there were any political, cultural, or ethnic basis for such an enterprise.[12] Inevitably, then, the Soviet army would face the choice between a reprisal policy to dissuade attacks on its truck columns, service units, isolated detachments, and flanks in general or the scattering of its forces to provide point defenses, flank guards, and search-and-destroy teams.

Although it is not uncommon for the same army to behave much more harshly with populations perceived as primitive than with those deemed more civilized, Soviet conduct in Afghanistan certainly shows a propensity for the most violent reprisals. It is generally agreed, for example, that the area bombing of nearby villages and towns is the normal Soviet response to guerrilla attacks, and there are many reports of executions of fighting-age men rounded up in the vicinity, even without evidence of their participation in those attacks. As it happens, some Afghan guerrillas—perhaps many—are transcendentally motivated, so that reprisals do not dissuade them. Even so, the bombing is effective in physical terms at least: in the new political geography of Afghanistan, where the rural population is undiminished, the volume of guerrilla action is very small; most guerrilla activity accurs in areas that have already been depopulated. Increasingly, guerrillas in the field no longer have their families and clans nearby, but rather in refugee camps inside Pakistan and Iran where they are safe from Soviet reprisals. By the same token, however, civilians are no longer in place to provide food and information to the guerrillas.

The implicit assumption of the resistance schemes—that the Soviet invasion forces in Germany would suffer ambush, raids, and sabotage without retaliating against the civilian population—is dubious, to say the least, and certainly obtains no validation from the Afghan experience. One wonders how long guerrilla-style attacks would persist after the executions begin and after the first violent reprisals against nearby civilian populations.[13] Nor is it realistic to expect that urban Germans would sustain the extreme hardships and heavy losses of guerrilla resistance as Afghan tribesmen are now doing.[14]

The Soviet Response

Even if we disregard political objections and all doubts aroused by their quasi-guerrilla element, as soon as we allow our still-picture view to evolve dynamically we discover that *none* of the defense-in-depth schemes could withstand the most obvious Soviet reaction. If the Alliance abandons preclusive security (forward defense) and the central front that is its instrument, it can hardly do so in secrecy or very rapidly. Parliamentary procedures, and the necessary relocation of some major armored and mechanized formations to new bases in the rear, would allow ample time for a responsive change in Soviet theater strategy. Actually very little time would be needed to prepare the most elementary Soviet reaction: to advance as quickly as possible in fewer, more concentrated columns aimed straight at the largest German cities (Hamburg, Frankfurt, Nuremberg, Munich) in order to induce the West German government to ask for an armistice.

No longer faced by the solid array of Alliance strength positioned for frontal battle, a Soviet invasion would not have to start by sending out probing regiments, to find unguarded gaps or fight their way through so as to open paths of advance for reinforcing divisions. Instead, Soviet forces could execute a "steamroller" theater strategy, with their entire strength massed into just three or four very powerful vectors of advance. Ignoring the defensive units spread out in depth, except for those that happen to stand directly in their path, Soviet columns would simply roll forward as rapidly as possible, to reach the major cities and invest them closely, thereby inhibiting nuclear counterattack.

As for Alliance counterattacks against the flanks of the Soviet vectors of advance, with so many Soviet divisions advancing together, the core of each penetration would be amply shielded. Finally, because the whole purpose of the defense-in-depth schemes is to avoid the mailed-fist strength of massed armor, the Soviet columns could not be blocked by head-on resistance without sacrificing the only justification for giving up the preclusive defense of the entire territory. And if that is done nevertheless, the ensuing fight could only lead to the destruction of the defensive forces hurriedly gathered to stand in the Soviet paths of advance, for they could not possibly outconcentrate the invaders already massed to begin with, given the prior dispersal of the defense. Reaction must defeat action in this case, and not because of any assumption of Soviet numerical superiority. On the contrary, even a perfect parity would assure that outcome. (Nor does the logic of strategy at the theater level condemn the *concept*; other things being equal and with fortune held even, the relational-maneuver defense should actually prevail.) The reason is that all the defense-in-depth schemes for West Germany and the Alliance contain a fatal flaw: they make no provision for German cities, which can neither be defended nor evacuated and which are not shielded by distance. (The center of Hamburg is a mere 25 miles from the nearest tract of the East German border; Frankfurt is within 75 miles of the border; Nuremberg is no farther from the Czechoslovak border; and even Munich is only some 100 miles from that border and just over 50 miles from the Austrian border.)

When Diocletian's strategy gave the Roman empire one more century of power and another of survival, precisely by thinning out the frontier garrisons to provide a defense in depth that held back the better units for counterattacks, the cities, towns, and even rural estates were all individually protected by fortified wall circuits. Invaders could take standing crops, seize loose cattle, pillage isolated farmhouses and lesser villages; but they could inflict no greater damage without pausing to undertake siege operations. Usually devoid of siege machinery and lacking in poliorcetic skills, the invaders could rarely do better than attempt to undermine walls while being pelted from above. Cities usually had garrisons and artillery to put up a more active defense, and even many land-lords armed their tenants in some sort of homeguard. When other emergencies, or the need to gather great strength from afar, delayed the Roman counterattack and allowed time for prolonged sieges, the delay did not favor the invaders. It was a crucial part of the scheme that granaries and other foodstores were protected especially well. Instead of being able to starve out the defenders, the invaders were themselves quite often driven away by starvation; they had no supply corps to sustain them, and indeed it was hunger that commonly induced their attacks in the first place.[15]

The Soviet army cannot be kept out of German cities by stones and boiling oil. It could be held off very handily by urban-defense forces, trained and equipped to turn suburbs into ambush grounds for enemy tank and mechanized units, with successive city perimeters opportunely fortified to compel Soviet forces to fight house to house. Formidable in open terrain because of its weight of armor, the Soviet army is short of infantry—and in street fighting a single row of office buildings can swallow the total dismounted strength of an entire division. But nothing could prevent Soviet tank guns from firing into buildings to quell resistance, Soviet combat engineers from blasting open corridors of advance to replace well-blocked streets, or Soviet artillery from barraging the urban space, however futile the results. To defend as in Stalingrad or Beirut is to destroy, albeit while consuming the attacker's strength as well.

No prospect is less attractive for an infantry-poor mechanized army of the Soviet kind than to wage war in city streets or even suburbs.[16] It is most improbable, however, that the government of West Germany would be willing to convert its largest cities into battle zones for urban warfare. If faced with Soviet forces about to drive into Hamburg, approaching Frankfurt, and on the edge of Nuremberg in the context of a denuclearized defense in depth, the West German government might agree to fight on according to Alliance plans, by means of long-range nuclear strikes against the invasion forces advancing across its own territory, moving up within the East German and Czechoslovak rear, or still inside the Soviet Union itself. But it would certainly not be willing to turn its cities into battlefields, repeating the experience of Berlin in 1945, when it was discovered that a few hours of artillery shelling and tank fire could be more devastating than a thousand-bomber raid.

With or without a guerrilla dimension, a defense in depth is therefore not the answer *for the central front*. Attractive as the notion is when we consider only the first-move response to Soviet theater strategy, it is revealed as very fragile when we consider the most likely Soviet reaction. Yet what holds for West Germany and the central front need not be true elsewhere. For we have here encountered the consequences of three specific characteristics of the particular theater of war: it is unshielded by any major geographic obstacles such as high mountains; it lacks depth as a whole; and it contains crucial values, large cities in this case, very near a threatened frontier.

The same theater strategy of defense in depth could be very satisfactory in the case, say, of an expeditionary American defense against a Soviet invasion of Iranian oilfields and ports in the Abadan area at the head of the Persian Gulf. With more than five hundred miles between the Soviet frontier and Abadan, and with a great deal of poorly roaded mountain terrain in between, there would be ample opportunity for delaying actions and disruptive attacks by light infantry and helicopters within a broad band of territory, and much room after that for counterattacks or simple blocking by heavier forces coming up from the coast. Indeed, we have recently witnessed the success of a defense in depth in the vastness of Iran, when Iraqi forces were first contained and later repelled after the initial invasion of September 1980. And we may recall that the Soviet regime only survived the war that attended its birth in 1917 because the huge expanse of Russia allowed much scope for both defense in depth and elastic defense, with the former favored to hold successive stations of the Trans-Siberian railway and the latter chiefly employed by the cavalry armies that fought White forces and local nationalists in the Ukraine. Again, during World War II, the Soviet Union became the scene of defense-in-depth as well as elastic-defense theater strategies, first by one side and then the other.

In the unsurprising conclusion that geographic expanse is needed for a successful defense in depth (with even more needed for an elastic defense), we encounter yet again the workings of the paradoxical logic: the less the parts are continuously protected, the more the whole can ultimately be defended, for protection in detail dissipates the very strength needed to overcome attack. In the resulting tension between priorities already noted, the vital interests of citizen and state can easily diverge, just as the interests of local inhabitants certainly diverge from those of the guerrillas who claim to fight in their behalf. Whereas the individual seeks uninterrupted protection for personal survival, the collective entity of the state may best secure its own survival in difficult circumstances precisely by suspending such protection, as guerrillas must always do if they are not to lose the elusiveness that is their chief strength. It is only under a forward-defense format that the divergence of interests is eliminated, since the goal of collective defense is equated to the protection of every part of the territory. As such, it is the format most congenial to individualistic democracies, even if it is not necessarily compatible with their survival.

CHAPTER 10

THEATER STRATEGY III: INTERDICTION AND THE SURPRISE ATTACK

We have seen that the different formats of theater defense are not in truth freely available options but are instead largely preordained by fundamental political dispositions and cultural attitudes. Normally it is always a preclusive forward defense that is desired, even if some shallow form of defense in depth is accepted in practice. As for its deeper versions, and certainly any deep elastic defense, these are hardly ever deliberately planned and only reluctantly adopted *in extremis,* to avert imminent defeat (Yugoslavia's official strategy is a prominent contemporary exception).

Actually there is a format even more desirable in theory than a preclusive defense, whereby the defense of a theater is not defensive at all but is instead accomplished by launching an immediate counteroffensive against the attacker. In its deliberate sacrifice of the inherent tactical advantages of defense, this choice must imply a judgment about the *current* balance of forces drastically at variance with the attacker's judgment. It also requires an offensive elan more likely to be encountered among aggressors than among victims. No modern example in pure form can be cited, and the nearest case, the advance of the French army and the British expeditionary force into Belgium in immediate reaction to the initial German offensive on May 10, 1940, is not an encouraging precedent.

The advent of long-range means of attack has made it possible to wage war deep in the enemy's territory as well, but certainly theater (or "strategic") depth continues to favor the defense, if that space is indeed disposable. France, though a large country by European standards, lacked theater depth in its railway-age warfare with

Germany because supremely valued Paris is not at the center of the country but rather in the northwest corner, a mere 100 well-roaded miles from the Belgian frontier, with no major terrain barriers in between. That being so, the size of the country was actually a disadvantage since most French reserves and garrison forces had to come from afar to stand between Paris and the frontier, and this obviously made France vulnerable to surprise attack. It was to compensate for this weakness that there was so much French fortress building at the frontiers long before the Maginot Line.

The same geography was by contrast favorable for French offensive action in a northerly direction, into the Low Countries and the German lands. With its political center so well positioned to serve as a forward command post, and with the frontier fortresses in place to serve as depots and jump-off bases, France could readily mount surprise offensives—and frequently did until the unification of Germany nullified the advantage.

The Soviet Union, like the tsars' Russia before it, has been in exactly the opposite situation. With almost 800 scarcely roaded miles to shield Moscow in a westward direction, measuring only to Warsaw, theater depth has been ample to absorb the strength of Swedish, French, and German invaders from Charles XII until Hitler. Nor did Peter the Great's foundation of his capital change matters fundamentally. While the city's defensive depth to the north was much smaller than Moscow's, by the time St. Petersburg was built, Swedish power was in sharp decline and no new northern great power had arisen in its place. As for westward depth, the shorter distance from East Prussia, still almost 500 straight-line miles, was offset by the watery terrain in between, which imposes large detours around swamps and lakes.

Moscow's geographic depth is even greater to the east, across a strategical vacuum of several thousand miles to the centers of Chinese power and Japan, neither of them in any case containing more than a peripheral threat, if that, to this day. Only to the south was Muscovy exposed, so long as what is now the Ukraine remained a no-man's-land, part of the steppe corridor open to Turkic and Mongol invasions—and that danger was finally removed by Russian expansion and Ottoman decline during the time of Peter the Great.

By the same token, however, the offensive potential of Russian armies mustered out of Moscow was greatly diminished by distance. In an age before railroads, their strength and supplies would be consumed in marching long before they even reached their own side of the frontier. Petersburg's foundation did not change matters very much, for Russian forces were still mostly mustered out of Moscow and the surrounding regions. Hence the preparation of any major Russian offensive before railways were built had to be a lengthy affair, with one year's campaigning season best used to prepare for the the next, by moving forward armies and their supplies to the frontier or not far beyond. Today, in spite of air transport as well as railways and paved roads, considerable time and large resources are still needed to overcome distance, and the long lines of communications are subject to a novel vulnerability, from air attack.

The other side of the coin of the Soviet Union's formidable defensive depth is, therefore, the inability of its armies to launch offensives *in full strength* from a standing start. In a westward direction, except for the forces already stationed well forward (such as the 30 divisions in Czechoslovakia, East Germany, Hungary, and Poland), even Soviet formations at full readiness must first make long transits before they can go into action. And to reach the war areas, most Soviet forces would have to depend on railways, with long unbranched segments, until they reach the dense networks of central Europe.

It is in this context that one more defensive concept for the Alliance central front mentioned at the start, chapters ago, can finally be considered to illustrate one more aspect of strategy: a deep-attack theater strategy, which would be superimposed on the present frontal defense, to delay, disrupt, and diminish Soviet reinforcements moving toward the combat zones by aerial strikes, while the Alliance frontal defense contains the first wave of advancing Soviet divisions. The peacetime array of Alliance forces stationed in West Germany might or might not manage to hold the first wave of Soviet armies. But it certainly cannot offer a reliable *and* nonnuclear defense against the mobilized Soviet formations that would next reach the scene, at a much faster rate than Alliance reinforcements could arrive; and then against the third wave of Soviet forces— even assuming, most optimistically, an invasion launched without any prior mobilization and without a preparatory buildup. And to the extent that the other Warsaw Pact forces are expected to take part, the prospects for the Alliance must be worse still (see Appendix 3).

INTERDICTION AS A SUBSTITUTE FOR DEPTH

A number of different deep-attack schemes are in circulation.[1] All of them, however, call for the use of cargo missiles armed with many small munitions, as well as manned aircraft and ordinary single-warhead missiles, to attack targets up to several hundred miles behind the front. There are three sets of targets: the bridges, viaducts, and railway marshaling yards that Soviet reinforcement convoys would have to cross to reach the zones of combat—all fixed targets; Soviet supplies and reinforcements in transit, both entrained and advancing on highways and lesser roads; and the airbases, command centers, and supply depots of the entire military infrastructure in eastern and central Europe as well as in the western Soviet Union—again fixed targets.

There is nothing new about the air attack of fixed targets in the rear, be they bridges or airfields, and only technical experiments and detailed cost calculations can evaluate the relative merits of doing so with guided missiles rather than manned aircraft. Certainly ever since 1945, the Soviet air-defense reaction to the technical superiority of Western airpower, once very considerable and even now persisting in some degree, has been exceptionally broad and intense. The great array of mobile antiaircraft weapons that continues to evolve within the Soviet ground forces, and the elaborate territorial air defenses with their many fighter-interceptors and larger missiles, have duly evoked an Alliance reaction in turn, both in the form of evasive tactics and a whole host of technical countermeasures. But after decades of reciprocal preparation, the most that can be said is that the ability of Alliance pilots successfully to attack targets deep in the rear is uncertain. Missiles of all sorts therefore offer an attractive alternative, but one that raises a number of technical, military, and political difficulties.[2] It is, however, the deep attack of the Soviet reinforcements themselves, as they move from the western parts of the Soviet Union toward the combat zones on rail and road that is the novel idea. It raises strategical questions of importance.

Artillery Interdiction

Again, there is nothing new about the interdiction of reinforcements as such. The systematic shelling of approach roads to the front was already much employed during World War I, when this long-range artillery tactic was an important element in both front-holding and front-breaking theater strategies.

Along with the unnatural obstacle of the no-man's-land between the opposed trenchlines, with its shell craters often filled with water and barbed-wire obstacles, and with the decisive arithmetical advantage of entrenched machine guns against troops advancing on foot, artillery interdiction helped to ensure that reinforcing defenders could outconcentrate the enemy's perpendicular thrusts, even if his forces had been secretly massed in great numbers just behind the front prior to the attack. Similarly, though usually with much less success in an era of warfare structurally unfavorable to the offense,[3] long-range artillery was employed in the attempt to break the front, by preventing the gathering of reinforcements into sectors under attack.

Artillery shelling against points on the map, typically crossroads on the approaches to the front, did not kill or wound many men or destroy much property. But neither did it have to do so in order to achieve the delay that was its purpose (heavy casualties by artillery interdiction did happen sometimes, as when thousands of troops converged each day for months on end into the small salient of Verdun).

Interdiction by Airpower

During World War II, and later in Korea and Vietnam, the much longer-range interdiction of supplies and reinforcements by air attack supplemented the shelling of approach roads. What is held to justify the deeper form of air attack, which requires larger and more costly aircraft or at least more fuel and therefore smaller bomb-loads, is the difference in the aspect the enemy presents behind and upon the front. Reinforcements moving to the combat zone in road convoys or by rail should offer much more visible, concentrated, and hence more profitable targets for air attack than those same forces once they are deployed for combat, dispersed, camouflaged, and gone to ground. But the richness of targets is one thing and the ability to exploit it quite another: the notion that fighter-bombers can range freely into the deep rear, flying along roads and rail lines to strafe and bomb military traffic, contradicts the logic of strategy: it implies a nonreacting enemy.

If the enemy's own airpower and antiaircraft forces are formidable, then his troops and supplies in transit can indeed be crowded in dense convoys, moving toward the front in broad daylight, offering targets potentially very lucrative. But then air interdiction is insecure and risky, and not likely to be attempted in any great depth by large numbers of attacking aircraft—partly because so many would be needed to escort those few armed for bombing and strafing. On the other hand, if the enemy's air defenses are clearly outmatched, allowing a free hand for interdiction aircraft, then they would rarely encounter dense military traffic to attack profitably. In that case the enemy would instead move troops and supplies at night, or in dispersed order, or both. Thus airpower too strong undermines its own potential effectiveness. To be sure, night movement and dispersal both impose delay in themselves, if not actual destruction, and the remaining question for the attackers is whether the time thus won is of sufficient value—tactically, operationally, or at the level of theater strategy—to be worth the cost of air interdiction. Will it delay the arrival of a particular body of troops that might tip the outcome of a given battle? Or will air interdiction merely lengthen a routine one-week transit by a number of days in the setting of protracted struggle?[4]

In the context of the Alliance defense of the central front, it is quite certain that Soviet reinforcements and supplies moving toward the front could not be seriously hampered by the bombing of the transport net itself, or rather its bridges, railway yards, roads, and viaducts. Soviet tank armies could hardly be supplied and reinforced by bicycle rigs, porters, and nighttime motor traffic on hidden tracks, as the North Vietnamese once were and the Chinese and North Koreans before them. But the increasing multiplicity of roads and greater rail density from east to west, from the Soviet Union to West Germany, and the Soviet Army's world primacy in combat bridging, would ensure the failure of any nonnuclear interdiction campaign aimed at the transport links rather than at what is transported.[5]

DEEP INTERDICTION SCHEMES

In the current deep-attack schemes, the bombing of transport links is only a secondary element, though it is argued that it could be far more efficient than before because of both precision and clustered munitions. The more important effort is to be made in bombing the moving traffic itself. The claim of deep-attack advocates is that scientific advances offer a possibility of breaking out of the strategic paradox, by nullifying the protection of the night and of dispersal. Satellite and high-altitude air observation instantly relayed, the rapid computerized assessment of targets and selection of the means of attack, and swift missile or manned aircraft strikes with advanced munitions, all certainly offer the technical possibility of attacking Soviet forces in transit, even by night, even if they are dispersed.[6]

There is nevertheless much controversy about the feasibility, economy, and resilience of entire systems that would identify and track moving targets, send missiles and manned aircraft of one sort or another toward them, and achieve the necessary aiming corrections as targets continued to move. Leaving detailed computations to others, we can examine the matter in strategical terms, discovering once more that Clausewitz has preceded us. There were no combat aircraft or guided missiles in his day, but the fundamental asymmetry between forces en route and forces already deployed for combat did of course exist. So did the attraction of striking at moving forces with deep-raiding cavalry, before the era of closed linear fronts. As usual, Clausewitz depicts the attractive prospect before revealing the difficulties:

An average convoy of three to four hundred wagons . . . will be two miles long; a major convoy will be considerably longer. How can one hope to defend this length with the handful of men that are normally assigned as escorts? Added to this difficulty is the ponderousness of the whole, which crawls slowly along and is always in danger of ending up in confusion. [The modern equivalent is more severe: a single mechanized division will include some 4,000 vehicles, requiring at the very least 60 kilometers of road track, so that congestion en route is a large danger.] Moreover, every part requires the same degree of cover, otherwise the whole train would stop and fall into disarray in any part were attacked. [The modern equivalent is the dilution of antiaircraft protection employed for route rather than point defense.] One may well ask how the protection of such a convoy is possible at all . . . Why is not every convoy seized once it has been attacked, and why is not every convoy attacked if it is worth an escort at all . . . ?

The explanation lies in the fact that most convoys are better protected by their general strategic situation [by the fact that they are in the rear] than is any other part of the army that the enemy may attack, and hence their limited means of defense are decisively more effective.

We may therefore conclude that while it may seem easy tactically, attacking a convoy is strategically not very advantageous. (*On War*, book 7, chap. 18, pp. 555–556)

In other words, once the operational disadvantage of any action performed outside one's own area of control, deep inside the enemy's space, is subtracted from the tactical advantage of engaging targets that are concentrated and visible as they move on roads and rail lines, the remaining benefit may not suffice to offset the initial technical cost and greater tactical risk of attacking at longer range in depth. Clausewitz thus reminds us of a third and somewhat more subtle consideration: the "general strategic situation" of convoys in the rear is operationally advantageous to the defending forces as a whole both because they can more easily observe the unfolding combat and because all their strength is in place. In the days of Clausewitz, the fate of a cavalry raid would not be known until the raiders returned to tell their tale; the rest of the army could not assist the raid in any way for lack of current knowledge of its vicissitudes. And only a small part of the entire army could be sent on raids: a few hundred horsemen would amount to a large raiding force even for an army of tens of thousands.

Today there are technical means of observation that can monitor the action as it unfolds, but it is still the defense that can best assess the ongoing results of aerial attack within its own area of control. Until destroyed—as they would be quite quickly—observation satellites can relay back imagery, but puffs of smoke and exploding debris would both reveal the effects of strikes and conceal them. High-altitude radar aircraft can look sideways to a considerable distance and aerial photography may continue throughout a war, but the totality of the information thus gathered can still not compare with the exact detail of a multiplicity of situation reports, if the defense can properly collate them. That information advantage, and the possession of all means in place, can enable the defenders to react with broad means against the deep-attack "system" of the attackers, where by engaging raiding cavalry with their own forces, as in the time of Clausewitz, or by today's air defenses, specific countering attacks, and technical countermeasures.

We cannot predict the state of play at any one time in the continuing interaction of measures and countermeasures that would ensue, if deep-attack systems were actually constructed by the Alliance. But of the complete array of initial sensors, transmission relays, control centers, primary air vehicles, and terminal munitions, we know that the latter at least must be vulnerable to countermeasures. Although the sensors that initially detect the targets for relay back to the control centers can have broad abilities on their varied platforms (satellites as well as aircraft, with radar, infrared, optical, and other sensors), the guidance of the individual munitions that finally attack each sparate tank or truck must be narrowly simple if the system as a whole is to be feasibly economical.

There is nothing to prevent the use of several different types of terminal guidance for as many different types of munitions, so that road convoys and trains could be attacked with mixed batches of guided munitions resilient *in toto* against any one countermeasure. But there is no obstacle either to the combined use of different countermeasures by the defense. Not all terminal munitions must be guided, of course; notably, the many small bomblets of cluster weapons aimed at an area as a whole need not be individually guided; but then it is their lethality itself that is a narrow capability, apt to be easily neutralized.[7]

The Fragility of Consecutive Systems

The technical contest between terminal munitions and terminal countermeasures is more or less symmetrical, except for the information advantage of the defense, but there is a fundamental asymmetry in the contest between deep-attack systems as a whole and the countermeasure effort bound to be made against them. To succeed, the raiding cavalry that Clausewitz evoked had to elude front-watching pickets, maneuver around larger forces in their path, find a convoy isolated on its own, and scatter its escort in order to attack effectively—all those things had to be achieved in sequence. Similarly, in deep-attack systems the initial sensors *and* the relay transmissions *and* the control centers *and* the missiles or manned aircraft *and* the terminal munitions must all function correctly one after the other, whereas the defenders can defeat the entire system's ability to attack any given set of targets by successfully neutralizing just one of the links. Again, redundancy can diminish the disadvantage, but only at a price—and even then the risks of friction, *requiring no effort by the defender,* will be compounded by the consecutive nature of deep-attack systems.

When we stand back from all technical speculations, what remains before us is the sheer uncertainty of the results that deep-attack systems may yield in war, as measures and countermeasures invisibly evolve over time. Uncertainty is war's constant companion, but there is a large difference in degree between the uncertainty that attends the use of a sword (which might break), a plain rifle or tank (which can jam or break down), and a complicated consecutive system of many separate devices, each separately fallible. Is it prudent for the Alliance to substitute deep-attack systems of uncertain effect for its present reliance on self-damaging but effective battlefield nuclear weapons? It would appear that to answer the question we should have to confront technical calculations we are unqualified to attempt, in order to estimate the reliability of whatever deep-attack systems are proposed. It might seem that, if we were persuaded that most Soviet reinforcements and supplies could be successfully interdicted, then the matter would be settled unequivocally, making it possible to abolish battlefield nuclear weapons altogether if only the frontal forces can repel the first wave of Soviet divisions. Conversely it would appear that, if we agreed with the critics who argue that deep-attack systems are too costly to be built on a sufficiently large scale and too fragile in the light of realistic countermeasures, then we should be thrown back on the present unhappy dependence on battlefield nuclear weapons, or else forced to demand a much larger effort of nonnuclear defense.

Although the answer appears to depend on complicated technical issues and elaborate cost estimates, this is not so: the logic of strategy and quite unexceptionable assumptions about Soviet conduct are sufficient to allow us to jump ahead in confident anticipation. If the Alliance does decide to construct deep-attack systems to cope with the reinforcing echelons of a Soviet invasion—in lieu of battlefield nuclear weapons and of such additional ground forces as might be acquired with the same funds[8]—then we may take it for granted that the Soviet armed forces would both develop all manner of technical countermeasures and also react in other ways to circumvent such systems, just as if it were quite certain that all countermeasures would fail.

For the Soviet Union, the most straightforward negating response to Alliance deep-attack systems in the event of war would simply be to attack them. Soviet antisatellite missiles and long-range fighters would be used to attack the platforms of the initial sensors (concurrently with electronic interference against their relay transmissions); manned strike aircraft, bombardment missiles, and commando raids would be launched against the computerized control centers, large facilities easy to find though heavily protected (concurrently with the attempt to confound their workings by camouflage and simulations); the missile "farms" and airbases of the primary vehicles would be attacked by the same combination of manned aircraft, missiles, and commando raids (concurrently with the attempt to jam or sever their communications from the control centers); air defenses of all kinds, in the form of fighters, missiles, and antiaircraft guns would seek to interfere with the delivery of the terminal munitions (concurrently with the use of deceptive and protective countermeasures against the latter); and in combining all these forms of attack, the asymmetrical vulnerability of consecutive systems could weigh heavily in the outcome. If fortune or a successful intelligence penetration assisted the Soviet neutralizing effort, the destruction of some sensor platforms, some control centers, and some primary vehicles at source or in transit might suffice to neutralize a complete deep-attack sequence, and then the next one, and so on.

The most obvious way in which the Soviet Union might circumvent any and all deep-attack systems, on the other hand, would be to adopt a one-wave *theater strategy,* whereby all or most of the formations needed to defeat the Alliance on the central front would be in place at the start of an offensive, eliminating any important reliance on reinforcements and thereby removing the prime targets of such systems. Actually it is possible, indeed probable, that such a theater strategy is already intended. The notion that the Soviet Union must choose between an unreinforced surprise offensive and a set-piece offensive preceded by a noisy mobilization implies a peculiar lack of artifice in an opponent not usually dismissed as naive.

THE SURPRISE ATTACK

For the Soviet Union to stake all on an offensive launched by only 30 of its 193 line divisions,[9] albeit the strongest and largest divisions already stationed in East Germany, Czechoslovakia, Hungary, and Poland, would be imprudent in the extreme, indeed frivolous. Actually, an offensive launched with such relatively small forces, not much larger than the Alliance forces kept in readiness to move into defensive positions, would also require battlefield nuclear strikes to achieve a quick victory—the only kind of victory the Soviet Union could hope for at all, should it start a war on its own initiative. This was probably what was planned during the

Khrushchev years, when troop reductions and the disestablishment of artillery formations resulted in large savings but also imposed a nuclear theater strategy on the Soviet army. The purpose of the entire armament program that has been so costly for the Soviet economy ever since the mid-1960s has been precisely to acquire war-winning strength without need of nuclear weapons, and that is a purpose now achieved which only the failure to use the full strength at hand can nullify.

If each Soviet troop transfer toward the West German border were bound to evoke a responsive strengthening of the Alliance forces in West Germany, by the mobilization of British, Canadian, French, and American forces and their deployment on the central front, then there might be a justification for treating seriously the prospect of an unreinforced Soviet surprise attack. But this is most unlikely. First, the Soviet army could move quite a few additional full-strength divisions westward, to the starting points of an offensive if not right up to the West German border, in the guise of a large-scale exercise. This should not give the secret away because such exercises are conducted twice a year, and they do involve the movement of complete divisions. Second, as it is, Soviet reservists are recalled from time to time to fill out cadre divisions for refresher training, and this offers the possibility of combining a certain volume of recalls with the transfers, to replace the ready divisions moved westward with new ones. Finally, under the current procedures of the Soviet army, new conscripts are inducted twice a year into the line divisions, replacing soldiers who have completed the two years of compulsory service; by simply retaining their seniors when the new conscripts arrive, divisional manpower levels can be increased by one quarter.

Combining all three measures, the war readiness of the Soviet army could be increased substantially, with some divisions already shifted to the west and others able to make the move at short notice, and all without arousing exceptional concern. Later on, to transfer more divisions to start lines in western Poland, Czechoslovakia, and Hungary, some sort of cover story would be called for, such as a simulated political crisis between Moscow and the Polish government, or the Czech, Hungarian, or even the East German. No riots or strikes would be needed: supposed discord between the Soviet Politburo and its Warsaw, Prague, Budapest, or East Berlin counterpart can be manufactured easily enough just by allowing Western journalists to inflate an indiscretion or two. The rather inglorious precedent by now well established is that punitive action by the Soviet army in the eastern half of Europe evokes some passing show of indignation in the western half—but certainly no responsive mobilization.

Satellites and the wizardry of electronic intelligence stand ready to issue warnings aplenty, and photography from space should certainly detect the transfer of the thousands of vehicles of each Soviet line division from east to west, at least if there happens to be a satellite on station (not an everyday event) and if the clouds are not too dense. But the desire not to know can overcome all. The first photographs and intercepts showing increased activity would no doubt be examined with interest by the specialists, but military commanders are not likely to demand mobilization just because a very strong army is becoming slightly stronger: maneuvers routine or not, or merely errors of interpretation, will seem sufficient explanation.

Next, if Soviet activity increases and more information comes in, the political leaders of the Alliance countries must be formally notified, but their likely reaction will be to seek innocuous explanations for the evidence, making them receptive for the cover story of the day. Otherwise they would have to order the transfer of units to frontal areas, the implementation of war-emergency controls on transport and much else, and, above all, the mobilization of civilian reservists, a colossal intrusion into the lives of millions of citizens. For political leaders who have never experienced the urgencies of warlike decisions, mobilization would require a drastic departure from all established habits of government. In the United States, which contributes a large part of the planned wartime reinforcement of the European central front, mobilization would of course mean the summoning of the National Guard to active federal duty, with the immediate shipment of its ready units overseas, so that a great many civilians suddenly in uniform would find themselves being transported thousands of miles away from their families in a matter of days. It would also require the evacuation of hundreds of thousands of military dependents from West Germany and other possible war zones. Hence the outset of a possible war, possibly catastrophic, would be marked by the abrupt separation of fighting men from their families, a thing perfectly ordinary in past wars but ordinary no longer when acute danger is also in prospect for civilians.

All these moves, moreover, would in themselves intensify the crisis. Actually they would appear to *provoke* the crisis because they would be dramatically evident as compared to the invisible progress of Soviet mobilization, manifest only in Western reports that some may choose to doubt. In the circumstances, the erstwhile readiness to explain away the evidence of a warlike Soviet buildup is quite likely to be followed by a widespread eagerness to alleviate the crisis by negotiation. At the moment of decision, or rather during the days of indecision, as Alliance consultations and political debate in many countries continue while more and more Soviet formations assemble at their starting lines, a Soviet undertaking to stop mobilizing if the Alliance does not begin its own mobilization may be irresistible, even if by then the balance of ready divisions had been drastically altered and the usefulness of deep-attack systems largely voided. To have a costly instrument for strikes in depth would be of little value to the Alliance, if the Soviet army were already massed just behind the front in sufficient strength to break its defensive array.

Soviet countermeasure efforts, attacks, and circumvention are not reciprocally exclusive alternatives, but rather complementary steps in a single process. After a one-sided mobilization had advanced as far as it could—if the Soviet Union's increased offensive strength were not just meant for diplomatic advantage but rather for actual war—missile strikes, bombing, and commando raids against Alliance deep-attack systems could inaugurate the fighting. The use of countermeasures would follow, further to diminish what systems already partly destroyed and largely circumvented could still nevertheless achieve.

THE LIMITS OF HIGH-TECHNOLOGY SOLUTIONS

We therefore discover that in the very large view of the level of theater strategy, which comprehends the interplay of armed forces within an entire zone of conflict, even such elaborate and complex technical means as deep-attack systems are reduced to the role of narrow instruments, all set to be outmaneuvered by the broad and varied abilities they seek to oppose. Just as the cheap antitank missile fielded against the costly tank will not nullify its strength once the complete armored formation responds, so too the creation of deep-attack systems cannot be expected to nullify the broad and therefore resilient strength that the Soviet Union derives from the conscription of its youth, the subsequent reserve duties of its trained men, and the mass production of heavy weapons in numbers that far exceed the combined production of the Alliance. The sacrifice imposed by military service on the Soviet population is large, and the expense of supporting 200 divisions accounts for a large part of the total costs of Soviet military power. The vast reserve-echelon strength thus generated in addition to the forces held in readiness will not be easily negated by novel devices, even if of remarkable technical ingenuity.

Their ultimate inability to decide the outcome of war does not mean that the construction of deep-attack systems cannot be advantageous for the Alliance. As earlier noted, only detailed calculations can evaluate costs and benefits, including the diversion of Soviet resources from primary offensive forces to defensive countermeasures. Certainly deep-attack systems will not be easily neutralized either. But the inherent limitations of the narrow instrument that would oppose broad strengths do mean that the question with which our inquiry began must now be recast.

We must ask not whether deep-attack systems can provide a reliable substitute for battlefield nuclear weapons—which they clearly cannot—but whether the risk of failure in containing Soviet reinforcements by means of deep-attack systems is preferable to the risk of doing so successfully with nuclear weapons.* As soon as we confront this question, we immediately recognize that it cannot be answered within the scope of theater strategy, for it transcends the considerations that arise from the spatial organization of military power. Instead it is the very meaning of security that must be defined, within the context of national policy and international diplomacy, and this can only be done at the highest level, of grand strategy.

*Many proposals have been advanced over the years to erase the difference between nuclear and nonnuclear weapons, by fielding "mini-nukes" so small that they would cause no fallout to speak of, indeed no effects appreciably different from those of any large nonnuclear explosion but obtained at far smaller cost. In other words, mini-nukes are meant to restore the military utility of nuclear weapons, whose larger specimens overshoot by far the culminating point of usability. There is no doubt that such weapons could make existing Alliance forces more efficient in producing firepower, and yet mini-nuke proposals have so far been rejected. The reason of course is that the logical response to very small nuclear detonations by Alliance forces are Soviet counterstrikes slightly larger, which would in turn impose the need for further nuclear attacks of still larger dimensions . . . and so on.

CHAPTER 11

NONSTRATEGIES: NAVAL, AIR, NUCLEAR

$\mathbf{B}$efore we can proceed to examine the level of grand strategy, we must first pause to dispose of the confused and confusing question of one-force "strategy," whether naval, air, or nuclear. In these matters, mere looseness of language and the innocent exuberance of enthusiasts who do not truly believe that their preferred instrument can encompass the total strategic predicament are both present, alongside vehement claims of just such an autonomy. The issue is not purely semantic, for if there were such a thing as naval strategy or air strategy or nuclear strategy in any sense other than a conflation of the technical, tactical, or operational levels of the same universal strategy, then each should have its own peculiar logic, or else exist as a distinct counterpart to theater strategy, which would then comprehend only ground warfare. The first is impossible, the second quite unnecessary.

To argue the matter in order, I will begin by noting that at the technical, tactical, and operational levels it is self-evident that the same paradoxical logic applies to all forms of military power. Accordingly, in exploring those three levels, I freely cited naval and airpower examples along with those drawn from ground warfare. At the level of theater strategy, it is true, the focus of the inquiry was on ground warfare, with airpower discussed only in reference to the latter[1] and no naval examples cited at all. But there is much less in this than meets the eye.

SPACE AND MOBILITY

The omission of naval examples and the slighting of air warfare in the discussion of theater strategy were not accidental, but neither did this reflect an arbitrary preference. There is no question that the same spatial manifestations of the paradoxical logic are present in naval and air warfare as well. Indeed one may think of theater strategy as "spatial strategy." In dealing with naval and air forces, too, one may distinguish between forward and rearward dispositions, forward defense and defense in depth, broad-front or deep-penetration offense—all of which could also apply to extra-atmospheric warfare for that matter. Air and naval forces interact spatially within the level of theater strategy exactly as ground forces do. But because of their technical superiority in mobility, the phenomena present within that level of strategy are simply much less important. Dispositions can be changed so swiftly that they do not precondition the spatial aspect of warfare, or do so in a manner transitory enough to be trivial (this is not true at the operational and tactical levels, of course, where momentary location can be decisive in itself).

Thus, for example, the concentrated battle-fleet concept associated with naval historian Alfred Thayer Mahan,[2] which was rigorously implemented by both the British and the American navies during World War I (and by the Japanese navy in World War II), amounted to an outright nullification of spatial considerations: the superior fleet was to control the oceans of the entire world while its main forces remained concentrated at some location of its own choosing, mostly quite inactive. With the torpedo boat already neutralized, and the submarine disregarded, the ultimate ability to defeat the enemy battleship squadron, if there were a battle in some location at some time, was to secure the benefits of naval supremacy everywhere and continuously, with free use of sea lanes for commerce and military transport while their use was being denied to the enemy—and without need for a blockade of his ports.

It was the hierarchic structure of naval strength that was to ensure such an outcome: being inferior, the enemy battleship squadron could not risk battle; nor could his battlecruisers venture out. Hence enemy cruisers could not steam about to attack shipping on the high seas, nor provide support for destroyer flotillas to do so, because if intercepted they would be defeated with ease by battlecruisers just as fast, of greater endurance, with bigger guns and stronger armor. The superior fleet's cruisers were therefore free to operate unchallenged, and the enemy could neither secure nor deny sealanes with his destroyers, even if they themselves happened to have an advantage of quality over the superior fleet's destroyers.

Thus the remote and inactive battleship squadron concentrated in one location could indirectly exert its domination over the oceans regardless of distance—as far and as wide as the unchallenged cruisers could reach. There was nothing to prevent an enemy destroyer from dashing out of secure harbors to intercept a stray merchant ship passing nearby, but that was all: except for sheltered coastal passages and traffic in closed seas such as the Baltic, the side inferior in battleships would find itself excluded from navigation on the high seas, as indeed was the case for the Central Powers during World War I.

In its pure form, the Mahanist concept was therefore based on the exploitation of an *operational-level* superiority in decisive encounters between capital ships, which if achieved or deemed achievable would confer supremacy without regard to spatial factors. Once the reality of the submarine was introduced into the scheme, however, the superior fleet could no longer ensure the safety of its own navigation. In the presence of strong enemy submarine forces, to focus exclusively on the hypothetical clash of battleships would condemn the fleet to passivity, since the capital ships that remained concentrated needed their escorting cruisers and destroyers, which could not be used to protect shipping from submarine attacks.[3] At worst, the result could be the symmetrical denial of navigation, a very poor outcome when there is an asymmetrical reliance on long-distance supply and troop transport. This indeed almost happened at the peak of the U-boat campaigns of the two world wars in 1917 and 1942, when Allied battle fleets prevented German maritime commerce, while the submarines of the Central Powers greatly impeded Allied shipping, *with both forces almost unlimited by spatial considerations.*

It is not the medium of warfare that makes the difference, then, but rather the degree of mobility of the respective forces: the greater the mobility, the less consequential the locations of the forces at any one time. If ground forces could move freely across the full expanse of theaters of war and between them, the level of theater strategy would lose its importance for them as well, in proportion to the speed and ease of such movements. This was precisely the advantage that motorization offered even before World War I, reducing the importance of theater dispositions for the forces involved far more than the railways had already done. With trucks to carry them, troops and weapons could move from one sector to another in "tactical" time, that is, in the course of a single battle, thereby diminishing the importance of prebattle deployments. Air transport intensified the effect for intratheater movements by the time of World War II, and since then its range has also been extended to intertheater movements, at least for those small and very light forces that can in fact be airlifted over long distances.

Important phenomena thus persist within the level of theater strategy only because of the mobility limits of ground motorization, the vulnerability, limited capacity, and airfield dependence of air transport, the geographic constraints, slow speed, and port-dependence of sea transport, and the even greater vulnerabilities and capacity limits of parachute and amphibious landings. A parallel may be drawn with the insignificance of the operational level of strategy if attribution is dominant at the tactical level. There is no basis for the conceptualization of distinct naval and air counterparts to theater strategy merely because it is the phenomena of ground warfare that are most important within that level. Nor can there be some other level of strategy that would apply only to a single form of military power and would stand above the operational level, yet below the level of grand strategy.

THE CONTENTS OF NONSTRATEGY

If there are no distinct phenomena encompassed, what then is the content of the many writings that carry "naval strategy" or "air strategy," "nuclear strategy" or, most recently, "space strategy" in their titles? With the interesting exception of Mahan's claim for seapower, we find that it is mainly technical, tactical, or operational issues that are examined in that literature, or else that it consists of the advocacy of a particular *policy,* usually at the level of grand strategy.[4]

Questions of *force composition* for example, which loom so large in what is described as naval strategy, like those evoked in the old debate between the advocates of battleships and aircraft carriers, or those that now arise in the endemic argument between the advocates of submarines and all other naval forces, clearly belong to the operational level of analysis, just as in actual warfare such forces would interact competitively at the operational level (as well as at the tactical level). As for even narrower debates over the merits of particular formats for given categories of ships, such as large aircraft carriers as opposed to smaller ones, they obviously belong to the technical level of analysis, just as in reality the matter depends on differences in technical performance and cost. To be sure, such seemingly technical preferences may reflect broader considerations, but then they will be considerations of grand strategy, as is certainly the case in the debate between large-carrier and small-carrier advocates. (Large carriers are better for offensive warfare, small carriers for defensive escort duty.)

In regard to airpower also, choices of force composition are conditioned at the technical, tactical, or operational levels, and it is therefore in those levels that analysis can uncover the relevant phenomena. This was true of the early debate between the advocates of balanced bomber forces, heavy, medium, and light, and those who saw merit in devoting all resources to heavy bombers alone; true of the later debate between the advocates of guided missiles and those who saw continued value in manned bombers; and true of the latest debate, in which remotely piloted vehicles have displaced guided missiles in the contention.

Questions of *targeting*, which have traditionally been important in what is described as air strategy,[5] also do not belong to theater strategy but rather to the level of grand strategy. The consequences of bombing the armed forces themselves as opposed to the industry that sustains them, or bombing the population whose will to work and fight sustains both, or the leadership and governing structures that direct the war as a whole, will be manifest at the level of grand strategy. Hence the choice between them is a fit subject for *national policy*, as indeed the victims' response will be a national response, again at the level of grand strategy.

The same considerations apply to the naval equivalent of targeting, that is, the purposes for which naval power is employed. The results of using naval forces to affect landings, for example, will be conditioned at the level of theater strategy, whereas in the case of blockade, or long-range sea denial nowadays, grand strategy will be the most relevant level of action and response—assuming that the denial is effective, which may depend on geographic factors pertaining to theater strategy but will mostly reflect the operational and tactical interaction of the forces on each side. Certainly if navigation is denied, the consequences will be determined by the self-sufficiency of the affected state, regardless of the particular nature of the forces involved; once again action and response will be manifest at the level of grand strategy.

Quite recently, for example, it has been suggested that the United States could respond effectively to a Soviet overland offensive in some continental theater of war by launching naval air attacks on Soviet naval installations in quite different theaters, and by seeking to destroy Soviet nuclear-missile submarines.[6] The proposal may or may not be politically feasible, depending on whether one assumes that the reaction in the United States to an outbreak of war in a given theater will be to try to restrict its geographic scope or to widen the war to include Soviet territory as well, thereby presumably inviting attack against American territory. And the proposal may or may not be advantageous, depending on how others react. Allies under attack by the Soviet army may regard large American efforts of any kind with approval, or else may view the diversion of means against the lesser threat of the Soviet navy with perplexity or even as presaging forthcoming abandonment. At the same time, allies in the regions into which the United States would extend the war may react by repudiating the effort, to avert retaliation.

As for the Soviet Union, it may be induced to reconsider its earlier aggression by American naval attacks against its own territory, or it may react symmetrically. Similarly, the envisaged campaign against its missile submarines may dissuade the Soviet Union from resorting to the use of nuclear weapons, by making that balance of forces less favorable; or, to the contrary, the Soviet Union might launch its own counterforce attacks, to offset any such adverse change in the nuclear balance.

Whatever one may think of the plausibility and desirability of the scheme, it is clear that its results occur at the level of grand strategy, wherein indeed the specifically naval origin of the envisaged attacks would be inconsequential: results and reactions cannot be substantially different if Soviet installations and nuclear weapons are attacked by other means.

CLAIMS OF AUTONOMY: SEAPOWER

There can be only one valid justification for conceptualizing an autonomous strategy, confined to just one form of military power: that it is decisive in itself. This was precisely Mahan's claim; in his interpretation of history, seapower was the determining factor in the rise and fall of nations.[7]

Mahan employed the term in two quite different senses, to mean dominant armed strength at sea ("which drives the enemy's flag from it, or allows it to appear only as a fugitive") and, more widely, to describe the full range of benefits that maritime endeavors could secure: commerce, shipping, colonies, and markets.[8] Mahan's sea-power I was the short-term determinant that decided the outcome of wars, even if largely fought on land, by blockade and sea raids. His seapower II, by contrast, was the long-term determinant of the the prosperity of nations, though of immediate relevance also by providing the means for seapower I as well as for subsidies to war allies. That Mahan overgeneralized from his interpretation of British history is obvious, for his equation of seapower in both meanings with power *tout court* ignored the continental empires that did not rely on navigation, of which the Soviet Union is the outstanding modern example.

Mahan's Fallacy of Composition

Somewhat less obvious perhaps, and more interesting from the viewpoint of our strategical inquiry, was Mahan's fallacy of composition in accounting even for Great Britain's success over its continental antagonists, which he attributed to the priority the British supposedly accorded to their strength at sea. That fallacy is present in sharper form in current Mahanist advocacy, which omits Mahan's qualifications and in which above all seapower I wholly displaces seapower II, as the upkeep of the strongest possible naval force is commended without regard to the state of overseas trade and commercial shipping.

That for Great Britain seapower I was an essential instrument, and seapower II the source of much of its disposable wealth, is beyond question. Yet the real cause of Britain's naval supremacy was the success of its foreign policy in maintaining a balance of power in Europe.[9] By intervening to oppose any one power or coalition that seemed on the verge of dominance, Britain ensured continued strife. This forced the continental powers to maintain large armies, which in turn prevented them from keeping large navies as well. To be sure, seapower I and II were both required to keep the continental powers "balanced" and at each other's throats. But the sequence and resulting priorities were the reverse of the ones Mahan depicted—and advocated for the United States of his day.[10]

It was a very active diplomacy and large subsidies to willing but impoverished allies that received priority in British policy, not the upkeep of the Royal Navy. Once the conditions that would ensure a relatively easy naval superiority were established by successfully upholding the balance of power, the navy was given the modest means it required to gain seapower I, which in turn yielded seapower II. Had the British gone the other way around, neglecting diplomacy in a straightforward attempt to achieve seapower I by simply outbuilding all seafaring continental rivals, the immediate result would have been to consume the capital needed for seapower II, and the longer-term result would have been to prejudice the upkeep of the balance of power. This in turn would have reduced the diversion of continental efforts to land warfare, and British resources could never have preserved naval supremacy in competition with all the seafaring talent of Western Europe, once its full potential had been unleashed.

Thus during the entire period that Mahan surveyed, British naval supremacy and the notoriously ungenerous funding of the Royal Navy, which often degenerated into outright neglect, were in full accord with the logic of strategy. By contrast, it would have wholly contradicted the paradoxical logic if Britain could have reached the goal of seapower I by merely adding more and more frigates to the Royal Navy, with no effective countermove from adversaries left free to react by that same exclusive concentration of purpose. Contemporaries who deplored the neglect of the Royal Navy given British dependence on both kinds of seapower, and the admirals who bitterly complained that British gold was being given to foreigners while their ships were in perpetual want, had commonsense on their side, but not strategy.

Ironically, even as Mahan's celebration of its past was published, Great Britain was about to abandon the historic policy.* When substantial funds were finally granted to the Royal Navy for the first time, in order to preserve seapower I in a direct shipbuilding competition with imperial Germany, commonsense and popular opinion were satisfied; the alternative of arming Germany's continental adversaries and especially the undersupplied Russians was excluded; and the balance of power was no longer exploited, to keep the strongest continental power entangled on land by subsidized allies.

---

*It was not as a guide but rather as the propagandist of a policy already formed that Mahan was so greatly acclaimed in Britain: the National Defence Act, which mandated "parity" with the combination of the two strongest continental navies, was passed in 1889—before Mahan's first "influence" book was published.

In the end, seapower II, the capital it had accumulated, and much blood were all sacrificed in fighting the war that followed. World War I was Britain's first truly costly continental engagement, which a less intense concentration on seapower I might have alleviated if not prevented. Whether it was the rigidity of public opinion that turned British leaders from emulating their predecessors (who would have financed railways and arsenals for tsarist Russia in lieu of building more battleships) or simply their own lack of strategic clarity, there is little doubt that Britain's agony of decline was much accelerated by a policy that reflected the Mahanist delusion.*

CLAIMS OF AUTONOMY: STRATEGY BY BOMBARDMENT

An entirely new claim of strategic autonomy was proclaimed just after World War I had exposed the marginality of navies in a modern continental conflict, with blockade agonizingly slow, sea raids scarcely possible, and the one large amphibious offensive at Gallipoli a costly fiasco. Because the tactical advantage of height was so universally understood, the heavier-than-air aircraft had been adopted for military use very soon after its first appearance. By 1914 aircraft for general observation and for artillery-fire correction were present in all the major armies, and by 1918 actual airforces had emerged on a very large scale (the Royal Air Force had 22,000 aircraft in its inventory by Armistice Day in 1918, and 293,532 men in uniform). Navies too had acquired their aircraft, mostly floaters precariously launched from aboard ship and recovered from the water; but the first true aircraft carrier was already completed before the end of the war.

The role of aircraft was therefore secure within both armies and navies, though only as an ancillary. Among the pioneer flying officers and publicists of military aviation who demanded independence for the new arm, some were content to do so on the grounds of efficiency, noting the savings that could be obtained if the acquisition of aircraft and the training of pilots were no longer fragmented between the two older services. Others, however, went much further, proclaiming the strategic autonomy of the new arm.

*The analogy with the navalist emphasis in current American policy need not be labored. The obvious alternative, the subsidization of the People's Republic of China, might be imprudent for more than one reason, but the diversion of the competition into other forms of military power should certainly be advantageous, given the asymmetrical dependence of the United States upon navigation.

Three men who promoted airpower as the wave of the future achieved wide resonance for their views, advancing similar arguments quite independently: Giulio Douhet, a leader of the Italian airforce even before World War I, who published his *Il dominio dell'aria* in 1921; William (Billy) Mitchell, also a flying officer whose most important work in a lifetime of advocacy, *Winged Defense*, was published in 1925, long before Douhet's book was translated into English (in 1942); and Hugh Montague Trenchard, founder of the Royal Air Force, whose views were mostly disseminated institutionally.

The common thesis of Douhet, Mitchell, and Trenchard was that aircraft offered the possibility of penetrating directly into the heart of enemy territory, overpassing slow troop advances and all topographic barriers; that large fleets of bombers could circumvent the processes of land and naval warfare by destroying the industry upon which all forms of military power depend; and that victory could be achieved quickly by superior airpower alone,[11] without the enormous casualties of land warfare and the long years of naval blockade. Douhet, Trenchard, and their followers in the embryonic bombardment branches of the major air services differed from Mitchell in claiming that the bombers could virtually disregard defenses, thereby equating airpower with offensive airpower.[12] But there was full agreement on the obsolescence of all other forms of military strength in the new era of airpower.

As already noted in another context, strategic airpower was undone both by its own shortcomings and by the reaction it evoked, all the more powerful because the largest claims made for bombardment had been generally accepted during the 1930s (especially after the Spanish civil war and the destruction of Guernica), while its shortcomings of precision and volume had been overlooked. One reaction to the prospect of massed air raids on capital cities (with gas-filled bombs, it was thought) was the intense search for a means of long-range detection that would give some hope of opposing the bomber effectively. By 1939 Britain, Germany, and the United States had developed long-range radar, which finally overturned the Douhet/Trenchard assumption that the bomber would always prevail.[13]

Air Defense

Because fighter defense had not been fully abandoned, on the fragile assumption that a multitude of telephoned air-spotter reports and sound-location devices would permit interception, both high-speed fighters and suitable organizational schemes for their effective direction by ground control were already in place to exploit radar, when it arrived on the scene. In the meantime, precisely because they were to be "strategic" and therefore required large weapon loads to destroy industry and cities, bombers had evolved into much larger and considerably slower aircraft than the fighters of their day, against which they could not maneuver at all.[14] For this recognized tactical weakness, the bomber advocates thought they had a guaranteed remedy, in the massed formation of armed bombers, which would greatly outconcentrate the stray fighters they might encounter on their way.

In accordance with classical military principles, the advantage of the initiative of bombers gathered for offensive action was to yield a net numerical superiority over enemy fighters within the time and space of the encounter. The concerted fire of the tail gunners, dorsal gunners, belly gunners, and front-firing guns of hundreds of bombers was to create a screen of fire that would negate the fighter's advantage in maneuverability, by closing off every vector of attack no matter how quickly the fighter could switch from one to another. In other words, the operational-level advantage of the formation was to overcome the expected tactical-level inferiority of the single bomber.

This is where radar-assisted ground control intervened in the sequence. By enabling the defense to direct fighters accurately, radar allowed the purposeful interception of bombers by groups of fighters[15] instead of having to rely on chance encounters or an inefficient system of standing patrols. Air space could now be defended as land space had long been defended, with the radar net forming a frontline and fighter squadrons acting as the mobile forces that can converge to match the degree of offensive concentration. The bombers' advantage of the initiative was thereby reduced to whatever delay radar limitations, deliberate countermeasures, and organizational frictions might impose on interception. The defense for its part would have the classic advantage of fighting within its own space, notably the ability to prepare the "terrain" with antiaircraft guns, searchlights, and baloon barrages. The defense, moreover, would be able to make repeated attacks with the same aircraft, refueled and rearmed for action while the offense remained exposed. Thus the spatially conditioned superiority of air defenses at the level of theater strategy could overcome the expected operational-level advantage of bomber formations, other things being equal.

This was the ultimate step in the vertical sequence that ensured the defeat by attrition of the Luftwaffe's 1940 bombing campaign against Britain: it had not broken Britain's will to fight, as no bombing campaign would ever break the will of any other nation; and the Luftwaffe's bombers lacked the explosive and fire-raising capacity to destroy British industrial capacity *quickly,* as no bombing campaign was ever to do against any other major industrial nation.

There was irony in the fact that it was the Luftwaffe that invalidated all predictions, because its leaders had not accepted the bombing of cities and industry as an overriding priority in building their forces.[16] German heavy-bomber projects had been canceled in favor of medium and light bombers whose design emphasized precision in small amounts for battlefield use, achieved by divebombing abilities that precluded the large bombloads needed for attacks on urban areas. Given the aircraft it had, the Luftwaffe's bombing of British cities, as of Warsaw and Rotterdam before them, had been improvisations. As an incidental consequence, Germany's losses greatly understated the vulnerability of bombers as such because— contrary to the thesis—its own bombers, smaller and more maneuverable to begin with, were always supposed to be escorted unless used for beam-guided bombing at night. Above all, the Luftwaffe had no four-engine heavy bombers, of the sort later produced in great quantity in both Britain and the United States. So the plain failure of the bombing campaign against Britain was not accepted as evidence of the error of the thesis by British and American bomber advocates, who continued to proclaim the strategic autonomy of their preferred weapon. It was only after their own formations of heavy bombers had full opportunity to attack Germany on a large scale that the Douhet-Mitchell-Trenchard thesis was finally abandoned, first by the British and then by the Americans. Bombing was not of course repudiated as an effective means of war, but evidently it could not offer a self-sufficient and swift instrument of victory. The long and bloody process of attrition by ground fighting and naval blockade that the bombers were to circumvent was instead translated into the air war, in which the chances of survival of bomber crews were actually smaller than those of the infantry in the trench warfare of World War I.

In the end, it was only the technical superiority of British electronic warfare and the quite unexpected performance of American escort fighters (which achieved a seemingly impossible combination of long range and great maneuverability) that enabled the bombers sent against Germany to destroy as much as they did, if only at the price of heavy losses. Even so, the result obtained was disappointing: as against the sheer scale and flexibility of German industry and infrastructures, even the vast British and American attacks, which dwarfed the Luftwaffe raids against Britain, could only have a slow cumulative effect, no more rapid than that of blockade. In a still sharper refutation of the thesis, bombing could not achieve *swift* results even against Japan's much smaller and less flexible industrial production, which suffered more from the lack of raw materials (caused by shipping losses) than it did from bombing.[17] Quite simply, the advocates of bombardment had grossly overestimated its physical effects and greatly underestimated the political and industrial resilience of its victims.

THE ADVENT OF NUCLEAR WEAPONS

When the atomic bomb exploded on the scene in 1945, it seemed that the claim of strategic autonomy for bombardment aviation, just recently disproved by the experience of war, had most unexpectedly been rehabilitated. Certainly all the shortcomings of the bomber, technical, tactical, and theater-strategic, and all the resilience of its victims would be nullified by the deus ex machina of the new weapon.

The bomber, it had been learned, would not always take off as planned because of technical failures; it would not always survive against air defenses; it would not always navigate correctly to reach its target; the bombs would not all be aimed accurately and would not all explode. It was the multiplication of these "degradation factors" that had made destruction by air bombardment so much more difficult to achieve than had been expected, even while the amount of the destruction needed was much greater than had been foreseen. But with atomic bombs the destruction of cities and industry became easy work. Douhet and his colleagues had thus been rescued from their greatest errors,[18] and it seemed that no obstacle could remain to the fulfillment of their prediction: once fission bombs were produced in reasonable numbers, the air arm—or whichever arm transported them—would become dominant, making all other military forces unnecessary and drastically reducing the scope of strategy to their use.

It was of course the nonuse of the new weapon for a diplomacy of dissuasion that was most congenial to the planners and thinkers of a satisfied status quo power such as the United States, for which it was enough to avert aggression in order to prevail. Upon this conjunction of the large destructive potential of the fission bomb—a universal fact of physics—with a particular view of the world shaped by political circumstances and cultural preferences, the entire conceptual edifice of deterrence was very quickly built, initially in the confident expectation that the "absolute weapon" could avert absolutely all forms of aggression, all wars.[19] If the Soviet Union had been the first to acquire the bomb, it too would no doubt have seen superior merit in nonuse, but then the diplomatic purpose would have been to impose changes in the status quo, and the conceptual edifice would have stressed "compellence."[20]

Naturally the paralyzing dissuasion that could satisfy the satisfied powers was not equally satisfactory to those who still wanted to change the state of the world. Their reaction guaranteed that even nuclear weapons would not be immune to the paradoxical fate of all technical innovations in the realm of strategy: the greater the increment of strength they offer when originally introduced, the greater the disturbance they create in the prior equilibrium, and the greater are the reactions evoked, defensive and competitive, which conjointly reduce the net effect of the new weapon over time, possibly quite dramatically. When originally introduced in the form of fission bombs that only one country could produce and only in small numbers, nuclear weapons promised to transform strategy. They were eminently usable: if the city centers of Hiroshima and Nagasaki had been devastated with no perceptible ill effects on the rest of the planet, the centers of five or ten Soviet cities could also be destroyed, and the United States was not exposed to comparable retaliation since it had the only nuclear weapons in existence. Hence the threat of nuclear attack, even if unformed in the minds of American leaders, could reasonably be expected to dissuade outright aggression.

Autonomy Diminished: Subversion

But inaction is the end point of success only for satisfied powers. While in the Soviet Union every effort was being made to react competitively, by developing not only fission but also fusion weap-

ons, an outmaneuvering reaction immediately developed. As it happened, Stalin's first priority at the time was to establish political
control over the eastern half of Europe by way of local communist
governments subservient to Moscow. The latter, however, could
not prevail in the early postwar elections, and the overt use of force
would have provoked the United States excessively. The wall of
dissuasion that stopped a simple military domination was instead
outmaneuvered by subversion.*

In the looming presence of Soviet occupation forces, between
1945 and 1948 the leaders of the majority political parties of Hungary, Romania, and finally Czechoslovakia were intimidated into
forming coalitions with local communist parties; police forces were
invariably placed under communist ministers. Very soon, noncom-
munist ministers, still in the majority but under personal duress,
voted in coalition decisions to outlaw the remaining political parties
of the right. Then a new coalition was formed, excluding a former
member party, which was outlawed in turn or dissolved by its
own leaders, in fear for their lives. The process was repeated, and
thus slice by slice the coalition was narrowed, until only Moscow's
communists remained in office. By the end of 1948, the process was
completed; the wall stood unbreached, but Soviet power had tun-
neled underneath it, to assert full control with no overt use of force.

At first, therefore, the strategic autonomy attributed to nuclear
weapons was only diminished in ways quite unmilitary, indirect,
and scarcely visible. As the United States and some of its allies
responded at first in Europe and then beyond through subversion
and countersubversion, more and more tunnels were bored under
the wall of the nuclear dissuasion of both sides. The pattern has
persisted to this day, assuming new and more varied forms as client
military forces and secret services, the stimulation and supply of
insurgencies, and the support of transnational terrorists have been
added to the repertoire.

The first and enduring effect of nuclear dissuasion was thus to
divert warlike energies into indirect or less visible forms of conflict,
always excluding direct American-Soviet combat but not armed
violence. Long before the indirect and deniable forms of conflict

---

*The covert manipulation of politics by the physical intimidation of leaders,
bribery, infiltration, secret subsidies, false-front propaganda, and deniable paramilitary action, to induce political groups in and out of office to act in a manner contrary
to their declared purposes.

became well established in the everyday reality of international politics, nuclear weapons evoked a much more prosaic defensive reaction. The Soviet response to their first appearance, as fission bombs for American long-range bombers, was to give a high priority to antiaircraft defenses. The organizational schemes of the war just ended, huge numbers of antiaircraft guns still perfectly adequate, radar at first copied from models originally supplied by the United States under Lend Lease, and later the first jet fighters and missiles—all were intended to resist American bombers.

Usually it is the defensive reaction that serves to diminish the net effect of new weapons, but that was not so with nuclear weapons. Even air defenses far more capable than any before seen could not be capable enough, because any one surviving bomber could destroy so much. With the inevitable bomber-protecting response in action as well, the net effect of the new weapon was scarcely diminished by antiaircraft defenses.

Autonomy Diminished: Inhibitions and Retaliation

Even before there was any danger of retaliation in kind, self-imposed inhibitions set limits to the use of the fission bomb. It was not a world destroyer, but several of them could devastate a large city, and the sheer dimensions of its destructive strength exceeded the culminating point of military utility in many cases, quite independently of the retaliation that might be evoked. Such great destruction inflicted even on declared enemies would be politically acceptable at home and abroad only if interests broadly recognized as highly important were at stake. Thus even while the American nuclear monopoly persisted, the excessive destructive power of the fission bomb left room for an entire category of possible wars that might have to be fought by "conventional" armed forces. They would be only small wars of course, in remote locations no doubt, against secondary enemies and for marginal allies, wars still worth fighting—but not with atomic bombs. Thus the strategic autonomy that some had eagerly attributed to the nuclear weapon, and which was of no avail against indirect and deniable forms of attack, was further diminished.

A much greater reduction in the strategic autonomy originally attributed to the atomic bomb was to come. The symmetrical reaction that the American monopoly evoked even before 1945 yielded its first fruits quite soon, and by 1949 the Soviet Union had tested its first fission device. Although there was no parity between the two bomber forces, one still small but the other no more than embryonic, the scope of nuclear suasion was immediately affected: whereas the present value of future money is discounted, in the forming of perceptions future military strength is anticipated.[21]

Once retaliation in kind became possible, war planners had to be more circumspect in their envisaged use of fission bombs, and political leaders much more careful in issuing threats meant to persuade. What suasion with fission bombs could achieve in imposing action (compellence) or inaction (deterrence) had always been limited by the other side's assessment of the likelihood of actual use—and that likelihood was inevitably much diminished when a nuclear attack in response had to be anticipated. Up to a point, opinions about the *character* of the leadership of the would-be persuading power had to figure in the assessment: those deemed especially prudent would be less intimidating than those deemed reckless. Speculation on the political uses of madness notwithstanding, what suasion could achieve would not be greatly influenced by variations in the prudence attributed to generally prudent American and Soviet governments.

Instead, the scope and limits of suasion with fission bombs would largely be determined by perceptions of the importance of the interests at risk *to the other party*. Exactly the same threat might be fully plausible in seeking to avert a direct Soviet attack on American territory, and much less convincing for shielding a marginal ally from a peripheral Soviet intrusion. The "balance of perceived interests" thus joined the balance of technical capabilities in defining what nuclear threats could achieve, breaking any simple relationship between the dimensions and quality of the forces in hand and their potentiality for suasion. Soviet assessments of American interests in American eyes, and American assessments of Soviet interests as the Kremlin saw them, might be manipulated on either side by skillful posturing,[22] but within limits: not every locality in danger could be made into a Berlin, and not every international connection of the Soviet Union could be elevated to the status of a sacrosanct alliance.

Thus some interests of each side could undoubtedly be secured by suasion with fission bombs, others might be, and many more than before would be beyond its scope, once the possibility of retaliation in kind was taken into account. A further category of possible wars that might have to be fought by conventional forces came into existence, reducing further the strategic autonomy once attributed to the nuclear weapon. True, the likelihood of a widening spiral of violence, and the possibility at least that the loser would resort to the use of fission bombs, virtually prohibited direct warfare even on the smallest scale between American and Soviet forces over interests regarded as secondary by both sides. Hence the expeditionary adventures, raids, and counterraids that might have marked the cold-war confrontation at its peripheries were all excluded: prior possession affirmed by a physical military presence became more important than ever before.

What was true for marginal positions and values, however, would not be true of interests truly important to both sides, over which war might erupt, notwithstanding the risk of an eventual resort to fission bombs by the loser. Those interests therefore had to be protected by conventional armed forces in place. The post-1949 stationing of American troops and airpower in Europe and the conduct of warfare in Korea after June 25, 1950, marked the retreat of suasion with fission bombs—and the extent of their loss of strategic autonomy.

The Excessive Weapon

The original atomic bombs were large, clumsy, and scarce. The transformation of nuclear capabilities during the early 1950s, with the development of fusion devices yielding fifty or even five hundred times as much energy as the first bombs, and with the mass production of smaller bombs, artillery shells, depth charges, mines, and warheads, had contradictory effects on the strategic autonomy of the nuclear weapon. On the one hand, the destructive potential of large fusion bombs, with retaliation in kind duly included, exceed by far any culminating point of utility *for suasion*. Indeed, the curve declined so steeply that less could be expected from those weapons than from fission bombs with only a fraction of their destructive energy: the interests that can warrant the risk of starting what might become a civilization-destroying war are naturally fewer than those that could justify the risk of a war with fission weapons, in which 1945 bombing results would have been duplicated, albeit much more rapidly. The incorporation of nuclear weapons into every part of the armed forces, on the other hand, greatly diminished the significance of nonnuclear imbalances. With nuclear weapons present in the inventory of air wings and army corps, larger warships and every submarine, a direct mechanism was in place to convert impeding nonnuclear defeat into nuclear combat, nullifying the victor's achievement up to that time.

Both effects have been evident in the experience of the nuclear powers from the start of nuclear abundance in the mid-1950s to this day. The Soviet Union has never been able to deny the nuclear intrusion into the balance of nonnuclear forces on land, in which its continued advantage has therefore remained without definite effect. On the other hand, the American attempt under the policy of "massive retaliation" to nullify the entire balance of nonnuclear strength, by instead relying "primarily upon a great capacity to retaliate, instantly, by means and at places of our own choosing,"[23] did not succeed either. Massive retaliation would certainly have been the fullest possible affirmation of the strategic autonomy of nuclear weapons, had it been successful. But it will never be known whether the Soviet leaders might have been dissuaded by nuclear means alone, since the policy was never implemented: the United States did not reduce its nonnuclear forces to the very low levels needed as tripwires for that "great capacity to retaliate." Instead, over the decades, through the cycles of rearmament, a losing war, disarmament, inflation, and more rearmament, the American nonnuclear military effort has tended on the whole to increase, at least in expenditure, in substantive proof of the eroding scope of nuclear suasion.

As the paradoxical decline in military utility caused by their own excessive destructive power shows so clearly, nuclear weapons are fully subject to the same logic of strategy that applies to all other weapons. A struggle fought with many large fusion warheads, say one in ten of those in current inventory, would certainly be different enough from all previous wars to warrant description in its own terms. War economics or war poetry, war propaganda or war legislation, and all the other familiar ancillaries of war would have no place in the resulting annihilation. But there is no distinct logic that would apply. The same logic we have explored so far, through the technical, tactical, operational, and theater levels, explains the self-negation of that kind of struggle very well, when we reach the level of grand strategy.

III

OUTCOMES:
GRAND STRATEGY

Introduction

Now at last we are ready to encounter grand strategy, the highest level of final results. This is also the everyday form of strategy, because the dynamic workings of the paradoxical logic continue even in the absence of warfare. Peacetime international politics are conditioned by the same logic, insofar as the use of force is still a possible recourse.

In examining the prior levels of strategy from the technical to the theater-strategic, convenient labels were at hand to differentiate between the normative *doctrines* promulgated by this or that military institution; the positive *analysis* of interested observers seeking to explain or even predict particular phenomena within a given level; and the objective *reality* of each level, as a slice of strategy whose logic has its conditioning effect, whether or not there is anybody to observe the process. This was so in the very plain distinction between the tactics prescribed by the manuals of a given army or navy, for a given type of force and perhaps in a specific setting ("urban tactics for armor"); tactical analysis performed to evaluate a weapon, explain a combat episode, or discern the implications of some institutional or environmental feature; and the tactical level of strategy itself, as it exists in reality, whether or not any particular tactics have been recommended for action at that level. It was the same for the trio of the techniques applied, the study of their results in technical analysis, and the technical level of strategy itself. Similarly, there was no great difficulty in differentiating between operational methods, such as "defense in depth" or "counterforce strike"; the operational-level analysis of, say, Patton's deep-penetration offensive in France; and the operational level itself—whose importance, we discovered, was a function of the relational-maneuver content. At the next level, the need for clarity imposed rather clumsier distinctions, as between the "theater strategy of the Alliance,'' for example, theater-level analysis, and the level of theater strategy itself, wherein military phenomena are conditioned spatially.

At the highest level of strategy, however, we have no convenient terms to differentiate readily between grand strategy as the doctrine declared by a given state or imputed to it (''Soviet grand strategy''); grand strategy as a level of analysis, whereby we examine the totality of what happens between states and other participants in international politics; and the reality of grand strategy as the conclusive level of strategy as a whole. Of course only the latter exists universally: very few of the states that participate in international politics have a thought-out grand strategy of their own. My purpose, as always, is to uncover the inner reality of the logic at the level of grand strategy, and not at all to recommend a course of action for the United States or any other country.

CHAPTER 12

THE SCOPE OF
GRAND STRATEGY

$\mathbf{I}$f we recall the earlier image of strategy as a sort of multilevel edifice, with floors set in motion by the waves and counterwaves of action and reaction, we would find that its highest level is very much more spacious than those below it, in a way that no feasible architecture would allow. For at the level of grand strategy, the interactions of the lower, military levels, their synergisms or contradictions, yield final results within the broad setting of international politics, in further interaction with the nonmilitary transactions of states: the formal exchanges of diplomacy, the public communications of propaganda, secret operations,* the perceptions of others formed by intelligence official and unofficial, and all economic transactions of more than purely private significance. On this disproportionate top floor, therefore, the *net* outcome of the technical, tactical, operational, and theater-strategic emerges in continuous interaction with all those dealings between states that are affected by, and in turn affect, what is done or not done militarily within any one state.

In a different image, which captures the dynamic nature of our subject, grand strategy may be seen as a confluence of the military interactions that flow up and down level by level—forming strategy's vertical dimension—with the varied external relations that form strategy's horizontal dimension at its highest level. In this

---

*Here employed as the generic term for all hostile intrusions into the territory of other states (except for outright military attacks and overt propaganda), usually categorized as *covert political action,* including undeclared subsidies, false-front propaganda, and the use of agents of penetration; and *paramilitary action,* including the support of local insurgents and all deniable forms of violence, from the intimidation of individuals to combat on a large scale. In subversion, as noted, both kinds of secret operation are combined.

image, the rivers and rivulets of international transactions would radiate from a central vertical flow, violating the laws of hydrodynamics in their reciprocal movement as military preparations and actions have their effects on the nonmilitary dealings of states, and as the latter in turn affect the military realm.

STRATEGY IN INTERNATIONAL POLITICS

The boundaries of grand strategy are therefore very wide, but they do not encompass all the relationships of all participants within the totality of international politics. Whatever dealings may exist between Sweden and Costa Rica, they are unlikely to be influenced in any significant degree by reciprocal fears of attack or by reciprocal expectations of warlike assistance. Hence they are not directly conditioned by the logic of strategy, even though neither the self-declared neutrality of Sweden nor the self-imposed disarmament of Costa Rica exempts either country from numerous other strategical relationships with potential enemies and allies that intersect at some point. Such indirect linkages, however, will scarcely affect the bilateral relations of the two countries. Grand strategy thus exists within international politics but does not coincide with its boundaries. We may note incidentally that one way of assaying international society on some normative index of progress is to examine how many of its relationships are significantly strategical.*

To be sure, grand strategy also exists outside international politics, for it comprehends the highest level of interaction between any parties capable of using unregulated force against one another. The

---

*Because so many intraregional quarrels have been suppressed by the emergence of fewer, larger, transregional confrontations, one might draw comfort from the improvement in the statistics, were it not for the concurrent emergence of the catastrophic nuclear danger: disregarding numerous actors capable of using force other than constituted territorial states, and accepting United Nations membership as an approximation of the number of states, multiplication yields more than 20,000 bilateral interstate relationships, of which not more than a few hundred are strategical to any perceptible extent. Within Europe, many historic quarrels, such as between France and Germany, have been made obsolete by the dominant impact of the East-West confrontation; it is the same in East Asia, and even in the quarrelsome Middle East, the Arab-Israeli confrontation and now the Iraq-Iran war continue to suppress many more intra-Arab quarrels.

same paradoxical logic is manifest at the level of grand strategy in domestic settings as well, insofar as the state's monopoly of force is incomplete, whether in civil war or in the doings of outlaws. Indeed one could identify the level of grand strategy even in a knife fight between two cutthroats in an alley: their grunts and screams may be seen as a form of diplomacy and propaganda conjoined; one or the other may attempt to employ economic inducements, offering money to stop the fight; some intelligence and deception will be present as they watch and try to misdirect one another by feints. And we may recognize in the fight a distinct level above the tactical, formed by their reciprocal thrusts and parries, or above the technical, defined by the qualities of their knives. Even the participants themselves recognize distinctions between the levels, insofar as they may plead, threaten, and bargain with each other as they continue to fight. So grand strategy may be present even on the smallest scale, insofar as individuals are acting as independent states, at least until the police arrive.

But if the logic at work here is the same as in the setting of international politics, the phenomena it conditions are very different, not merely because of their trivial scale but because they are made of individual acts and individual thoughts. The entire institutional and political aspect that characterizes the conduct of states is thus absent, and with it the permanent contradiction between linear-logical political arrangements and the paradoxical logic that rules in the external conflictual realm. My inquiry will be confined to the dealings of states with one another not because strategy has a more natural place within them, but precisely for the opposite reason: only states ruled by strategist-kings could emulate the spontaneously strategical conduct of two cutthroats going at each other in an alley, for whom paradoxical action to deceive and outmaneuver comes quite naturally.

Whether we imagine it in static terms as an edifice in the odd shape of a pedestal table or in dynamic terms as a sort of very complicated fountain, grand strategy is the conclusive level, where all that happens in the vertical and horizontal dimensions finally comes together to acquire a definite meaning. Brilliant achievements at the technical, tactical, operational, or theater-strategic level, or for that matter diplomatic blunders, may translate directly, or have quite the opposite effect, or even remain without consequence in the confluence of grand strategy.

LINEAR GOALS IN A PARADOXICAL MEDIUM

Of course whether the results that grand strategy yields are deemed good or bad is a matter of subjective interpretation: how outcomes are seen depends on what goals are being pursued, and whether they are set by tradition, dictatorial whim, bureaucratic preference, or democratic choice, the logic of strategy has no say in their making. At the level of grand strategy, some governments above all seek power over other states or actual territorial expansion; other governments desire only to keep what external power and influence they have, while dedicating their greater efforts to domestic purposes, including the increase of prosperity; some are active on the world scene primarily to claim economic aid in various forms and can measure their achievement with rare precision; others see a fullness of success if they are simply left alone, and still others seek external support precisely to be left alone by states they fear. Each has its own goals, if only implicit, and each therefore assays results differently so that the same outcome, say the preservation of an unchanged status quo, may be deemed highly successful by one government and a crushing failure by another.

What is true of failure and success within the compass of single questions is also true of all the other goals that are formed domestically before being thrust into the conflictual medium of strategy. That "national interests" are subjectively defined in a political process that owes nothing to strategy's logic is obvious enough: when contending parties in domestic politics seek approval for their own goals by presenting them as national interests, they must usually do so in terms of commonsense, linear logic, where good is good, bad is bad, and the larger gain is better than the smaller; and "national security" must also be defined within the linear logic of domestic politics, where more is more and less is less.

There is no need to cite an infinity of examples to show the consequences of this pervasive contradiction. If history is to a large extent the record of the follies of mankind, then the faultline between the two kinds of logic has been instrumental in a great many of them (as many a political leader successful in domestic governance has discovered when venturing to apply his talents to foreign matters, and as many a conquering hero of war or diplomacy has learned when attempting to govern at home). In a few specific matters, the repetition of tragic error time after time over the centuries has left some impression, so that the projection of linear, logical goals on the conflictual scene is questioned. If x army divisions or y missiles are thought necessary for national security as currently defined, it is now possible that it will not be taken for granted that twice as many must be even better, except for the cost. It may at least be suspected that the formation of additional divisions or the construction of additional battleships could evoke adversary reactions either competitive or worse still preemptive, which can make more divisions or battleships less desirable than fewer would have been. It is fittingly ironic that such enlightenment has been advanced by way of the simplistic, indeed mechanistic, notion that "arms races" are self-propelled, closely interactive, and without a valid purpose at each remove, as the image of "two apes on a treadmill" suggests. The clash of political ambitions that is the true cause of competition in all categories of weapons, and in many other things as well, is thus ignored, as is the role of purposeful innovation: the ape who is chased by another has good reason to step ahead, on a treadmill or not—for there is no staircase to salvation in any case, so long as the political confrontation persists.

A more obvious category of exceptions to the unthinking translation of linear logic across the faultline is evident to every traveler in lands once much contested. Around the Mediterranean countless villages are perched on mountainsides, now picturesque and easily reached by car and tractor, but for centuries most uncomfortably removed from their own fields and from the highways in the valleys below. The ruins of lowland settlements dating back to many different periods show that it was only through bitter experience that survivors learned that the good site is bad and the bad site is good, when conflict arises. In secure Roman times, mere commonsense had favored convenient valley sites. In recent times, when war if it comes will not spare the high ground, the valley can again be chosen for its convenience. But during the centuries in between, the hilltop villagers were constantly exposed to the fatal temptation of settling in the lowland, where the weary climb would no longer be added to the end of each day's labor; and that they sometimes yielded is shown by the ruins still visible.

Matters are no different for those nations most uncomfortably entrapped in the realm of conflict, divided by common interests that are not mutual, usually in perfect agreement on the goodness of peace and the badness of war, on the undesirable costs of armament and the superiority of disarmament, and yet prevented from acting on these commonsense findings by the lively expectation that the one-sided pursuit of peace and disarmament would be a powerful incentive to the adversary effort that will overcome their defenses—as indeed it is, and by the full force of the paradoxical logic.

But if that is the rule of survivors, it is not the universal rule. Frequent are the attempts to project linear logic across the faultline, in search of commonsense cooperative solutions whose merits seem exasperatingly self-evident to those who propose them. If we want peace, why not simply have it? If we agree that weapons are costly and dangerous, why not simply disarm? And if there is a quarrel over substantive interests, why not resolve it by all the procedures of law, arbitration, and bargaining that daily resolve such quarrels within the domestic sphere? The persistence with which such cooperative solutions are proposed is not surprising, for the notion that the very pursuit of peace or disarmament logically leads to their opposites is simply bizarre in the perspective of linear logic.

But of course it is not intellectual error that induces these attempts to descend into the comfortable valley, but rather the acute temptation to escape from the paradoxical logic, wherein simple inaction is prohibited by the plain need to confront danger while action is always costly and can easily become self-defeating. The modern annals of diplomacy are replete with attempts to evolve commonsense solutions and to dissolve hostility by demonstrations of good will, as if expressions of hostility were not a mere symptom of conflict caused by some substantive clash of purposes. When the *causes* of conflict have been removed, not only cooperative diplomacy but also gestures of goodwill can be productive.

In this vein, post-1945 Franco-German diplomacy has been successful in propelling joint initiatives in many fields, and the many summit meetings, state visits with mass participation, youth exchanges, and more such have all helped to dissipate an outdated hostility. But it was only the suppression of the old conflict by the new, much wider East-West conflict that ensured the success of Franco-German diplomacy, and of all the gestures of goodwill, by translating the entire relationship across the faultline, where good is indeed good, bad is bad, and common interests can also be mutual. When exactly the same procedures were tried before World War II, with continuous formal diplomacy, summit meetings (notably at Munich), arms-control negotiations, and a great many gestures of goodwill, including friendly reunions of veterans of the trenches, the only effect of so much gazing at the tempting valley below was to increase the felt discomfort of conflictual precautions.

From this famous failure of statecraft, and the parallel British-German case that was to cast the ancient and honorable practice of appeasement* into disrepute, a most influential exception arose to the proclivity of projecting linear-logical solutions into the conflictual realm. The arms-control negotiations of the interwar years, the summit meetings, goodwill gestures, and even the process of diplomatic communication itself were all condemned as harmful to preparations for a war they did nothing to avert, because of their supposedly intense soporific effect. Accordingly, for many years after World War II, when it was the clash of purposes with the Soviet Union that was its object, Western diplomacy was conducted with great, perhaps excessive circumspection in the shadow of the "lesson of Munich." It is possible to argue that in the process useful opportunities for mutual accommodation may have been missed, at least during the Khrushchev years. But it has rightly been said that history teaches nothing except that it teaches nothing, for of course the various Soviet leaders were not intent on war as Hitler had been, and their timetable in the pursuit of their own ambitions was certainly devoid of Hitler's urgency.[1]

To be sure, diplomacy can serve many purposes in all situations however conflictual and indeed can be especially productive in the midst of war, not necessarily to bring it to an end. The intermingling of warfare and *direct* negotiations in the Korean and Vietnamese wars was a return to classical procedures. It was rather the absence of direct diplomacy during the two world wars that was untypical. In the case of World War I at least, the renunciation of diplomacy was generally regarded in retrospect as an elite concession to mass sentiment (inflamed from the start by elite-directed propaganda) and as evidence of the special ferocity of "democratic" war.

* A term useful enough to be worth rescuing from the pejorative connotations that derive from the Munich debacle. Appeasement implies that the causes of conflict can be identified and removed by cooperative diplomatic surgery, a procedure impossible when the salient cause of conflict is the very character of the negotiating partner.

THE CASE OF ARMS CONTROL

If confined to narrow and well-defined issues, even an outrightly cooperative, linear-logical, diplomacy can coexist with the persistence of unresolved conflict over larger interests. Such diplomacy can serve one side or all sides to gain some advantage, perhaps of propaganda, by channeling continuing rivalry away from paths deemed undesirable by all. In territorial conflicts, the best expression of such cooperation has been the reciprocal acceptance of buffer states, left alone by both sides even as they continue to seek expansion at each other's expense elsewhere. In the context of the largely nonterritorial American-Soviet conflict (a warlike struggle without war), the 1955 State Treaty that left Austria as a buffer state is a less typical example of cooperative diplomacy than the 1962 atmospheric test-ban treaty. The energies engaged in the nuclear competition, which is a manifestation of the struggle *and also its most important substitute for war,* were not diminished, but the agreed channeling of competitive efforts away from nuclear detonations in the atmosphere has been of benefit to both sides and to third parties as well.

The error hidden in the wake of such success is to misconstrue the diversion of conflictual energies as a partial solution of the conflict itself, thereby suggesting that a progression of further partial agreements might bring the conflict to an end. Thus arms-control negotiations are often misinterpreted as a form of conflict resolution, whereas they only affect a symptom of conflict, namely the derived military competition. On the other hand, it is possible to argue that the process of negotiations itself can have a calming effect.

Because arms control as such does not restrain the competitive impulse but merely diverts it, the consequences of agreed limitations depend on the features of the particular weapons effectively restrained and of the new weapons for which developmental resources are thereby released. Insofar as the former are known and the latter are not, the pursuit of arms control is a gamble for each participant, though one that systematically favors the side best placed to innovate (generally the United States in the American-Soviet case). The accelerated development of new weapons caused by agreed prohibitions on the multiplication of the old will periodically generate further stresses in the conflictual relationship as a whole—when, that is, the new weapons have novel configurations that disturb established patterns of interaction between the forces on each side. Such "innovation shocks" should also be anticipated when evaluating the calming effect that arms-control negotiations may have.

The pursuit of arms control is itself conditioned by the paradoxical logic, insofar as *effective* agreements that limit the competition in some way are actually negotiated. (Agreements merely cosmetic are not substantive phenomena in the strategic sense and therefore escape such conditioning.) Specifically, as with any other activity in the realm of strategy, arms control steadily pursued must eventually become self-defeating after a culminating point, in this case reached after a certain accumulation of agreed limitations.

It is the mechanism of "verification"—the procedures and devices used to assure compliance with negotiated restrictions—that is the vehicle (not the cause) of the self-annihilation of arms control. Dependent on satellite observation, radar tracking, signal intelligence, and such, verification is the sine qua non of arms control: what cannot be verified cannot be limited—and not all weapons are sufficiently stable and visible to be detected and reliably counted, and not all forms of performance are sufficiently transparent to be assessed. If all existing weapons whose number and characteristics can be verified were successfully restrained by mutual agreement, developmental energies and production resources would be diverted to the acquisition of new weapons not yet controlled, some sufficiently stable to be counted and whose performance can be assessed remotely, and others not. If the new weapons that are verifiable are then limited in turn, the result would be a further diversion of effort into newer weapons, some verifiable and others not. Eventually, as the process continues and all verifiable weapons are duly subjected to effective limitations, all developmental and production resources will have been diverted into the acquisition of weapons that cannot be verified for one reason or another and therefore cannot be subject to limitations. At that point, the competition in arms would continue. But arms control would have come to an end, annihilated by its own success, just like the perfect antitank weapon that would cause the disappearance of tanks from all battlefields or the army that advances so far that it marches to its own self-destruction.

That arms-control diplomacy can as best achieve only specific restraints on particular weapons hardly condemns its pursuit, for this is precisely its declared purpose. Certainly the process itself cannot be blamed for the chronic propensity to misconstrue it as a device for the resolution of the underlying hostility and as a prelude to disarmament. Yet no error is more natural in the domestic politics of prosperity-seeking countries of consensual government, where the reconciliation of conflicting interests is the everyday business of politics.

The tension between goals formed domestically by linear thinking and the conflictual aspect of international politics is not a universal condition. Governments that rule by warlike methods at home are much less likely to pursue linear goals on the international scene. Their leaders need not have any greater intellectual understanding of the paradoxical logic;* indeed they may be primitives who do not think in such terms at all. But habitual reliance on secrecy, deception, intimidation, and force for domestic control engenders its own education in strategy, as patterns of failure and success themselves suggest the outlines of its logic. Just as consensual politics at home inspires a linear-logical outlook in foreign policy, the domestic politics of imposed control prepares its authors for the logic of conflict abroad. No particular predisposition to aggressive conduct follows. There is simply no connection between the form of domestic politics and the propensity to wage war by choice.

As the historical record shows, dictatorships can be impeccably peaceful and democracies can be fiercely aggressive. It was an increasingly democratic Britain that was increasingly aggressive during the nineteenth century in subduing much of south Asia and all of southern Africa, and its leading competitor in imperial expansion was France, especially with the advent of democratic government after 1871. Nor can the spirit of the times be invoked to explain all: the electorates of both countries still heartily approve the use of force overseas when the opportunity arises.

There is no asymmetry of intentions, therefore, but there can be one of effectiveness. Its consequences are manifest in the struggle of prosperity-maximizing countries of consensual government to contain power-maximizing governments that choose to apply

---

* Although the Hegelian dialectic contained in Marxist doctrine certainly favors a strategical outlook. There is an obvious similarity between the dialectic and the paradoxical logic here proposed.

abroad what they daily practice at home. The former breed a greater ingenuity in production and easily prevail in scientific advancement, but in the use of secrecy, deception, intimidation, and force, the more practiced governments naturally show greater skill. War can nullify the difference, and in World War II the Anglo-American democracies were clearly superior precisely in secrecy and deception, to the point of making the Germans and Japanese seem almost naive in retrospect. Yet in coping with the conflictual aspects of peacetime international politics, linear-logical attitudes are an undeniable source of weakness that can weigh heavily in the balance of power.

CHAPTER 13

ARMED SUASION

$\mathbf{N}$o matter how they are interpreted, in the light of goals inappropriately linear-logical or properly conflictual, the results emerging at the level of grand strategy are only "final" in the sense that they mark a completion of the interactive process in both its horizontal and vertical dimensions, when all other external transactions have had their impact on the military levels. Because the dynamic logic of strategy has no end, at least for those who survive its workings, all outcomes—even victory and defeat sealed by formal treaty—are only interim results, destined to be changed by the reactions that they themselves immediately begin to induce. Subject to that, the *normal* results manifest at the level of grand strategy, those of "armed suasion" as opposed to combat, are no less substantial for the absence of any visible clash of arms: indeed armed suasion is nothing less than power, or rather that portion of the power of states that derives from their military strength.

Although this neologism was first introduced in conjunction with the novel impact of nuclear weapons upon world politics, armed suasion is as old as violence itself: there can be no capacity for violence that does not evoke some response from those who hope it might be used on their behalf or from those who fear it might be used against them. As we saw, the new term is necessary to overcome the political and cultural bias that so greatly emphasizes just one of its forms, obscuring the more general phenomenon: armed suasion is to "deterrence" (or "dissuasion") what strength in general is to defensive strength. And having introduced the general concept, now I can revert to plain language to describe its various forms, with *dissuasion* being the negative form of power as *persuasion* is the positive, manifest both when adversaries feel themselves compelled to act as they are bid to do and when friends are encouraged to persist in friendship by their expectation of armed help in time of need.

Thus both adversaries and friends may be persuaded, as adversaries alone may be dissuaded, but always by their own doing: the suasion is not in the keeping of armed strength, but rather in the response of others to such strength, the result of decisions *they* make, shaped by *their* calculations and emotions—decisions that reflect their view of the world, including their own opinion of the armed strength before them, their vision of the likelihood and circumstances of combat, and their estimate of the willingness to use it, for or against them. Descriptions of this or that force as a deterrent (or presumably "compellent"), which imply that the act of dissuasion is accomplished by the upkeep of a given force, entail a confusion between subject and object that can be dangerously misleading. The would-be deterrent is the passive object, and the party to be influenced is the sentient, active subject, who may or may not choose to be dissuaded.[1]

Perceptions of both actual and potential military strength can evoke suasion. Subject to the envisaged duration of whatever warfare is deemed possible, the economic and demographic capacity of nations that is thought available for mobilization can induce anticipatory suasion at par, at a discount, or not at all. For example, the widespread belief common in the 1950s that any American-Soviet war would be nuclear from the start and very short had the effect of undercutting the suasion that the United States might otherwise have derived from its then vastly superior capacity for industrial mobilization. Since then, in a manner doubly ironical because Soviet military policy has increasingly emphasized preparations for a protracted nonnuclear war,* American mobilization capacity has been revalidated, at a time when it is in rapid erosion.

In combat, force is an objective reality in action, whose only valid and totally unambiguous measure is in the results achieved. With armed suasion, however, there is only the subjective estimate of a given potential for combat in the eyes of others, friends and enemies alike. The accuracy of such estimates is not merely uncertain but actually indeterminate, because that combat potential is only measurable in the reality of war—which may never happen

---

*As the changing structure of the Soviet army reveals, notably in the restoration of higher-echelon artillery formations, intended to provide costly but nonnuclear firepower. See Appendix 2.

and whose outcome if it does happen will be influenced by all the unpredictables of time, space, and circumstance. To be sure, it is easy to think of extreme cases in which uncertainties and indeterminacy alike are simply nullified by overwhelming material imbalances, as in the case of a nuclear war between the Soviet Union and nonnuclear Albania or in a naval war between the United States and land-locked Nepal. But the record of military history shows conclusively that as soon as one contemplates less extreme cases not wholly absurd, uncertainty and indeterminacy begin, and far sooner than any reasonable reading of the precombat evidence would suggest. But then, if the outcome of combat were less uncertain, there would be very much less combat and much more accommodation to avoid its test.[2]

There is no help for the essential indeterminacy of combat, but great efforts are made to reduce uncertainty. Numbers are dutifully counted for men, weapons, and supplies, and there is much striving to evaluate the quality of weapons and their ancillaries. But there still remains the far larger part of the unknown, the intangibles of organization, morale, cohesion, and leadership that count for so much more than the material factors and that can only be guessed—and no greater accuracy is assured in evaluating the fitness of tactics, operational methods, and theater strategies in the envisaged setting of combat, given those material factors and those intangibles.

DIPLOMACY, PROPAGANDA, AND DECEPTION

In the absence of any objective measure for armed strength unused, strategy outside war is therefore a commerce conducted in as many currencies as there are interested parties. Inevitably, different values—sometimes greatly divergent—are assigned to the same military forces, and an important function of both diplomacy and propaganda is precisely to manipulate those subjective evaluations. Sometimes, very rarely, the aim is to devalue forces about to be unleashed so that they may be launched with unexpected strength,[3] but much more often the purpose is to evoke as much suasion as possible. This is why even a pervasively secretive Soviet government has long chosen to stage public flying displays and Red Square parades to which Western military attachés are invited, as is photography—to view the latest aircraft, tanks, guns, and missiles—in a country where otherwise even railway stations cannot be photographed. If secrecy can undercut the potential for evoking suasion and appropriate advertisement can secure it in true proportion, even more can be obtained by outright manipulation.

It was thus that, during the 1930s, the diplomacy of Mussolini's Italy was greatly enhanced by a stance of restless bellicosity and by a mirage of great military strength: an army of "eight million bayonets," whose parades were dashing affairs of *bersaglieri* on the run and roaring motorized columns; an air force greatly respected, not least for its spectacular long-range flights to the North Pole and South America; and a navy that could acquire many impressive ships because so little of its funding was wasted on gunnery trials and navigation. By a military policy in which stage management dominated over the sordid needs of war preparation,[4] Mussolini sacrificed real strength for the sake of hugely magnified images of what little strength there was—but the results of suasion that those images evoked were very real: Britain and France were both successfully dissuaded from interfering with Italy's conquest of Ethiopia, its intervention in Spain, and the subjection of Albania; and none dared oppose Italy's claim to be accepted as a Great Power, whose interests had to be accommodated sometimes in tangible ways (such as the licenses obtained by Italian banks in Bulgaria, Hungary, Romania, and Yugoslavia). Only Mussolini's last-minute decision to enter the war in June 1940—when his own considerable prudence was overcome by the irresistible temptation of sharing in the spoils of the French collapse—brought years of successful deception (and self-deception) to an end.

What Mussolini did, and many others before him, has also been done since his day, with Nasser of Egypt being his closest imitator and Khrushchev during the missile-gap years an even more successful practitioner. As we now know, between 1955 and 1962 the Soviet Union's supposedly great strength first in bombers and then in "atomic rockets" consisted of a few bombers and later a mere handful of huge, unworkable missiles that could hardly be aimed at all, carefully orchestrated talk, and the spectacular imagery of pioneering space exploration, which was also manipulated to amplify very real achievements.[5] But that is how matters stand with armed suasion: when there is no objective truth manifest in action, but only a mass of impressions to be construed as best one can, there is room for much error, and deception as well.

NATIONAL WILL

Because military power cannot dissuade or persuade except insofar as its actual use is deemed possible, that great subject of metapolitical speculation, the "will" of leaders and nations, is reduced to simple mathematics in the phenomenon of suasion: aside from all else that is of consequence, the effect that armed forces induce in others depends on their perceived strength multiplied by the perceived willingness to use that strength—and if that willingness is deemed absent, even the strongest forces, whose strength is fully recognized, may not dissuade or persuade at all. The meaning of the matter for nations who successfully present themselves as relentlessly peaceful to the outside world is plain: they can hope to obtain but little in the way of suasion from the forces they keep. Sweden, for example, although a considerable military power by European standards, has been quite unable to dissuade frequent violations of its territorial waters by Soviet submarines in recent years. At least from the narrow viewpoint of suasion, a demonstrative peace policy can be too successful.

But very few countries are content to display an easily provoked bellicosity, to maximize their potential for suasion at the expense of their other priorities. The rest, the vast majority of countries dedicated neither to peace at all costs nor to war at the merest opportunity, are confronted by one of strategy's typical dilemmas, the other side of the paradoxical coin: in order to avoid the actual use of force and still protect their interests, they must maintain a reputation for violence if they are to persuade or dissuade by armed strength—and this is not the sort of reputation that those most intent on avoiding war care to present or are well placed to keep up. Often enough, domestic political imperatives and urges derived from unstrategical sentiments and self-images greatly undercut suasion potentials, not necessarily without tangible effect. The usual way out of the dilemma is to present two Janus-like visages, proclaiming both a dedication to peace that rules out all aggression and a great readiness to fight if attacked. Valid enough for countries that have to protect only themselves, this simple formula will not do for great powers that remain great only by protecting others as well. Instead they are forced back into the dilemma and accordingly must keep a declaratory stance carefully qualified to strike a delicate balance between a reassuringly peaceful attitude and one that reassures precisely because it is not wholly peaceful.

In multilateral alliances, this striving to avoid the need to use force by obtaining the results of suasion must be in perpetual crisis, with some marginal allies contemplating separation because they are frightened off by an excessive bellicosity, while others are in exactly the same state because of exactly the opposite reason. Ultimately, by the usual paradox, it is those considered most willing to use force who are least likely to have to use it—and this indeed has always been the secret of military empires, whose widespread intrusions upon other nations could only result in endemic war on all fronts were it not for the eagerness with which their desires are accommodated without war.

Overt attempts to induce suasion, positive or negative, by declared demands and expressed refusals to tolerate this or that are quite rare, and it is *latent* suasion that is the common phenomenon. Indeed, the suasion that the perceived existence of armed strength silently elicits is largely the preserver of world order such as it is, just as the ultimate existence of courts and policemen is the preserver of private property. That silently continuous effect is not only quite undirected but may also be unconscious. Armed forces are usually maintained to preserve institutional continuity for possible future war, for internal repression, or even for tradition's sake, and only rarely for any deliberate purpose of suasion.[6]

THE PARADOXICAL LOGIC IN SUASION

Whether or not there is conscious intent, if there are countries that choose to see the military strength of others as reassuring and therefore persuade themselves to reciprocate in some way, or if there are adversaries who consider it a threat and are therefore dissuaded from some hostile act, armed suasion is at work. Because it is a conflictual phenomenon—whose existence derives entirely from the possibility of war, even if most improbable—armed suasion is conditioned by the paradoxical logic, and as soon as it actually happens in the minds and deeds of others, linear logic is displaced. Just as warlike actions lead to reactions that set in train strategy's distinct logic, so too armed suasion elicits not only desired responses but also confounding reactions, and it matters not at all if the suasion is spontaneously induced by the imagined reflection of military strength meant for quite other purposes.

With linear logic out and paradoxical logic in, the usual results follow. In the static view, more can be less and vice versa, as commonly in the case of the less destructive threat that elicits more in the way of suasion because the less catastrophic action is that much more plausible. In dynamic terms, on the other hand, we encounter again the coming together of opposites that may reach the point of a full reversal. The more a given striving for dissuasion is effective in achieving its particular goal, the more likely it is that it will be circumvented or even directly attacked by the frustrated would-be aggressor: if the Soviet Union had not been so well dissuaded in the immediate postwar period from the outright use of force in Eastern Europe, it would not have engaged in so much subversion. And today, if the Soviet Union were not so well dissuaded by the Alliance in Europe, it would adventure less in the Third World.

More generally, we have already seen how nuclear dissuasion has been circumvented on a global scale, by means of all the indirect and deniable forms of aggression, both quasi-political and paramilitary, both bloodless and very bloody indeed. While the United States and the Soviet Union have each been dissuaded from direct warfare because of the presence of nuclear weapons, their hostility has found an outlet in the wars fought by their allies, clients, and transitional agents. The counterpart of the unprecedented peace of the great powers has therefore been the unprecedented gravity of small-power wars.[7] They are no longer desultory affrays fought with secondhand weapons, but rather very intense surrogate fights, exemplified by the post-1967 Arab-Israeli wars in which weapons of the first quality have increasingly figured; or else endlessly protracted conflicts of attrition, as in Kampuchea and between Iraq and Iran at this writing. Thus the triumph of nuclear dissuasion is paradoxically manifest in nonnuclear violence that seemingly cannot be dissuaded.

Second-Strike Attack as a Paradoxical Remedy

The attack of imperial Japan on the United States fleet kept at Pearl Harbor after May 1940 embodied the confluence of success and failure in suasion. Had the presence of the fleet at that forward base been less effective in its intended aim of dissuading the Japanese from invading British Malaya and the Dutch East Indies, it would not itself have been attacked.[8] Understandably, the Pearl Harbor attack left a deep and enduring impression, even though it was not deemed a "lesson" of Pearl Harbor that antagonists should not be deprived of choices other than war—as Japan was after the April 1941 trade embargo that essentially cut off its oil supplies— unless war is actually intended and fully prepared; and even though no "lesson" was seen in the refusal of the United States to wage war in order to oppose Germany's conquests or Japan's, as they subjected most of continental Europe and much of China—until the Tojo cabinet made that decision on America's behalf.

What was eventually learned from the experience was that an armed force sufficiently threatening to dissuade attacks aimed at other targets positively invites attack upon itself—unless even its residual *postattack* strength is calculated by would-be aggressors as great enough to dissuade them. Out of this came the concept of "second-strike capability," which has played a large role in shaping American military policy for the construction and deployment of nuclear weapons.[9] Its insight is that only postattack, and not preattack, strength can safely be used to threaten, for otherwise it is provocation and not suasion that might be elicited. Its practical consequence has been the physical protection and abundant multiplication of nuclear weapons and of their means of command, to achieve the survival of a rather large number even in the wake of an all-out attack.

Patterns of Suasion

Aside from its everyday effects, silent, undirected, and mostly opaque, armed suasion also has its clear-cut victories and defeats, whose consequences can be identical to those of war, once its destructions are mended and its victims buried. The Romans had to fight for two centuries to subject North Africa and every part of Iberia, while their domination of the Hellenistic lands was obtained by very few battles and much intimidation.[10] Similarly, Hitler won Czechoslovakia without a fight entirely by armed suasion, whereas the Germans forcibly invaded Poland. But aside from the damage inflicted in the process, there was no difference in the aftermath so long as both remained conquered. In a contrary vein, we may note the equality of results between the successful defense of Korea by war in 1950–1952 and its equally successful and far less costly protection in all the years since, by armed dissuasion. The Korean example is especially instructive, not because it typifies dissuasion at work but precisely because it does not: in the Korean context, the distorted, quasi-mechanical, view of "deterrence" as an *action* of one's own, rather than an intended political response, is much less misleading than usual, so that the extent of the usual distortion is fully revealed.

In the first place, the perceived danger that emanates from North Korea is not a conceptualized threat, derived from computations of the enemy's military potential under selected assumptions and from rarefied conjecture as to the hypothetical circumstances in which a hypothetical political leadership might choose to attack. Instead the danger is manifest in immediate physical form: much of the huge North Korean army is massed very near the frontline, visibly ready to attack. As for the intent of the North Korean leaders to invade, that has frequently been declared over the years, receiving persuasive confirmation from actual invasion preparations (including tunnels dug underneath the demilitarized line), commando attacks, and repeated assassination attempts against South Korean officials[11]—a form of war that even the Arab states and Israel have always avoided despite all their other excesses. Moreover, the South Korean view of the threat is not a self-centered mental construct, imposed on hostile energies that might be directed in many other directions. Because of geography alone, the North Korean forces can only fight on a serious scale against the South; they can serve no other external purpose.

Thus the North Korean threat can actually be described accurately by that word, since it is continuous and can only by aimed in one specific direction—just as the mechanical view of deterrence always implies and as is so seldom the case. Normally of course, the danger is *not* continuous, but rather a possibility that could materialize in the hypothetical circumstances of a severe crisis; and it is *not* specific in form, intensity or direction, so that no countering effort is self-evidently appropriate—and is rather planned on the basis of idealized threats that sometimes correspond to limiting cases.[12]

In the Korean case, dissuasion is unusual in another respect as well. Although the possibility remains of bombardment even with nuclear weapons, to punish North Korea after the fact, it is primarily the prospect of a successful defense of the South that is meant to dissuade invasion. An element of dissuasion by denial, as opposed to dissuasion by punishment (or "retaliation"), is inherent in any defensive strength, just as an element of persuasion is inherent in any offensive strength. But the two forms of intended dissuasion are separable in principle and the difference can also be reflected in the detailed composition of the forces.

A policy of dissuasion by denial seems at first glance altogether preferable to the alternative of dissuasion by punishment, not only in the particular case of Korea but in principle—and therefore also for the Alliance in Europe, which now relies on a combination of denial—by the frontal forces first and battlefield nuclear weapons second—and punishment, by the American, British, and implicitly French long-range nuclear forces. Similarly, a policy of nonnuclear dissuasion by denial seems even more clearly preferable in principle to dissuasion by nuclear punishment. That indeed is the goal of the various proposals for nonnuclear Alliance defense that we have examined.

In the first place, under a policy of dissuasion by denial, all available military resources can be used to provide the most effective defense possible against invasion. If those preparations dissuade the attempt, so much the better—but if they do not, the invasion can still be resisted physically in full force. In other words, no military resources have to be diverted from the defensive effort in order to maintain retaliatory forces, of vast destructive capacity perhaps but of small value in physically resisting advancing enemy forces (as opposed to the punishment of those who sent them).

Second, dissuasion by denial does not have to rely on the tenuous psychological calculus that is the essential mechanism of dissuasion by punishment. In the classic formulation, in order to dissuade, the punishment has to be certain and capable of inflicting "unacceptable damage." Aside from its physical requirements, namely the ability to strike after an attack, this certainty of punishment also implies a peculiar and indeed paradoxical reversal in the usual characteristics of victims and aggressors. The victim has to proclaim his will to attack most destructively, and because counterpunishment is to be expected, the victim must actually appear reckless, ready to act in a self-destructive manner, in order to dissuade. The aggressor by contrast has to be prudent in order to be dissuaded, and certainly must not be self-destructive. In the case of the European Alliance, a gathering of democratic countries on the defensive, the simulation of a reckless collective personality is especially dubious, and its individual nuclear members are not much better placed in this regard.

Further, the classic formula leaves open the question of what damage, and how much, will be deemed unacceptable and by whom. The targets of a failed defense by denial are obvious: the invading forces that must be defeated in battle. But what is the proper target of punishment? The easiest targets are cities, which can be attacked with the smallest, simplest, least accurate punishment forces. To attack cities, however, means to kill innocent civilians, especially so in the case of the Alliance confronted as it is by a bureaucratic dictatorship that would hardly need popular sanction for an invasion. Industry at large is of some military relevance if the war is long. Moreover it offers targets only slightly more demanding by way of accuracy and weapon numbers than cities. But as a practical matter, to attack industry usually means attacking the population as well because industrial areas rather than single factories would be the targets. Next there are the military facilities, forces and bases, less innocent and more relevant to the ongoing invasion but also much more demanding, to the point where it may be impossible to differentiate between a punishment force and one actually meant for a disarming first strike. Finally there is the leadership itself, or rather the sum of political and military headquarters, command centers, and communication facilities. These targets are not innocent, and it would not be impossible to maintain punishment forces with the accuracy needed for the task, which at the same time would not be numerous enough for a first strike. If the leadership is attacked, however, there is no possibility of negotiating an end to the war. Indeed, no purpose of strategy can be served because all residual restraint would presumably come to an end once those who would have to exercise it are directly attacked.

Then there is the question of the magnitude of the punishment. It must be large enough to be "unacceptable," we have seen, but how much is that and for whom? Hitler at the end declared that the destruction of the German nation was acceptable and even desirable, because the Germans had shown themselves decadent by failing to win the war for him. Stalin was never driven to the point of self-destruction, but he not only deemed the deaths of many millions of his subjects acceptable but actually contrived that result deliberately. Mao likewise presided over the deaths of tens of millions, and not before a war as in Stalin's case but afterwards, so that those millions of Chinese who were killed because they were two-acre landlords died just a few years after many other Chinese had been killed in war merely because they were Chinese. Hitler, Stalin, and Mao have each found their emulators in Africa—and in recent years Pol Pot of Cambodia successfully emulated all three.

How much damage, then, must be threatened in order to exceed the limits of the acceptable? Here the paradox is central and not to be lightly dismissed: it is precisely the Hitlers, Stalins, Maos, and Pol Pots who must be dissuaded, not gentler souls who would find aggression unthinkable anyway; and yet such men are the very ones who might find any amount of damage acceptable as the price of aggression, so long as their own power survived and perhaps even if it did not. Because moderates are excluded from consideration in any event, Hitler, Stalin, Mao, and Pol Pot are not unrepresentative cases that may be overlooked. They are typical of those who must be dissuaded—and clearly only attacks on leadership targets are apt to be unacceptable to them. But to attack the leaders, as we saw, precludes any realistic hope of dissuasion to stop a war before its destruction exceeds all limits.

As for leaders and governing groups not so murderous, for whom the destruction of, say, a few cities would be quite unacceptable in normal circumstances, they too may not be dissuaded by such punishment in the course of an intense crisis. Prudence can be undermined by the sheer dynamics of commitment making, as each side is maneuvered into positions from which retreat is emotionally difficult and politically dangerous. Crises are unusual, and those with any large element of emotional intensity have been few indeed,* but again it is not for normal times that dissuasion is needed, but precisely for abnormal times when even quite reasonable leaders may act unreasonably.

As against all the weighty defects of nuclear dissuasion by punishment, nonnuclear dissuasion by denial has one shortcoming: it fails, or rather it has often failed before and is apt to fail again, simply because an aggressor comes to believe, rightly or wrongly, that he can win. Of course he might lose, but a war must still be waged and suffered—a war that dissuasion by punishment could have avoided, albeit at the risk of catastrophic failure.

---

*Recognized crises of the postwar period that involved the United States and were serious enough to raise nuclear considerations were: Iran 1946, Berlin 1948, Korea 1951, Korea 1953, Quemoy/Matsu 1954, Indochina 1954, Suez 1956, Quemoy/Matsu 1958, Berlin 1959, Berlin 1961, Cuba 1962, Pueblo/Korea 1968, India/Pakistan 1971, Arab-Israeli 1973. Of these, only the three Berlin crises and the Cuban missile crisis can unambiguously be placed in such a category.

NUCLEAR DISSUASION IN EUROPE

In Korea, demography and geography allow the defense to man a narrow front in great strength. But in the case of Europe, the ratio of ground forces is not favorable for the defense, and the advantage in battlefield and airpower is not large enough to offset the deficit, once Soviet air defenses are duly included in the calculation. Even if the Alliance were greatly to increase its forces, it would still be at a disadvantage at the level of theater strategy, as we saw, because it must provide a forward defense of the entire territory, while the Soviet offense could concentrate against narrow frontal sectors of its own choosing. Even if the forward defense were abandoned (an Alliance-breaking step) *and* the ratio of forces were greatly improved, nonnuclear dissuasion by denial could still fail, if Soviet military and political leaders were to evaluate the matter differently. Like others before them, Soviet leaders might come to believe that a cleverly prepared surprise attack could defeat even Alliance forces much stronger than those now in place, and they could be right.

With dissuasion by denial so unreliable, and with dissuasion by punishment riddled with baffling uncertainties, it is not surprising that the Alliance has attempted since 1967 to combine both forms of dissuasion. Actually the Alliance relies on a combination of means: inadequate nonnuclear frontal defense forces, a rather vulnerable complement of battlefield nuclear weapons (also meant for dissuasion by denial), an array of theater-range nuclear forces also somewhat vulnerable, and American long-range nuclear forces, very large indeed and much less vulnerable than either battlefield or theater nuclear weapons, but whose use on Europe's behalf cannot be certain.

What seems a congeries of inadequacies is congruent with the paradoxical logic. It is precisely because the nonnuclear frontal defenses are inadequate that the use of battlefield nuclear weapons is credible. In the course of a desperate losing fight, with Soviet invasion columns breaking through after days of stalwart resistance, the firing of nuclear artillery and short-range nuclear missiles about to be overrun is plausible. By contrast, if stronger frontal-defense forces successfully contain the initial wave of invaders, creating a pause for deliberation, Alliance governments are unlikely to be able to resist opposition to the use of nuclear weapons, even as the impending arrival of Soviet second-echelon formations makes it a necessity. If, on the other hand, the nonnuclear forces for frontal defense were to become much stronger than they now are, making the use of battlefield nuclear weapons unnecessary, the Soviet Union would no longer be able to plan for a quick nonnuclear victory and would revert to its theater strategy of the 1960s, based on the early use of its own battlefield nuclear weapons to break open gaps in the front.

In the usual paradoxical way, therefore, if the strength of Alliance nonnuclear forces is increased beyond the culminating point of a defense that can stop intrusions and a less than all-out offensive, the result would be to weaken dissuasion, by undercutting the credibility of battlefield nuclear use. If the strength of the nonnuclear forces is then further increased to much higher levels, to solve the problem by making the use of battlefield nuclear weapons unnecessary, the result would not be to avoid nuclear warfare in that form but rather to ensure it in the event of war, albeit by Soviet initiative. Of course the Soviet Union would lose a great deal in the process, namely the possibility of winning a clean, nonnuclear victory, but this is only significant if it is believed that the Soviet Union could attack the Alliance as a matter of calculated choice rather than in desperation. It is possible, then, that the refusal of Alliance governments to keep larger nonnuclear forces reflects an awareness, however unsystematic, of strategy's paradoxical logic, and not merely economic considerations: once again, more can be less.

Similarly, the vulnerability of the theater-range missiles and nuclear strike aircraft of the Alliance is not necessarily a disadvantage; nor is the insufficiency of their range, which does not reach very far into the Soviet Union. As matters now are, the theater nuclear weapons of the Alliance threaten punishment, which is meant to dissuade Soviet nuclear attacks against airbases, entry ports, command centers, and other military targets, including battlefield nuclear weapons. But they could not reach all Soviet cities in the way that their Soviet counterparts could reach all European cities. Besides, at this acute stage of a war, when the Soviet Union would be threatening cities in order to dissuade the Alliance from using its own nuclear weapons to resist invasion, that ultimate threat could not be negated by the parallel counterthreat of Alliance attacks against Soviet cities without the high risk of precipitating a Soviet first strike against the theater nuclear weapons themselves.

Only American intercontinental nuclear weapons can present a fully persuasive counterthreat because they have the range, protection, and numbers to destroy all Soviet cities even after absorbing the full impact of a first strike. It is precisely this specific counterthreat that forms the substance of the American nuclear guarantee to the European countries of the Alliance: American cities are placed at risk by the threat against Soviet cities, in order to dissuade Soviet threats against European cities, meant in turn to dissuade the use of Alliance nuclear weapons against an invading Soviet army.

The fundamental bargain that sustains the Alliance is therefore the exchange of the European promise to resist Soviet military intimidation in peacetime, and to oppose invasion in wartime, for the American promise to share in the risk of nuclear warfare should it exceed the scope of battlefield nuclear attacks. The theater nuclear weapons of the Alliance have the capacity to extend nuclear war to the Soviet Union, but they are not sufficient to counter all Soviet nuclear threats to Europe. Hence both strength and weakness sustain the linkage of American and European survival. If the theater nuclear forces were made much stronger and more self-sufficient, this would weaken the linkage and the Alliance. More would be less, as the paradox dictates.

ASYMMETRICAL NUCLEAR SUASION

As the unusual Korean case reveals by implication, in the majority of cases dissuasion is anything but a mechanical application of potential military strength against an ongoing threat of attack. In many settings where deterrence is said to obtain, there is no current threat to be averted but only a possibility, perhaps very remote, of an eventual threat. This is certainly true of the central axis of the worldwide balance of military strength, the reciprocal striving for nuclear suasion of the Soviet Union and the United States.

Images such as Oppenheimer's "two scorpions in a bottle" and the very notion of the "balance of terror" imply symmetrical threats, implicitly to the respective populations, whereas actually it is asymmetry that dominates. For the Soviet Union, the threat of an American or Alliance nuclear attack against targets such as military bases can only become a danger in the event of some prior Soviet attack, nonnuclear perhaps but not resistible by nonnuclear forces alone and aimed against interests the United States will not give up. An invasion of Europe is the most important example, and a Soviet offensive across Iran to the Persian Gulf has been cited as a possibility. For the United States, on the other hand, the threat of a Soviet nuclear attack against military targets can become a danger only in the event of a prior American nuclear attack against Soviet targets, such as military bases, in the context of impending defeat in Europe or in some expeditionary theater of war.

It is only in a second stage that nuclear attacks against cities would become an imminent danger, with American and European cities threatened by the Soviet Union in the attempt to dissuade the United States and the Alliance from launching further nuclear attacks (not against cities), and Soviet cities threatened by the United States to affirm that very response, nuclear but not aimed at cities. Thus the underlying asymmetry in the *nonnuclear* forces governs the interplay of implicit nuclear threats step by step. Because of their nonnuclear weakness, it is the Alliance and the United States, although on the defensive, that must be the first to threaten nuclear attack, though not against cities. And because of that, in turn, it is the Soviet Union, though devoted to the accumulation of operationally usable military power, that must be the first to threaten nuclear attacks against American and Alliance cities.

The sequence outlined so far has not explicitly addressed the intermediate stage of reciprocal "counterforce" threats, which is actually the engine of the American-Soviet nuclear competition. For the majority of their nuclear weapons are aimed at each other's nuclear weapons, and it is for this function that the most accurate missiles and the largest warheads are produced. But once again there is no symmetry, and the competition is not driven by "mindless" instincts of supremacy but rather by substantive motives. The salient purpose of the Soviet counterforce threat to American nuclear weapons of intercontinental range is to dissuade their *selective* use (in response to a Soviet nonnuclear invasion or to Soviet nuclear attacks upon military targets overseas), by threatening to destroy them en masse if any are employed at all. In this way the Soviet Union seeks to deny all flexibility in the use of American nuclear forces of intercontinental range, *thereby eliminating their usefulness except for self-defense.* (No Soviet counterforce attack could possibly deprive the United States of a residue of functioning weapons amply sufficient to destroy Soviet cities.) The salient purpose of the American threat against Soviet nuclear weapons of intercontinental range is precisely to affirm their selective use, by threatening to offset Soviet counterforce attacks by destroying Soviet weapons in turn.

It is thus mainly over the freedom of action of the United States to use a few nuclear weapons, selectively and not against cities, that the nuclear competition unfolds. Were it not for the counterforce targeting requirements of each side, the intercontinental-range nuclear forces of the Soviet Union and the United States could not possibly have become as large as they are, with almost 20,000 warheads on both sides at present.[13] For if the nuclear weapons themselves were removed from the target lists, there would simply be no worthwhile targets for most of the intercontinental nuclear weapons now in place.

It may then seem that there is an easy, unilateral American solution to the arms race: to renounce the use of intercontinental nuclear weapons except in the event of a prior Soviet nuclear attack upon the United States, but then to use them against Soviet cities. With such a declared policy, the United States could directly proceed to reduce the number of its intercontinental weapons unilaterally, down to a mere fraction of the present inventory—the number required for a second strike against Soviet cities. Counting fifty cities at most, making a healthy allowance for a prior would-be disarming Soviet attack and all technical malfunctions, a maximum of, say, 500 nuclear warheads distributed for safety among bombers and missiles, cruise and ballistic, land-based and sea-based, should suffice. In this way an American policy of "no first use" might rapidly undo the consequences of decades of accumulation: out of more than 10,000 American intercontinental nuclear weapons, all but 500 would be dismantled by order. And even without any negotiated agreement, most Soviet weapons would eventually be dismantled in turn, or would simply not be replaced when their machinery deteriorates, because they would no longer have worthwhile targets.[14]

What prevents this ready solution is the very *structure* of the military balance, in which it is only the asymmetrical American threat to use nuclear weapons selectively, in response even to a nonnuclear Soviet attack, that links nuclear strength with the nonnuclear, allowing the former to offset the weakness of the latter. And it is that same threat of selective use, in response even to a Soviet strike against non-American targets, that embodies the willed connection between the United States and its European allies, which offsets the natural, territorial proximity of the Soviet Union that would otherwise be decisive. The relatively few warheads involved thus have a significance that wholly transcends their numbers. They are the small cause of the very large counterforce competition that has resulted in today's huge nuclear inventories. But this small cause could not be removed without effects even larger, on the overall military balance and on the Alliance connection that both exposes the United States and makes its strength relevant on the world scene. Once again, linear reasoning is revealed as misleading in strategy's paradoxical realm: if it were the aim of the United States to bring about a drastic reduction in the size of the respective nuclear inventories, to pre-counterforce levels as it were, it is only by *increasing* its own nonnuclear strength that the United States could succeed, if other things—including the Alliance—remain equal.

Nuclear war is frequently imagined in just one of its possible forms, as a relentless escalation of move and countermove that reaches the ultimate stage of all-out attacks on the respective populations. In that extreme eventuality, the conditioning effect of the paradoxical logic is correspondingly extreme: the use of nuclear strength in this manner overshoots the culminating point of utility so completely that the result evolves to a full reversal, with the most devastating attacks equivalent to no attack at all from the perspective of each attacker-victim. Certainly as a practical matter, once the destruction of all population centers large enough to attract a warhead is accomplished, neither side could identify any benefit from the parallel catastrophe inflicted on the other, even if there were survivors interested in calculating the matter.

CHAPTER 14

HARMONY AND DISHARMONY IN WAR

$\mathbf{W}$e may have recognized that there is no automatic harmony among the vertical levels of strategy, but we have yet to confront the full meaning and implications of disharmony. When a weapon is technically inefficient, tactically inadequate, of slight operational value, and almost ineffective at the level of theater strategy, we can safely predict what will happen at the conclusive level of grand strategy, where that particular weapon along with everything else in the armed forces achieves its final effect within the much wider context of all state transactions with the outside world, in peace as in war. Subject to errors of assessment by others, and subject also to deliberate and successful deception, this weapon should add very little to the suasion that the armed forces as a whole can hope to evoke. And subject to all the contingencies of combat, the weapon will not do much to increase the chances of victory in war.

Obviously a harmonious sequence of success will have an opposite effect, of greater or lesser significance within the level of grand strategy depending on the scope of the matter in the context of the times. When first introduced at the end of the seventeenth century, even the humble bayonet made a perceptible difference, by finally allowing all foot soldiers to be equipped with firearms. Until then, each infantry formation had to have a proportion of pikemen to hold back cavalry charges while the musketeers tended to the slow reloading of their weapons. For the French army, which was the first to make large use of the new device, the bayonet actually won battles at first because its infantry could have more firepower than equal numbers of enemy troops so long as many of them still trailed the puissant pike. The latter had its defenders no doubt, but evidently they did not form a social group powerful enough to save the old by blocking the new, as the Mamelukes of Egypt once saved their swords by resisting the introduction of firearms.

Above all, the innovation was fully compatible with unchanged tactics, operational methods, and theater strategies as well as the prior regimental organization. Former pikemen could quickly be drilled to become musketeers, and the strain on supply was insignificant at a time when a hundred rounds per man was ample allowance for an entire campaigning season. Hence the technical advance was not contradicted or diminished at the higher levels of the vertical interaction, and its effect could be fully manifest at the level of grand strategy—until the bayonet was in due course universally adopted and the French advantage was entirely lost.

In our own century, the introduction of the British "chain home" network of radar stations in time for the 1940 battle of Britain had similar results. The task of air defense did not change at the level of theater strategy, and there was no difference at the operational and tactical levels: whether or not an intercept was made as a result of a prior radar detection, the mission itself, the nature of combat maneuvers, and the teamwork of squadrons and groups were exactly the same. Once again, the technical innovation was unimpeded at the three higher levels of strategy, and once again its effect was fully manifest at the level of grand strategy, in the form of a numerical gain. Because they could be sent where and when they were needed on the basis of radar information, the fighters of the Royal Air Force did not have to patrol the skies in search of enemy intruders. Instead the aircraft could remain on the ground until they were sent toward their targets by the radar-informed tracking room of Fighter Command. The Luftwaffe could be resisted in full force with all machines fueled and ready, and pilots as rested as combat would allow. Just as the number of French musketeers was effectively increased by the bayonet, so too the number of British fighters ready to fight was increased by radar, whose technical effect reached up to the level of grand strategy at full value.

But what about disharmony? We have already encountered its simple and conclusive form, that of achievement at one level *totally* negated at the next, as in the case of the French mitrailleuse of 1870, a significant technical innovation whose effect was nullified at the tactical level because of self-inflicted organizational reasons. The result of such extreme disharmony was that the effect of the gun was not perceptible at all at the level of grand strategy. Especially in regard to new weapons, such total negation is not rare; technical innovation and organizational change proceed at different paces, driven by different impulses, and it is easy enough for a fatal dissonance to persist between the two.

Still by far the more common experience, indeed the normal predicament of those who strive in the realm of strategy, is a disharmony much more subtle and measured, which results not in absolute negation but in a complex *interpenetration* of failure and success. In terms of our earlier image of strategy, the waves and counterwaves of action and reaction at any one level can intrude on the levels above and below at the extremes of failure and success.

INTERPENETRATION AMONG THE LEVELS
IN WORLD WAR II

Consider a classic case of disharmony in recent military history, that of the German expeditionary force that fought in North Africa during the middle years of World War II. By the time Lieutenant-General Erwin Rommel was sent to Tripoli, capital of Italian Libya in February 1941, at first with just one mechanized division, Hitler had decided that Egypt was not worth conquering and preparations for the Barbarossa plan, the invasion of the Soviet Union, were far advanced.[1] Accordingly, Rommel's task was strictly limited: he was to help the Italians resist the British offensive that was seemingly on the verge of expelling them from their North African colony (a debacle that would damage the prestige of the Axis), but he was not to advance into Egypt. Even the reconquest of Cyrenaica, the huge but empty eastern half of Libya, was not to be contemplated until the autumn, if then.

Such restraining orders should hardly have been necessary. Rommel's force was much too small for offensive action; he himself had never been in North Africa before and had no experience whatever of desert warfare; and the German army was in any case wholly unprepared for that harsh environment, having neither the necessary equipment nor desert training.[2] (Vehicles did not have sand filters, and the Germans did not even know that a low-fat diet was essential to keep troops healthy in the torrid desert climate.[3]) The German Army High Command (OKH) had already calculated that an offensive to conquer Egypt would require at least four armored divisions with commensurate airpower—forces that could not be spared from Barbarossa and could not have been supplied anyway by scarce motor transport across the vastness of Libya, along the one and only road, the Via Balbia, which followed the coast for more than a thousand miles from Tripoli to the Egyptian frontier.[4] Moreover, the sea route from Italian embarkation ports was precarious, with steady losses of shipping to British submarines as well as aircraft based in Malta. Finally, the handling capacity of the only port at Tripoli was insufficient for the tonnage that would have been required.[5]

At the level of theater strategy, the British were in a vastly superior position. The region under their control extended across Egypt to Palestine, Transjordan, Iraq, and the Persian Gulf to the east, and into the Sudan to the south—indeed all the way from Cairo to Capetown. British forces, moreover, with their Indian, Australian, New Zealand, and South African contingents, were already much larger than any Germany could possibly send, even before Barbarossa, and on the whole their quality was superior to that of the Italian forces with Rommel. The British advantage in supply was even greater, with a safe if long sea route around the Cape, access ports at both ends of the Suez Canal, good roads and railways from the canal to Cairo and Alexandria, well-equipped bases and workshops, and ample motor transport unaffected by fuel shortages. At the level of theater strategy, therefore, given the means that Rommel could count on, nothing more than a limited defensive effort could have been expected.

Rommel arrived in Tripoli on February 12, 1941, with a very small staff and the title of Commander-in-Chief, German Troops in Libya.[6] Two days later, troopships brought the reconnaissance and antitank battalions of the Fifth ''Light'' Division, some 2,000 troops in all with guns and armored cars but no tanks; in spite of the danger of air attack, Rommel ordered the ships to be unloaded overnight, under floodlights. On the next day, February 15, the small German force paraded through the streets of Tripoli before driving directly to the east. The British had taken Benghazi, capital of the Cyrenaican half of Libya, 600 miles from Tripoli, had moved another hundred miles beyond it, but showed no inclination to advance any further. (The Greek campaign was about to begin, and British units were being withdrawn for shipment to Greece.) Rommel could have carried out his mission without attacking at all. At this point Rommel was supposed to wait for the second division promised to him, the Fifteenth Panzer, due in mid-May, before attempting an offensive, and even then he was not supposed to go beyond Agedabia, at the gates of Cyrenaica, without further orders.

Rommel did not obey: without waiting to stockpile supplies and arrange for their transportation, with no pause to acclimatize the troops, he drove his small force forward as fast as it could move. On February 26, 1941, the Germans encountered the British for the first time and a skirmish ensued, already 470 miles east of Tripoli. One week later, the only Panzer regiment of the Fifth Division arrived, with some fifty tanks in all. It too was paraded through the streets of Tripoli and sent directly to the east. One month later, on April 2, 1941, Rommel had fought his first battle to seize Agedabia, 500 miles east of Tripoli, at the base of the great bulge of the Cyrenaican peninsula held by British forces stretched out along the coastal road, where desert tracks that cut across the bulge to the coast next to Egypt began and where he was supposed to stop.

Acting directly against an order from Hitler himself,[7] Rommel divided his already small one-division army to press the British retreat along the interminable coastal road; in the meantime a stronger force was sent onto rock-strewn camel paths to cross the desert. Actually Rommel did not send but rather led his troops in person, often riding in an open car at the head of the column, even though the Fifth had a perfectly competent commander of its own. Two days later, on April 4, 1941, the Germans advancing along the coast were in Benghazi capital of Cyrenaica 600 miles from Tripoli, and by April 9, the outmaneuvering force emerged from the desert to stand before Tobruk, the port of eastern Cyrenaica that was by then the main British base, all of 1,000 miles from Tripoli. Rommel was still supposed to be in Tripoli awaiting the arrival of his second division. To reach the coastal road and Tobruk so quickly, Rommel had driven his forces long past the breaking point of the embryonic supply lines that originated in Tripoli. His units had to obtain their fuel by sending back scarce troop trucks for them and later by capture; half of the tanks were by then broken down along the way, the men were so exhausted that they could hardly stay awake, and the entire force, very small to begin with, was scattered across the desert.

But paradoxical action earned its reward, just before the offensive was totally self-defeated by excess. Because the Germans had moved so much faster and farther than the British had expected,[8] all their forces in Cyrenaica west of Tobruk were outmaneuvered, cut off, and forced into a panic retreat during which they left behind much more equipment than the Germans had to begin with, along with large quantities of food, fuel, and ammunition. Again and again, small German task forces of motorized infantry and artillery with a mere handful of tanks would emerge unexpectedly out of the desert to surprise and capture, destroy or scatter British truck columns, artillery trains, and infantry units retreating along the coastal road. British armor units, though numerically superior, never seemed to be in the right place at the right time to assist the infantry and artillery; and they would fall prey to German antitank guns when attacking on their own without infantry and artillery support.[9]

It is clear that Rommel's method of command and his sheer dynamism conferred a huge operational-level advantage on the German forces. With Rommel leading them in person, the Germans could act much faster than the British could, much as a better fighter pilot with a better machine can turn inside the circle of a more sluggish opponent in a classic dogfight, to fire at his tail with impunity and then turn to fire again, while his opponent is still trying to react to the first turn. The Germans' advantage at the operational level went a long way to overcome their extreme disadvantage at the level of theater strategy, and this penetration of success from one level to the next sufficed to modify the outcome that could reasonably have been expected.

But Rommel's headlong advance in the spring of 1941 did not end with victory in Cairo, but instead inaugurated almost two years of dramatic offensives and hurried withdrawals by each side—as one and then other overshot their culminating point of success—up to the final German defeat in 1943. Great as it was, the German operational-level advantage in North Africa obviously could not penetrate through to the level of grand strategy, to achieve a decisive victory. The obvious reason is that the entire North African campaign was a mere sideshow in the wider context of the world war. Its outcome was bound to be dominated by what would happen in the more central theaters of war, on the eastern front where the Germans had almost a hundred times as many troops; in Western Europe, to a lesser extent after the Normandy landings; in the Asian-Pacific theaters that detained additional American strength; in the North Atlantic theater where the contest between Allied shipping and German submarines would determine how much supply the Allies could have; and in the air theaters over all the Axis countries, where the war of the bombers against industry would unfold.

Vertical Success and Horizontal Failure

Actually even those much more important military struggles in the vertical dimension, as I have named it, were dominated by Hitler's utter failure of statecraft in the horizontal dimension—a failure of diplomacy, intelligence, and propaganda that made defeat virtually certain, even amid great battlefield successes, by uniting the strongest industrial powers of the world against Germany and its distant Japanese ally. It would have taken exceptional success in the vertical dimension to overcome the consequences of that colossal error, and so much military success was impossible because of Germany's inferiority in material resources—the most obvious consequence of its weakness in the horizontal dimension.

In the confluence of the two dimensions at the level of grand strategy, the early German and Japanese success in the vertical dimension did diminish, at first, the impact of fundamental error in the horizontal dimension. Specifically, the occupation of much of Western Europe and the western regions of the Soviet Union with their large industrial capacity, as well as the Japanese seizure of Malayan rubber and tin production and of oil output in the Dutch East Indies, correspondingly reduced the imbalance in material resources caused by the failure of German and Japanese foreign policy. At the level of grand strategy, therefore, during the early phase of the war the Axis advantage in the vertical dimension, derived from war preparations and superior competence, was reducing the Allied advantage in the horizontal dimension (in which the successful cooperation of a conservative British government with Stalin's Soviet Union may be compared to Hitler's gratuitous declaration of war upon the United States after Pearl Harbor, and to Japan's own colossal miscalculation that led to the attack on the American fleet when it was Southeast Asia that was Japan's objective).

As the Allies mobilized their human resources, as well as the larger part of their material resources still intact, their superiority derived from success in the horizontal dimension began to condition the military struggles of the vertical dimension within one theater of war after another, thus preventing the Axis from achieving further gains at the level of grand strategy. At a later stage, the rising competence of Allied soldiers, sailors, and airmen, the emergence of able military leaders, and the development of appropriate tactics and methods deprived the Germans and Japanese of their former superiorities at the tactical and operational levels of the vertical dimension, in one form of war after another, in one theater after another.

With quality in their favor in addition to quantity, the Allies no longer lost in battle the advantage they were obtaining from their superiority in the horizontal dimension. In the confluence of grand strategy, the opposite was happening, with some reoccupation of territory, some damage to Axis industry by bombardment, and much later the submarine interdiction of Japanese shipping routes. Thus the countries that had picked the wrong allies and made the wrong enemies to begin with started to lose what they had earlier gained by the bold aggression that expressed their conjunction of military talent and incompetent statecraft. In the end, the final victories of 1945 were so absolute because of the mutually reinforcing effects of superiorities in both dimensions: Axis forces increasingly outmatched technically, tactically, and operationally were also in sharp numerical decline within each one of remaining theaters of war, both because of their prior losses in that particular theater or form of warfare and because of cumulative losses in all other theaters—whose multiplicity expressed their complete *and continuing* failure in the horizontal dimension.

But where was the logic of strategy in such an outcome? Certainly no single error of decision could have a continuing effect in the continuing dynamics of grand strategy. After all, the increasing weakness of the Germans and Japanese in the vertical dimension should actually have been advantageous to them in the horizontal dimension, so as to slow down or even interrupt their decline. As the Allies were progressing toward total victory in the major theaters of war, as the profile of the postwar distribution of power was beginning to emerge, the alliance itself was ripe for fragmentation: for if the war simply continued on a straight path, it would eventually leave the British and Americans facing the Soviet Union in a new confrontation, where each side would be in great need of the Germans and Japanese as allies.

For the Soviet Union, technically and industrially inferior, it was German and Japanese industrial talents that would be especially needed. For the British and Americans, it would be German and

Japanese troops that would make all the difference, in facing a continental power as rich in ground strength as the Soviet Union. And neither side could hope to have what it would need in the emerging postwar world if Germany and Japan were completely defeated and destroyed as major powers. This was the opening that German and Japanese statecraft might have exploited, had the two regimes not previously followed paths so extreme that any such accommodation was excluded. Had it not been for the effect upon Americans of the traumatic Pearl Harbor attack, with all its connotations that racism amplified; had it not been for the effect on the whole world of all the Nazis had done, the Germans and Japanese could have auctioned their remaining strength and future potential, so as to induce one side or the other to make a separate peace. Such was the breakdown of statecraft in Berlin and Tokyo that they did not even seriously try, although Japan did succeed in remaining at peace with the Soviet Union until the very eve of surrender.

Stalin, it appears, was more or less certain that the British would strive to persuade the more innocent Americans to secure an alliance with Nazi Germany, before its defeat became complete and German support against the Soviet Union would be useless. From Stalin's point of view, it was simply illogical for the British and Americans to come into the forthcoming confrontation without securing a valuable alliance that they could so easily obtain; *he* had been preparing for the new postwar conflict since 1943 at least and had overlooked Nazi crimes easily enough to make a profitable alliance with Germany in 1939. Stalin therefore assumed that the British and Americans would do what he might have done in their place, probably behind the figleaf of a new German military government that would remove Hitler while continuing the war—but only against the Soviet Union. This is why news of the abortive military coup against Hitler of July 20, 1944, merely aroused Soviet suspicions, as did any British or American contacts whatever with German officers (which did eventually take place during the last weeks of war, in conjunction with localized surrender negotiations).*

---

*After being informed *by the British* of the American negotiations in Berne with commanders of the German forces in Italy intent on surrender (nothing better than unconditional surrender was offered), the Soviet government denounced the talks as an anti-Soviet conspiracy in a note of March 22, 1945, from Molotov to the British ambassador in Moscow. In a message of April 3, 1945, to Roosevelt, Stalin wrote, "I also cannot understand the silence of the British . . . although it is known that the initiative in this whole affair with the negotiations in Berne belongs to the British." Churchill, *Triumph and Tragedy*, p. 446.

Stalin was wrong in his suspicions of the British and Americans, but perfectly right in his conscious understanding of the logic of strategy. The American alliance with the Germans and Japanese did materialize just as he (and Hitler in his final days) had expected, though only after the war was long ended and the political character of the new partners had entirely changed. During the war itself, however, the alliance-breaking tendency manifest in the horizontal dimension was willfully resisted, so that no contrary force intervened to impede the Axis defeat, eventually fully accomplished in the vertical dimension of each form of war, in every major theater of war.

The Limits of Interpenetration

Thus if Rommel had won his own fight in North Africa, he would merely have shared the fate of the unchallenged German garrisons in the Channel islands, Denmark, and Norway, which had to surrender anyway on May 7, 1945. But of course Rommel did not win his own fight. Great as it was, the operational-level superiority of the German forces over the British did not *fully* overcome the conditioning effect of the spatial factors at the level of theater strategy. One must look beyond North Africa to recognize the magnitude of the spatial factor against which the Germans were striving. We may speculate that if Rommel had received larger forces and if they had been properly supplied, he might have reached his own ultimate objectives, Cairo and the Suez Canal, 1,500 miles from Tripoli. That would have been a very great victory indeed for a general whose talents did not extend beyond the operational level and who obviously did not comprehend theater strategy at all, at least in the case of North Africa.[10] But that would still have been only a battle victory, or rather the result of several such victories, and not a campaign victory, for the campaign would not have ended.

The British would have continued to fight, no doubt forming a new front south of Cairo from bases in Upper Egypt and the Sudan, and another on the Sinai edge of the Suez Canal, from bases in Palestine and Transjordan, with resupply for both fronts by way of the Red Sea. If left alone, the British would have developed bases, workshops, field hospitals, roads, rail lines, and ports with American assistance, in order to accumulate reinforcements for an eventual reconquest. Unable to force a British surrender, which could only be obtained in London and not in Cairo, the Germans would then have had to choose between waiting passively as the British buildup increasingly threatened their hold on Egypt and undertaking further offensives, to capture the large area in which the counteroffensive was being prepared against them. Such epic conquests would have made Rommel even more famous than he is, but so long as London did not surrender, a campaign victory would still have eluded him. Just as they did when the loss of Malaya, Singapore, and Burma to the Japanese threw them right out of Southeast Asia, the British would no doubt have continued to fight, resisting in the vast deserts of eastern Transjordan as well as in Syria and in the vaster expanse of Sudan or even Ethiopia, with supply to the eastern front by way of the Persian Gulf and Iraq, and supply to the southern front by way of the Cape and East Africa. As before, the British would have started to accumulate reinforcements, eventually going over to the offensive, just as they reinforced in India after 1942 and then set out to reconquer Burma in 1944, on their way to Malaya and Singapore (whose impending reconquest was made unnecessary by Japan's surrender).

With their forces by then stretched out across a huge area, the Germans would once again have been faced with the choice of indefinite fighting on two fronts against an enemy of growing strength or another round of offensives in order to advance into the space from which the British would have continued to threaten all their conquests. So long as the campaign did not end, everything from Tripoli onward would still be at stake and could only be held by more fighting—which had to be offensive fighting for the Germans, swimming as they were against the tidal wave of material strength coming upon them, the result of their fundamental failure in the horizontal dimension of statecraft. Ultimately Rommel would have had to advance through East Africa all the way to Capetown, and also eastward beyond Iraq and across Iran to conquer the whole immensity of India, in order truly to win his campaign. Only then would there be no more open fronts for the British to fight on. Unless they were totally expelled from Africa and squeezed out of India by a German advance to meet the Japanese on the Burmese frontier, the British would have continued to challenge all previous conquests, still with faraway Tripoli as their final objective.

When Rommel seemed to be at the very peak of his success in the late summer fighting of 1942 inside Egypt, at a time when the Japanese seemed to be on the verge of invading India, there were fears in some Allied circles of a concerted Axis offensive on a scale more than Napoleonic, which would achieve a link between Germany and Japan inside a conquered India. As we now know, the Germans and Japanese had no such plan or indeed any other plan of concerted action, fighting as they did as co-belligerents rather than jointly as allies in the full sense. As we also know, both offensives had already passed their culminating point of success: what was actually to be found at the spearheads of those spectacular advances of 1942 were Rommel's badly outnumbered tanks running out of fuel and starving Japanese infantry at the end of grossly overstretched supply lines.

But even if there had been real strength in both offensives, even if they had somehow been supplied to advance much farther than they did, even if India had been conquered from either side, the Allies would not have been defeated, and their major war efforts would have continued undiminished. No matter how enormous its scale, the entire fighting from Tripoli to India would still have been a mere sideshow. To be sure, much would have been lost to the Allies: the manpower of the Indian army, whose well-drilled regiments added significantly to British strength outside India as well; the oil of Iraq and Iran, insofar as the tanker shortage allowed it to be used outside the Middle East itself and insofar as the Germans could have shipped it away for themselves; and the small but rising industrial war production of India itself. Still, most of what the Middle East and Indian regions added to Allied resources was consumed within them, while both required strength from the outside to defend them. Hence the overall balance of forces and resources for the main Allied efforts against Germany and Japan could even have improved.

This transformation of failure at the theater level into a net gain at the level of grand strategy—so long as the defeat is not too costly in forces lost in the process—is inevitable when efforts are being expended on secondary theaters that cannot yield victory. This was true for both sides during World War II, as in any war, but more so for Germany and Japan than for the Allies, owing to the fundamental asymmetry in their situations at the level of grand strategy.

Victory and Defeat in Two Dimensions

Because of their great superiority in war resources, the Allies could benefit from *any* military encounter that reduced German and Japanese military strength even if their own losses were distinctly higher—so long as the loss ratio did not exceed the overall ratio of strength in their favor or, more precisely, so long as those losses would not reduce the gap in the respective growth rates. For example, at a time when Germany was producing, say, 500 fighter aircraft per month while British and American fighter production destined for the European theater was three times larger, even the loss of three Allied fighters for every two German fighters shot down would be a gain that would eventually accumulate to yield victory, if one disregards inequalities in pilot recovery rates. For the Allies, moreover, such attrition could be profitable anywhere: there are no sideshows in attrition. It was nevertheless undesirable for the Allies to divert efforts from the main theaters. To do so would not make victory less certain, inasmuch as cumulative attrition could proceed anyway, but it would slow down the Allied progress toward victory simply because it was not in the secondary theaters that any enemy forces could be encountered in the greatest numbers. Further, it was only in the most important theaters of all, the Axis homelands, that military strength in the vertical dimension of strategy could be applied to intensify German and Japanese weakness in the horizontal dimension, by the bombardment of industry and infrastructures.

The Germans and Japanese were in a very different situation. Military victories, that is, successes in the vertical dimension, could only help them to win the war if those victories affected the horizontal dimension as well. The defeat of Allied forces in combat, which happened over and over again during the war, was not enough because it did not affect the central Allied strength along the horizontal dimension: this was the alliance itself, which in turn resulted in a superior conjoint ability to generate trained men and equipment for the fighting forces.* In other words, the Axis could truly benefit from military success only when it served as a substitute for statecraft, notably by undoing alliances that enemy diplomacy had secured. This in fact did happen, when Germany totally

---

*In theory, the Axis countries *could* have won the war by battle victories alone, but only if they could have inflicted more and more losses as time went on, until reaching a level that corresponded with the maximum ability of the Allies to field new forces. Britain and the Soviet Union did not reach their maximum force-generating capacity until late 1943 or early 1944, while the United States never reached its limit at all. And of course the Axis ability to win victories and impose losses was already in sharp decline by 1943.

defeated Poland, Belgium, and France, forcing them out of the war altogether and thus changing the situation in the horizontal dimension. No such vertically induced gains in the German position could be achieved in North Africa, which contained neither states that could be overwhelmed in place nor war resources of value.

Hence the German Army High Command was quite correct in initially opposing Rommel's adventure in Egypt. When Hitler overruled it, even he provided only limited means to Rommel, appreciating his exploits mainly for their publicity value: the dashing general in the romantic desert made for excellent copy, especially in contrast to events on the Russian front, sinister even in victory.[11] The advance to Egypt could serve no greater purpose, and it did not help the Germans that they absorbed disproportionately large British forces in North Africa; the British had no main theater of battle in 1941 or 1942, whereas the Germans did, soon after Rommel's arrival in Tripoli.

It was only on the eastern front that Germany could have achieved definitive results in grand strategy. By fighting the Soviet Union, the Germans did have at least a possibility of victory, since vertical success could have horizontal consequences in that theater: any German conquest of inhabitants and resources would diminish the Soviet Union just as if an ally were being detached by diplomacy, and simultaneously enhance Germany just as if an ally were gained, to the extent that people and resources could both be harnessed to the German war effort. A total conquest of the Soviet Union would of course have removed the consequences of Hitler's greatest failure of statecraft, enabling Germany to cope with the additional failure of statecraft represented by the American entry into the war alongside Britain. In that case, success in the vertical dimension could have been dominant at the level of grand strategy.

While the German investment in the North African sideshow was at least kept quite small, imperial Japan compounded fundamental failure in the horizontal dimension—a failure of intelligence in the largest sense—by dissipating its military strength in secondary theaters. After the Pearl Harbor attack, the Japanese did proceed to occupy Malaya, Singapore, and the Dutch East Indies, realizing vertically induced gains in the horizontal dimension. Though there were no Allies to defeat and detach in those countries, there was a commensurate gain in important resources, the rubber and tin of Malaya and oil in the Dutch East Indies. As for the conquest of the

Philippines, accomplished as it was with small forces, that too could be justified, primarily because it might serve as a base for heavy bombers that could attack Japan, as indeed had been the American intention. On the other hand, the invasion of Burma that followed, the fleet raid into the Indian Ocean, the southern Pacific invasions as a whole, the attempt to conquer New Guinea especially, and above all the continued war in China were all diversions from the one and only theater where in theory the Japanese could have won the war: the United States itself.

Having done for the Americans what the Americans could not do for themselves, bringing them unequivocally into the war, the Japanese could have overcome their failure of statecraft only by invading a country they should never have challenged in the first place. Only by defeating the United States in its own territory, therefore incapacitating its rising strength at the source, could the Japanese have converted a temporary superiority in the vertical dimension into a conclusive victory at the level of grand strategy. The one campaign that could have secured victory for the Japanese after Pearl Harbor would have been an invasion of California, followed by the conquest of the major centers of American life and culminating with an imposed peace dictated to some collaborating government in Washington. To be sure, the forces of imperial Japan, even if pulled back from China and everywhere else, could never have been successful in that venture, and of course no such invasion was even contemplated. So the best Japanese option after Pearl Harbor was to sue immediately for peace, bargaining away Japan's ability to resist eventual defeat for some years in exchange for whatever the United States would concede to avoid having to fight for its victory.

In the negotiations before Pearl Harbor, the Roosevelt administration had demanded much from imperial Japan, including the withdrawal of its forces from China. After Pearl Harbor, the United States would undoubtedly have demanded Japan's withdrawal from Manchuria as well, and very likely from the older colonies of Korea and Taiwan. Moreover, having discovered how effective Japanese military power really was, American leaders would have certainly insisted on some partial disarmament. Such was the true value of the tactical and operational success of the Pearl Harbor attack: in the context of its best course of action after the fact, Japan would have been better off if its pilots had lost their way or missed their mark. At the level of grand strategy, in the confluence of the vertical dimension and the horizontal, the latter was so adverse for Japan that tactical and operational success at Pearl Harbor was actually worse than failure would have been.

The case is far from unique. It is indeed common for tactical achievement, even when quite brilliant, to become counterproductive at the level of grand strategy. All that is needed to make less out of more in this way is a sufficient disharmony between the dimensions. If, for example, the diplomatic and propaganda effects of a bombing campaign are adverse, more bombing is worse than less bombing, and accurate destructive bombing is worse than ineffectual bombing. If there is a severe disharmony between the *levels* of the vertical dimension, then military actions simply fail, as we have seen. But when there is disharmony *between* the dimensions, vertical success can be worse than failure.

Because imperial Japan was defeated to begin with, once it failed to march on Washington after Pearl Harbor, there were no genuinely decisive battles in the Pacific war. The only difference that the naval and ground battles of the Coral Sea, Midway, New Guinea, Guadalcanal, and so on, could make was to modulate the speed of Japan's defeat. None of those battles, dramatic as they were, could be decisive at the level of grand strategy because they could not determine the outcome of the war, as several of the German-Soviet battles on the eastern front certainly did. Even a complete victory of the Japanese navy in the 1942 battle of Midway could not have had more than transitory results: had American aircraft carriers been destroyed instead of the Japanese, it would not have deprived the United States of the naval supremacy that its ships and aircraft in production and its pilots in training would have ensured in any case by 1944. And had the Japanese defeat at Midway been even more decisive than it was, it could have done no more than hasten an outcome that was already inevitable once the fully mobilized military forces of the United States arrived on the scene.

Even without an invasion of the United States, Japan did have some chance of negotiating an acceptable settlement. If the Japanese had avoided large battles instead of seeking them so assiduously, if they had evaded American strength and kept the fighting at a desultory level in those remote islands of the southwest Pacific, they might have been able to prolong the war, year after year. As it happens, the United States would have interrupted the process anyway with its heavy bombers and the atom bomb. But were it not for that, and if we imagine a quite different Japanese style of war, Japan might well have been able to obtain a negotiated settlement by exhausting not American material resources but rather the patience of the American people, thereby fragmenting the post-Pearl Harbor consensus that sustained the war effort. Thus Japan's failure of intelligence and diplomacy could have been redeemed within the horizontal dimension itself, by way of a propaganda effect of modest military achievements that would have confronted Americans with the prospect of indefinite warfare.

THE REWARDS OF HARMONY

The North Vietnamese, who did not have to live down a counterproductive initial military exploit like Pearl Harbor, won their war in just this way, precisely by modest but sustained achievements in the vertical dimension, exploited in the horizontal dimension by propaganda and diplomacy guided by good intelligence (in its broadest meaning). Nor were they altogether unsuccessful in the vertical dimension either, being at least equal at the tactical and operational levels and only slightly inferior at the level of theater strategy.[12] As for the technical level, their style of war made it of scant importance for both sides, in spite of the peculiar American enthusiasm for action just at that level. But still they could not win by success in the vertical dimension alone, once the United States intervened. No accumulation of tactical victories could have won the war for the North Vietnamese simply because Vietnam was not the main theater of the war, but merely the scene of the fighting. The strength ranged against them was coming from a quite different theater, the United States itself, the primary source of equipment and supplies for the South Vietnamese from start to finish as well as the source of American military forces between 1966 and 1972. Even if the North Vietnamese could have defeated every force sent against them, victories in the vertical dimension alone would have enabled them to resist only until the arrival of more forces, eventually to lose.

Nor did the North Vietnamese have the ability to interdict the flow of forces sent across the Pacific. They had no submarines or aircraft to operate on the open ocean, and their ground strength in Vietnam itself did not suffice to close South Vietnam's ports and major airfields until the very end of the war. Still less could North Vietnam have applied strength in the vertical dimension against the United States itself: while the United States bombed North Vietnam from time to time, it was of course itself immune from bombing. But North Vietnam's diplomacy and propaganda were not similarly limited in geographic reach: they began by damaging the relations of the United States with its major allies of Europe, and the effect reached into the United States itself, with powerful consequences.

Without ever defeating any large body of American forces in battle, without exhausting American material strength, the North Vietnamese won by successfully exploiting diplomacy and propaganda to fragment the American political consensus that sustained the war, first to induce the withdrawal of American forces and then to bring about a drastic decline in the flow of equipment and supplies to South Vietnam—while their own flow of equipment and supplies from the Soviet Union and China continued without interruption. Military achievement was indispensable for the North Vietnamese, not to win battles that were bound to be inconclusive anyway, but simply to continue the war so as to create the conditions in which diplomacy and propaganda could be successful.

As the example of North Vietnam's victory shows, in the confluence of grand strategy even modest achievement in the vertical dimension is sufficient to yield victory, if it occurs in harmony with the demands of the horizontal dimension—just as even the greatest achievements of war will avail little, and may even be counterproductive, if the two dimensions are in disharmony. The success of Anwar Sadat's war of October 1973 is an even sharper demonstration of the principle.

As the Egyptians recognized, they had no possibility of winning by straightforward military action, by crossing the Suez Canal to engage and defeat the Israeli army in the Sinai, then to impose a settlement of their liking or simply proceed to invade Israel proper. Although the deployed forces of the Egyptian army were very much larger than the active-duty standing forces of the Israelis, when the latter mobilized their reserve formations they could field as many as seven divisions of ground forces and send enough of them to the Sinai to defeat the eight Egyptian divisions that could be fielded, given Israeli superiority in airpower at every level and in armor-mobile power at the operational level.[13]

On the other hand, the international situation was potentially very favorable for Egypt in 1973. The United States had just disengaged from Vietnam and was in no mood for conflict. The Soviet Union was far more inclined to be active, seemingly to claim in the reality of world politics the "strategic" parity that the United States had conceded, rather lightly, in the 1972 strategic-arms limitation accords. With rising worldwide demand for oil and falling production within the United States, the Arab exporters of the Persian Gulf had become the price-setting marginal suppliers whose output was now irreplaceable—and any interruption of supplies would immediately reveal their dominance. Israel for its part was in a weak position diplomatically because it appeared to be content with the status quo and uncooperative in resolving the conflict.

Action in the vertical dimension, as we have seen, can have very limited effect in adverse circumstances, but potential strengths in the horizontal dimension need not have any effect at all. If Egypt had done nothing, it might nevertheless expect that rising diplomatic pressure would eventually induce the Israelis to give up conquered territory without the diplomatic recognition they demanded in exchange. And the sheer passage of time would further increase American as well as European and Japanese dependence on Arab oil, further increasing diplomatic pressure on Israel in the long run. This, however, was a process not only prolonged but uncertain: if the United States were to revert to activism while the Soviet Union were distracted in turn by its own difficulties, the Arab producers would not brave the consequences of trying to exploit their control over oil supplies on Egypt's behalf. Nor was their control over the oil market bound to endure forever.

Only military action could activate Egypt's potential strength in the horizontal dimension—not industrial strength, like that of the Allies in World War II, but rather diplomatic strength, the ability to use the strengths of others, both the Soviet Union's weight in world affairs and the Arab "oil weapon." Yet, as we have seen, the Egyptians could not actually win a war, and they knew it. To be sure, they did not need a total victory to activate diplomatic pressures on Israel; indeed, if the Egyptians could have marched all the way to Tel Aviv they would not have needed diplomatic support in the first place. But neither could they hope to interest the Soviet Union and the United States, by the minor pressure of desultory raids or artillery shelling. Only a crossing of the Suez Canal could do it, and not an overnight affair either, since that would be followed by an Israeli counterattack and the Egyptians would be expelled in humiliating fashion. Sadat therefore needed an actual battle victory, even if it would not result in a campaign victory at the theater level.

The Suez Canal, a hundred yards of calm water, was not itself a serious obstacle, and the Israelis no longer manned their canal-side fortifications, having gone over to an armor-mobile defense based on the prompt deployment of a reinforced tank division against a crossing. They also relied heavily on their airpower.[14] So the Egyptians could cross the canal easily enough, although this would not solve the immediate problem of coping with the Israeli tanks waiting for them. Still less could they hope to resist the full force of the Israeli counterattack that would be mounted as soon as the Israelis mobilized their reserve forces, that is, within three days or so of a crossing. In the meantime, the Israeli airforce, which Egyptian fighters could not successfully engage in air combat, would systematically bombard the Egyptian forces, assuming they had somehow prevailed over the Israeli tanks guarding all the likely crossing points.

The Egyptian plan to solve this seemingly insoluble problem is a model of its kind because of the harmony it achieved both within the vertical and horizontal dimensions and between them. In the horizontal dimension, one important element was diplomatic: the Syrian government, with which Egypt's prior relations had been far from close, was nevertheless persuaded to launch a simultaneous offensive, so that Israel would have to divert part of its reserve forces to the Golan Heights instead of sending most of them to the Sinai front. In the event, two of the five full-strength reserve tank divisions were sent to fight the Syrians during the first week of the war. Another element of the plan, also in the horizontal dimension, combined intelligence, propaganda, and deception in the attempt to achieve total surprise for the planned offensive, even though the massing of Egyptian forces and bridging equipment by the canal could not be masked. The attempt was successful: the Israelis did not decide to mobilize until 9:20 on the morning of October 6, the same day as the Egyptian offensive. According to the standard theory, surprise is achieved in such conditions because "signals" conveying true information are masked by "noise," or the greater mass of outdated, erroneous, and deceptive information; a variant of the theory stresses the importance of deliberate deception.[15] But there may be a deeper truth in the matter, as already suggested:

deception deceives when there is a strong predisposition to self-deception.

The Israelis could and did monitor closely the Egyptian buildup for months before the October 6 surprise, just as Stalin could follow German preparations for months before the surprise of June 22, 1941, and the United States knew that Japan would attack somewhere, long before December 7, 1941. But the Israelis did not act to disrupt Egyptian preparations, for both domestic and external political reasons.[16] Once a situation is accepted in which the enemy is allowed to build up a threat, it only remains to justify inaction by an appropriate rationalization. For the Israelis it was the belief that Sadat was bluffing, as he had bluffed before, just as for Stalin it was apparently the belief that Hitler would issue an ultimatum and make demands (which he intended to accept); and for the Roosevelt administration it was the conscious calculation that war had to be started by the Japanese to start well from a political point of view (though of course the attack on Pearl Harbor itself was unexpected). As it happens, the Israeli rationalization was so powerful that it dominated even the clearest warnings—as such things are seen in retrospect.

Not too much should be made of *any* theory of surprise, however. True warnings, which are not ignored because of any political inhibition and are not suppressed by any rationalization, can simply become false warnings after the fact, in an especially direct version of strategy's reversal of opposites. In the circumstances of October 1973, if the Israelis could have placed a spy or a microphone in Sadat's office to overhear what was planned weeks in advance, if they had therefore mobilized their reserves to send two or three divisions to the front, Sadat would have had to cancel his offensive. So nothing would have happened on October 6, converting the true information into a false warning. Next time, of course, the surprise might succeed, *because* it had earlier failed.

As it was, with the mobilization of Israeli reserve divisions delayed by surprise, the Egyptians still had to face Israeli tanks and airpower. In fact, Sadat's planners did not believe that the Egyptian army would be able to withstand a counterattack once Israeli reserves were fully mobilized, even if belatedly, even if in part diverted to the Syrian front. For that seemingly insurmountable problem yet another horizontal-dimension solution was at hand: after several days of fighting, once the oil producers and Soviet diplomatic support were both activated and the United States was duly alarmed, Egypt would obtain an imposed cease-fire in the Security Council of the United Nations, which would freeze the post-October 6 lines and secure its conquests. But there still remained the problem of the ready tanks just across the canal and the ever-ready Israeli airforce. At this point the harmony of the dimensions was not enough, and planning solutions had to be found within the vertical dimension alone.

This too the Egyptian plan achieved successfully, by coordinating action at each level. Most visible was the provision of many antitank weapons and antiaircraft missiles, a technical-level solution. As it happened, the antiaircraft missiles were much more successful than expected, and the antitank weapons also outperformed expectations at least at the very beginning of the war. Still the weapons themselves could not have made the difference. The Egyptian planners also had a tactical-level answer for the threat of the Israeli tanks. Tank-hunting teams of tough foot soldiers were to attack Israeli tanks in their firing positions at short range with hand-held rockets, exploiting their lack of an infantry escort for close-in defense; in the event, Israeli tanks were late in moving into their positions, so that the Egyptian teams found themselves ambushing the tanks in conditions even more favorable than expected.

More important still was an operational-level solution, aimed at Israeli airpower as well as the tanks. The Egyptian crossing force consisted of foot and motorized infantry rather than armored units. By deviating from the textbook approach, whereby the infantry wins bridgeheads for fast-moving armor columns that cross within a day or so, the Egyptians hoped to deprive the Israeli tanks of the best targets for their guns and also to dilute the effect of Israeli air strikes. As it happened, the Israeli tanks were reduced to firing at infantry with armor-piercing rounds, after quickly running out of machine-gun ammunition. As for Israeli fighter-bombers, instead of being able to attack well-delineated armored vehicles, they found themselves under constant threat from the missiles while scattering their bombs among dispersed infantry. The effect was compounded at the level of theater strategy because the Egyptians did not attempt to concentrate their effort but crossed at many points all along the 70 miles of the Suez Canal. Thus the Israeli airforce was unable to attack the crossing medium itself: instead of a few heavy bridges for armor columns easily seen, easily destroyed, and hard to repair, its pilots were confronted by many light pontoon bridges whose damaged sections could be easily replaced, as well as by a large traffic of boats and amphibious vehicles hardly worth attacking at all.

In the event, the harmonies of the Egyptian plan yielded a large success. The crossing of the Suez Canal was duly accomplished on October 6, and the Egyptians did withstand both the resistance of Israeli tanks on the line and the attacks of the Israeli airforce. On the rising curve of success, they even defeated the first counterattack of the mobilized Israeli forces on October 8.[17] By now the "oil weapon" was being activated, the United States was alarmed, and the Soviet Union was playing its appointed role. But having achieved such unexpected success, the Egyptians who had resisted both tanks and aircraft could not resist temptation. Instead of accepting the favorable cease-fire in place they could have had, they decided to strain the fortunes of war. On October 14 they launched a classic armored offensive, attempting to fight above their limits of competence and overshooting the culminating point of success. Prompt defeat of the offensive marked the turning point of the campaign. By October 15, 1973, the Israelis had crossed the Suez Canal in turn, and within a week it was the Egyptians who were reduced to pleading for a cease-fire in place that left much of their army surrounded and the Israelis just 70 miles from Cairo. Of course this was only an operational-level victory, not a victory of grand strategy, because the Israelis could not go on to occupy Cairo and impose a peace on their terms.

Instead it was Egypt that achieved a *conclusive* if strictly limited victory in grand strategy, formally marked by the 1974 disengagement agreement that left Egypt in control of both banks of the Suez Canal. Thus, once again, results achieved within the vertical dimension alone are seen to be of limited effect for grand strategy when the transactions of the horizontal dimension intrude—just as potential strengths in the horizontal dimension need not develop at all without some transaction in the vertical dimension. War without statecraft must almost always fail, but statecraft cannot always succeed without war.

CHAPTER 15

CAN STRATEGY BE USEFUL?

$\mathbf{M}$y purpose has been to uncover the workings of the paradoxical logic in its five levels and two dimensions, offering in the process a general theory of strategy that describes but does not prescribe. As for the derivation of rules of conduct, practical implications, or even a complete scheme of grand strategy, that must be left to those who have powers of decision in a specific time and place, even though the theory clearly suggests how outcomes can be optimized: not by narrowing down complex issues to extract clear-cut choices for one action at a time, but by making concerted decisions carefully iterated through the five levels and two dimensions, to ensure a tolerable harmony among them all; and not by pursuing success without limit, but by exercising deliberate restraint in success, to avoid exceeding culminating points at each remove.

Yet there are reasons to hesitate in applying the general theory. The first is the sheer complexity of the required labors of harmonization. If the theory is considered, even the choice of a single weapon becomes an elaborate undertaking. Cost calculations and technical tests, themselves elaborate, no longer suffice. The weapon has to be evaluated at the tactical level also, to examine how it would be employed initially, to anticipate enemy reactions, and then to ascertain its net effect in the aftermath. And this is only the prelude to analysis at the operational level, and next at the level of theater strategy—to be repeated for each separate theater of interest. If the weapon is important enough to be noticed beyond narrow specialist circles, because of its novel characteristics, dramatic aspect, or simply its size, or if it is nuclear, the likely diplomatic and propaganda repercussions in the horizontal dimension have to be evaluated as well before an assessment can be made at the level of grand strategy. Even that is only an interim assessment, pending an evaluation of the range of possible future reactions by allies and enemies alike. If the new weapon is acquired, it is no longer only the *current* forces, weapons, countermeasures, and attitudes that have to be considered, but also the new configurations that its appearance may elicit.

To be sure, some of these considerations already figure in military decisions. Even the most feckless pragmatism could not allow nuclear matters to be decided on operational grounds alone; nor is it likely that technical choices in weapon design would entirely ignore the needs of tactical employment. There is still a wide gap, however, between current practice and the full iteration through levels and dimensions that application of the theory would require. Often enough, what happens is that advocates of this or that decision focus on just one or two levels, the ones that correspond to their own expertise or where analysis is apt to yield congenial results. The annals of military history are replete with cases of technically impressive weapons that would never have been built had elementary tactical reactions been considered (as in the case of the costly Ferdinand tanks lost in the 1943 battle of Kursk by the Germans because they lacked machine guns to resist Russian infantry); of weapons both technically and tactically successful whose decisive operational failure should have been anticipated (the antitank aircraft tried out on all sides in World War II, and now revived at great expense, which in searching for massed tanks encountered massed antiaircraft guns as well); of weapons successful at all military levels but counterproductive at the level of grand strategy because of the reaction of other powers (the German pre-1914 battleships that gained for Germany only Britain's lethal hostility).

Far greater complications await if the theory is to be used not to guide a single choice but to define an entire scheme of grand strategy. First the goals of *national policy,* whether set by tradition, bureaucratic compromise, a dictator's whim, or expressed democratic choice, must be congruent. It matters not if they are deemed wise or foolish, but they cannot be mutually exclusive or ranked inconsistently, for otherwise the definition of a normative grand strategy cannot even be conceived. Next, precise norms of conduct must be worked out for both the vertical and the horizontal dimensions of strategy, that is, in the full detail of *military policy* at every level and of *foreign policy* toward all relevant countries.

Whatever elegant ingenuity the grand scheme may contain, its implementation depends on a myriad of detailed policy decisions. In military policy, priorities set by the scheme between immediate readiness for war and future strength have to be affirmed in the hundreds of different line items of the budget; priorities between what forces to keep, on the other hand, are likely to involve much more than merely administrative complication, since branches and services will resist any scheme that would diminish them to permit other forces to grow. On the output side of the military equation, the envisaged use of forces must be defined at both the theater-strategic and the operational levels, to lay down theater goals and congruent operational methods, for each theater of interest. In the conduct of foreign policy, the scheme's guidelines will similarly require implementation just as detailed, by the separate bureaucracies responsible for diplomacy, propaganda, secret operations, and economic action—with the latter especially likely to encounter resistance or simply fail when strategic purposes collide with domestic interests.

Even if there is no elected parliament to contest the will of the executive and its scheme of grand strategy, even if there are no interest groups outside the government capable of challenging its policies, the diversified bureaucratic apparatus of modern states is itself a powerful obstacle to the implementation of any comprehensive scheme of grand strategy. Each civil and military department is structured to pursue its own distinct goals, rather than the optimization of national policy goals across the board. Consciously or not, those who populate the separate departments are likely to resist a concerted scheme whenever it clashes with their particular bureaucratic interests, habits, and urges; besides, they may lack skills or means not needed till then but now required by the scheme. For the implementation of a normative grand strategy, then, the organization of modern states is both the essential instrument and a powerful impediment.

A second reason for diffidence in applying the general theory is substantive rather than procedural. It is not easy to devise properly strategic solutions that are also superior to mere pragmatic improvisation. Insight into the paradoxical logic of strategy in its five levels and two dimensions can readily expose the error of making decisions on one level alone or of formulating unidimensional policies that ignore the reactions of others. But to proceed from the negative to the positive it is necessary to contend with all relevant aspects of a problem, at each level, in both dimensions and all at once. Procedural difficulties can now become the cause of misinformation in decision making and of distortions when the time for action arrives. In other words, the elaborate procedure of decisions and the tight policy coordination needed to apply the theory allow that much more scope for error. The theoretical superiority of properly strategical conduct may thus be overturned in practice, just as in combat a complex plan of maneuver far superior in theory can be so burdened with added frictions that it turns out to be worse than a brutally simple frontal attack.

The problem of substance is obviously at its peak when it is an entire scheme of grand strategy that must be devised. We now know that the frequent appeals heard in public life for a "coherent" or "consistent" national strategy are not merely vacuous but actually misleading. They suggest that the policies of each department should be tightly coordinated into a national policy that is logical in commonsense terms, whereas in strategy only policies that are seemingly contradictory can circumvent the self-defeating effect of the paradoxical logic. If, for example, during the consideration of a scheme of grand strategy a point is reached when some growth in current war readiness is deemed necessary (although military spending cannot grow), manpower levels, stocks, and training would all have to be increased at the expense of long-term weapon development, facility construction, and so on. Because the result is to enhance present strength at the expense of future strength, such a military policy would mandate a conciliatory foreign policy, so as eventually to reduce the intensity of the conflict by a placating diplomatic stance, restraint in propaganda and secret operations, perhaps, or even outright concessions. Subject to many other variables here ignored, a "hard" military policy of immediate strength would thus require a "soft" foreign policy. As a result, the overall conduct of national policy would seem neither coherent nor consistent, precisely because it does achieve harmony in both dimensions of strategy.

This particular example suggests another grave obstacle to strategical conduct at the national level: it would be hard for democratic political leaders to follow policies that can so easily be branded as illogical and contradictory (and in this example, as so often, the charge of appeasement might be made as well).

More generally, it would be hard to maintain public support for paradoxical policies when the latter, inevitably, could only be explained through the adverse medium of commonsense discourse.

This is not a universal difficulty, however. Dictatorial governments have the advantage of being able to pursue deliberately contradictory policies with little need for explanation. They can combine conciliatory diplomacy, and even concessions meant to relax the vigilance of their adversaries, with an accelerated armament effort; they can thunder and threaten in one direction while preparing to act in another; and they can launch surprise attacks even on the largest scale. Democratic governments can also have their military buildups, of course, but cannot mask them because a public atmosphere of fear or hostility must be created to justify the sacrifices; they can threaten other countries, but only after their action has been justified in the open; and they cannot achieve political surprise if they attack, only tactical surprise in the circumstances of a crisis that has already prepared their people for war.

Still, all the complications, obstacles, frictions, and political objections that impede the practical use of the general theory do not in any way diminish its validity or prohibit its application. They simply mean that the conduct of strategy at any level is burdened with difficulties, just as war and diplomacy themselves are. In many cases, no doubt, all difficulties could and should be overcome to implement the logic and thus obtain better outcomes in matters large and small, from the formulation of theater strategies and operational methods to the development of specific weapons, from tactical choices to the conduct of some conflictual aspect of foreign policy.

Even if the aim is much more ambitious, to devise and implement a national grand strategy that will harmonize policy on all levels, it is possible that the impediments could be overcome by great intellectual effort, a strong tenacity of purpose, and much political ingenuity. There is, however, a sinister danger that threatens such exceptional achievement. Huge uncertainties of fact must be involved in devising any substantive scheme of grand strategy. Success in both formulation and implementation therefore entails the lively possibility that error will be systematized. The shortsighted pragmatic decisions and uncoordinated improvisations that mark the daily conduct of government result in many errors, to be sure, but most of them will be small and with luck many of them will cancel each other out. The successful application of a normative grand strategy should greatly reduce the prevalence of small errors of disharmony, but only at the risk of focusing energies to perpetrate much larger errors.

ENVOI

In spite of obstacles, friction, and risk, the general theory here presented does offer some scope for practical application. It may not help soldiers and statesmen as explorers may be helped by a good topographic map, but it can serve them at least as jungle explorers are served by a guide to poisonous plants; negative advice can also be valuable.

First, once it is understood that the paradoxical logic conditions all that is conflictual, strategic practice can be freed from the systematically misleading influence of commonsense logic. For the conduct of foreign policy, this offers the prospect of an eventual liberation from the false discipline of consistency and coherence, to allow scope for concerted policies that are purposefully contradictory. Military leaders have always been able to pursue paradoxical tactics and operational methods (so much so that unconventional moves now coincide with commonsense notions of how war should be fought), but a new recognition of the pervasive reach of the logic can release them from the imposition of linear-logical thinking on peacetime military policy, with its harmful derivatives and misleading criteria of efficiency.

Second, once the dynamic consequences of the logic are understood, the exercise of restraint in pursuing success in war or peace, in the conduct of an offensive or in the building of weapons, will no longer depend on vague instincts of moderation but can instead be sustained by a compelling rationale as culminating points are approached. Mere awareness of the endless dynamics of the logic can serve as a warning against excess, to provide a stout wall of caution against the momentum of animal desires for unlimited success.

Third, once the structure of strategy is understood, with its distinct levels and dimensions, an entire class of errors can be exposed, resisted, or directly inhibited—those frequent errors that arise from decisions made at some level chosen arbitrarily with other levels ignored, and from the pursuit of success in one dimension alone in disharmony with the other.

But a discipline need not be of practical value to merit our attention: the study of strategy should be its own reward because it alone can explain the tantalizing continuities and baffling contradictions that pervade the human experience of conflict.

APPENDICES

WORKS CITED

NOTES

INDEX

APPENDIX 1

Definitions of Strategy

It is my purpose to demonstrate the existence of strategy as a body of recurring objective phenomena that arise from human conflict, and not to prescribe courses of action. Most current definitions are exclusively normative, as if it were assumed that no such objective phenomena exist or else that they are too obvious to be worth defining. This of course raises the question of what basis there can be for generic prescriptions, as opposed to specific advice on how to deal with a particular question in a given context.

Clausewitz, the greatest student of strategy, was simply uninterested in defining anything in generic, abstract terms; he regarded all such attempts as futile and pedantic. His own characteristically offhand definition of strategy occurs by distinction from tactics and is presented as no more than common usage: "Everyone knows fairly well where each particular factor belongs . . . Whenever such categories are blindly used, there must be a deep-seated reason for it . . . We reject, on the other hand, the artificial distinctions of certain writers, since they find no reflection in general usage. According to our classification, then, tactics teaches *the use of armed forces in the engagement;* strategy, *the use of engagements for the object of the war.*" *On War,* book 2, chap. 1, p. 128 (Princeton edition).

As in the case of many scientific terms, the word "strategy" (French *stratégie,* Italian *strategia*) is derived indirectly from the Greek *strategos* (general), which does not carry the connotation of the modern word. The Greek equivalent for our "strategy" would have been *strategike episteme* (generals' knowledge) or *strategon sophia* (generals' wisdom). Cognates such as *strategicos,* as in the title of Onosander's work, or much later *strategikon* (of Mauricius), have a didactic connotation. On the other hand, *strategemata* (*Strategematon* is the Greek title of the Latin work by Frontinus) describes a compilation of *strategema*, precisely "stratagems" or tricks of war (*ruses de guerre*). Much more commonly used by the Greeks, from Aeneas in the fourth century B.C. to Leo after the seventh century A.D. and beyond, was *taktike techne*, which described an entire body of knowledge on the conduct of warfare, from supply to exhortatory rhetoric, including both techniques and tactics proper as well as petty diplomacy. *Taktike techne*, or rather its Latin translation *ars bellica*, resurfaced by 1518 in Machiavelli's use of "arte della guerra" in the *Discorsi* on Livy (who in fact uses that term) and later in the title of his *Dell' arte della guerra*, and it spread quite widely (*Kriegskunst, art de la guerre*, art of war). See Virgilio Ilari, "Politica e strategia globale," in Jean, ed., *Il pensiero strategico* (1985), pp. 57–59.

For Clausewitz "strategy" was normative, and so it remains in the following contemporary American definition: "A science, an art, or a plan (subject to revision) governing the raising, arming, and utilization of the military forces of a nation (or coalition) to the end that its interests will be effectively promoted or secured against enemies, actual, potential, or merely presumed." King, ed., *Lexicon of Military Terms* (1960), p. 14.

Characteristically, a modern American definition of official military origin is much more inclusive: "The art and science of developing and using political, economic, psychological and military forces as necessary during peace and war, to afford the maximum support to policies, in order to increase the probabilities and favorable consequences of victory and to lessen the chances of defeat." U.S. Joint Chiefs of Staff, *Dictionary of United States Military Terms for Joint Usage* (1964), p. 135.

Even broader, yet equally prescriptive, is the standard definition of strategy from *Webster's Third New International Dictionary*: "The science and art of employing the political, economic, psychological, and military forces of a nation or group of nations to afford the maximum support to adopted policies in peace or war."

The definition found in the collective and exceedingly official *Soviet Military Strategy*, attributed to the authorship of Marshal V. D. Sokolovsky, which reveals both Marxist and bureaucratic preoccupations, differentiates between the descriptive and prescriptive meanings: "Military strategy is a system of scientific knowledge dealing with the laws of war as an armed conflict in the name of definite class interests. Strategy—on the basis of military experience, military and political conditions, economic and moral potential of the country, new means of combat, and the views and potential of the probable enemy—studies the conditions and the nature of future war, the methods for its preparation and conduct, the services of the armed forces and the foundations for their strategic utilization, as well as foundations for the material and technical support and leadership of the war and the armed forces. At the same time, this is the area of the practical activity of the higher military and political leadership, of the supreme command, and of the higher headquarters, that pertains to the art of preparing a country and the armed forces for war and conducting the war.'' Scott, ed., *Soviet Military Strategy* (1975), p. 11.

General André Beaufre's succinct definition, normative but based on the descriptive, is congruent with my own purpose in this book: "l'art de la dialectique des volontés employant la force pour resoudre leur conflict" (the art of the dialectics of wills that use force to resolve their conflict). *Introduction à la stratégie* (1963), p. 16.

APPENDIX 2

The Soviet Army: A Note

The habit has persisted of measuring the Soviet army by the number of its divisions. There have always been a great many of them, partly because of the general conscription of Soviet youth, and more because released conscripts are assigned to structured and equipped reserve units, held at varying states of readiness. Indeed, to a large extent the Soviet army may be viewed as a reserve-producing operation, very much on the lines of the Israeli army. The results are impressive: at this writing, for example, it is estimated that there are 51 tank divisions, 142 "motor-rifle" (actually fully mechanized) divisions, and 7 airborne divisions, three-quarters of them containing only cadres on active duty but all capable of being fielded in short order. Western estimates of Soviet mobilization delays are unreliable: it is not in the Soviet military style to insist on the elusive mirage of units fully manned by fully qualified soldiers fully equipped; the Soviet army is much more likely to send units into action as soon as they have minimal competence and the basic equipment. And the format of armored warfare favors this approach: while forces of high quality are needed at the spearheads, the armored thrust as a whole can gain mass and momentum from forces of lower quality as well.

For war operations, however, it is not by divisions that the fighting would be done but by "armies," groupings of four or five divisions under a single command group, with their own extradivisional organic support. At present, for example, each army is supposed to include a large artillery complement, a surface-to-surface missile unit, a large antiaircraft complement, a 64-helicopter regiment, an elite air-assault battalion, and a tank regiment with as many as 150 tanks (some Western *divisions* have only 200).

Armies are in turn grouped under "fronts," the unit of planning for large operations, which again have their own organic support. Currently, for example, each front is supposed to include a complete artillery division with almost as many guns, howitzers, and heavy mortars as some of the smaller Western armies (240 in all), antiaircraft units on a comparable scale, surface-to-surface missiles with nuclear warheads, two helicopter regiments, an elite air-assault brigade, and an independent tank brigade with up to 200 tanks.

It follows, therefore, that the counting of divisions is doubly misleading in the case of the Soviet army. On the one hand, its divisions are smaller than those of the main Western armies, notably including the American; on the other, the procedure overlooks the great strength contained in the support elements of the forty-odd "armies" and sixteen "fronts" now estimated.

Another significant factor in the warmaking power of the Soviet army is also slighted by divisional (and equipment) counts: the elite forces that offer distinct quasi-commando capabilities to the otherwise all-mechanized Soviet army. Recruited, trained, and inspected by a separate Vozdushno Desantnye-Voyska (VDV) organization, these troops serve for much longer terms than other conscripts (five years) and are parachute-trained (although in most cases they would be air-landed or delivered by helicopters). A family of air-portable, tracked light-armor vehicles has been specifically developed for the VDV, whose forces currently include: 7 airborne divisions, with 7,000 men each and organic, airmobile light-armor vehicles and artillery; first-line air-assault brigades, with 2,000–2,500 men and some light-armor vehicles; airmobile assault brigades, with 1,700–1,850 men and some light-armor vehicles (they could be a transitional type or intended for secondary fronts); and army-level air-assault battalions, with less than 500 men each. In addition, there are commando (Spetsnats) forces, some of which can operate in disguise. At present, there are reportedly 19 Spetsnats "brigades" and "regiments," but these designators greatly exaggerate actual force levels. Finally, the Soviet navy has a total of 18,000 men in its elite naval infantry.

Sources: International Institute for Strategic Studies, *Military Balance, 1985–86,* pp. 22–23, 188–189, and *Military Balance, 1986–87,* p. 37. David C. Isby, "Air Assault and Airmobile Brigades of the Soviet Army," *Amphibious Warfare Review* (1985). Norman Polmar, "Soviet Naval Infantry," idem.

APPENDIX 3

NATO, the Soviet Army, and Other Warsaw Pact Armies: Terms of Comparison

Comparative estimates of military power based on numerical comparisons of formations and equipment are systematically misleading because they ignore the larger part of the whole: the intangibles of morale, discipline, cohesion, and leadership, as well as the quality of tactics, operational methods, and theater strategies. But NATO and Warsaw Pact ground-force comparisons on those lines are even more misleading than usual, since the normal unit of account, the "division," is not valid in principle for the Soviet army (see Appendix 2) and in any case conflates a multitude of formations that are radically different in purely numerical terms, even when they are supposed to be of the same type.

At present, for example, Soviet first-line "tank" divisions at full strength are estimated to contain a total of 10,500 men and 322 tanks (others are significantly smaller); the counterpart American armored divisions, by contrast, have 16,500 men but only two more tanks (324). Likewise, Soviet first-line "motor-rifle" (mechanized) divisions at full strength have 12,500 men and 271 tanks, while the counterpart American mechanized divisions have 16,000 men and 270 tanks. West German divisions, which are the most important in the NATO array, have fewer tanks, with 300 in the Panzer divisions and 250 in the Panzergrenadier divisions, but more men, with 17,000 and 17,500 men respectively. British armored divisions with 16,300 men have only 285 tanks, just a few more than first-line Soviet *motor-rifle* divisions, while French divisions are very much smaller than the latter even in manpower.

Actually there is a fairly consistent structural difference between Soviet and NATO ground forces: Soviet four-regiment divisions contain fewer men and more heavy weapons than three-brigade NATO divisions, notably the tanks and combat carriers especially needed for offensive operations, but also artillery and antiaircraft weapons. NATO forces, because they are equipped with more costly weapons produced on a much smaller scale, have fewer of them—even in the case of weapons especially suited for defensive tactics, such as antitank missiles. Thus the poorer Soviet Union has capital-intensive forces while the ground forces of the richer NATO armies are manpower-intensive.

If manpower levels are taken as the salient measure of combat strength, Soviet divisions should be counted at 60 percent of their number, as compared to their American and West German counterparts. But if judged on their equipment holdings, Soviet divisions should be counted at par. If so, the numbers estimated at this time for each side upon full mobilization are not very reassuring for the Alliance: 110 Soviet tank and motor-rifle divisions as against 89 NATO armored and mechanized divisions. If the comparison is broadened to include nonmechanized divisions (foot/truck infantry, airborne and mountain forces), the divisional count is much more favorable for NATO: at present it could field up to 54 such divisions upon full mobilization, as opposed to only 6 for the Soviet army. But while the former are mostly plain infantry, and poorly equipped reserve infantry to boot, the latter are elite airborne divisions, albeit very small with only some 7000 each.

In fact, another systematic difference between the Warsaw Pact ground forces as a whole and those of NATO is the *structural* homogeneity of the former and the very great diversity of the latter. In the complete array of divisions that each side could mobilize for war on current estimates, 143 for NATO and 180 for the Warsaw Pact, only three basic types (tank, motor-rifle, airborne) account for almost all Pact divisions, as opposed to an entire menagerie of diverse types in NATO, including Italian high-mountain infantry (Alpini), American marines, German Panzer divisions, Turkish foot infantry, Greek reserve divisions that exist largely on paper, and British divisions manned by long-service professionals. To the extent that diversity reflects adaptation to local terrain requirements and variant comparative advantages on a national basis—the Turkish army can count on excellent infantry, the West German excels in armor, the Italian leads in mountain troops—it actually favors NATO. But the great mass of nonmechanized divisions in the Alliance is suspect; it suggests not an adaptation to varying circumstances but a severe shortage of armored vehicles in the poorer armies.

Geography accounts for one more asymmetry. All Warsaw Pact divisions can reach the front by overland movement, but American (and Canadian) reinforcements must cross the Atlantic, almost entirely by slow and insecure sea transport. At present, 13 of NATO's fully mobilized total of 89 armored and mechanized divisions, and 15 of its 54 nonmechanized divisions, are supposed to come from the United States.

A final difference between NATO and Warsaw Pact ground forces is the presumed Alliance loyalty of the former and the presumed potential disloyalty of the latter. This need not be as significant as is sometimes suggested. First, the Soviet army in any case accounts for a large part of the Warsaw Pact total (41 out of 57 tank divisions and 74 out of 112 motor-rifle divisions, according to current full-mobilization estimates). Second, the format of armored warfare would allow even forces of dubious loyalty to be profitably used; they could not serve reliably in the spearheads of penetration, but they could be used to hold secondary fronts, add mass and momentum to the vectors of penetration, occupy axes successfully opened, and attract Western counterattacks that would otherwise be aimed at the Soviet forces themselves. Nor is it reasonable to expect that armed forces that are now obedient enough would suddenly revolt in war, precisely when the number of Soviet divisions (and the mass of extradivisional forces) deployed in the client states would be sharply increased, from 53 to 115 tank and motor-rifle divisions according to current estimates. The safest assumption is that Warsaw Pact forces would obey Soviet orders if the Soviet army were winning the war and be inclined to disobedience if it were losing. In other words, if NATO does well, it would receive the added advantage of Warsaw Pact defections—but if it does poorly, it could not expect relief from that quarter.

Source: International Institute for Strategic Studies, *Military Balance, 1986–87*, pp. 226–227.

Works Cited

Adan, Avraham. *On the Banks of the Suez*. Novato, Calif.: Presidio Press, 1980.

Addington, Larry H. *The Blitzkrieg Era and the German General Staff, 1865–1941*. New Brunswick: Rutgers University Press, 1971.

Bartov, Hanoch. *Dado, 48 Years and 20 Days*. Tel Aviv: Ma'ariv Book Guild, 1981.

Beaufre, André [General]. *Introduction à la stratégie* (Introduction to Strategy). Paris: Librairie Armand Colin, 1963.

Betts, Richard K., ed. *Cruise Missiles: Technology, Strategy, Politics*. Washington: Brookings Institution, 1981.

Bond, Brian. *Liddell Hart: A Study of His Military Thought*. London: Cassell, 1977.

Botti, Ferrucci, and Virgilio Ilari. *Il pensiero militare italiano dal primo al secondo dopoguerra, 1919–1949* (Italian Military Thought from the Aftermath of the First World War to the Aftermath of the Second). Rome: Stato Maggiore dell'Esercito, Ufficio Storico, 1985.

Brodie, Bernard, ed. *The Absolute Weapon*. New York: Harcourt Brace, 1946.

―――― *Strategy in the Missile Age*. Princeton: Princeton University Press, 1959.

―――― *A Guide to Naval Strategy*. New York: Praeger, 1965.

Brossollet, Guy. *Essai sur la non-bataille* (Essay on the Nonbattle). Paris: Belin, 1975.

Burrel, Raymond E. *Strategic Nuclear Parity and NATO Defense Doctrine*. Washington: National Defense University, 1978.

Canby, Steven L. "Territorial Defense in Central Europe." *Armed Forces and Society*, 7 (Fall 1980).

―――― "New Conventional Force Technology and the NATO–Warsaw Pact Balance, I." *New Technology and Western Security Policy*. IISS Annual Conference Papers, Adelphi Papers 198. London: IISS, 1985.

Churchill, Winston S. *The Second World War: Triumph and Tragedy*. Boston: Houghton Mifflin, 1953.

Clausewitz, Carl von. *On War* (1833, 3 vols.). Ed. and trans. Michael Howard and Peter Paret. Princeton: Princeton University Press, 1976.

Cooper, M. *The Phantom War*. London: Macdonald and Jane's, 1979.

Cotter, Donald R. "New Conventional Force Technology and the NATO–

Warsaw Pact Balance, II." *New Technology and Western Security Policy.* IISS Annual Conference Papers, Adelphi Papers 198. London: IISS, 1985.

Couteau-Bégarie, Hervé. *La puissance maritime: Castex et la stratégie navale.* (Naval Power: Castex and Naval Strategy). Paris: Fayard, 1985.

Craven, Wesley F., and James L. Cate. *The Army Air Forces in World War II.* 6 vols. Chicago: University of Chicago Press, 1948–1955.

Crowl, Philip A. "Alfred Thayer Mahan: The Naval Historian." In Peter Paret et al., eds., *Makers of Modern Strategy: From Machiavelli to the Nuclear Age.* Princeton: Princeton University Press, 1986.

De Seversky, Alexander P. [Major]. *Victory through Air Power.* New York: Simon and Schuster, 1942.

Douhet, Giulio. *Il dominio dell'aria.* Rome, 1921. English translation: *The Command of the Air,* trans. Dino Ferrari. New York: Coward McCann, 1942.

Enthoven, Alain C., and K. Wayne Smith. *How Much Is Enough? Shaping the Defense Program, 1961–1969.* New York: Harper and Row, 1971.

Erickson, John. *The Road to Stalingrad.* London: Weidenfeld and Nicholson, 1975.

Fitzsimons, Bernard, ed. *Encyclopedia of 20th Century Weapons and Warfare.* New York: Columbia House, 1971–1977.

Gabriel, Richard A. *The Antagonists: A Comparative Combat Assessment of the Soviet and American Soldier.* Westport, Conn.: Greenwood, 1984.

Garthoff, Raymond L. *Soviet Military Doctrine.* Glencoe: Illinois University Press, 1953.

Gilbert, Martin. *Finest Hour: Winston S. Churchill, 1939–1941.* London: Heinemann, 1983.

Graham, Gerald S. *The Politics of Naval Supremacy: Studies in British Maritime Ascendancy.* Cambridge, Eng.: Cambridge University Press, 1965.

Guenther, H. K. "Der Kampf gegen die Partisanen" (The War against the Partisans). *Wehrwissenschaftliche Rundschau,* 1968.

Harris, Arthur. *Bomber Offensive.* London: Collins, 1947.

Hastings, Max. *Das Reich: The March of the 2nd SS Panzer Division through France.* New York: Holt, Rinehart and Winston, 1981.

—— *Bomber Command.* London: Pan Books, 1981.

Hillgruber, A. *Hitlers Strategie.* Frankfurt am Main: Wehrwesen, Bernard und Graefe, 1965.

Hinsley, F. H., et al. *British Intelligence in the Second World War: Its Influence on Strategy and Operations.* New York: Cambridge University Press, 1979 (vol. 1), 1984 (vol. 3, pt. 1).

Horelick, A. L., and M. Rush. *Strategic Power and Soviet Foreign Policy.* Chicago: University of Chicago Press, 1966.

Horne, Alistair. *The Price of Glory, Verdun 1916.* London: Penguin, 1961.

Howard, Michael. *The Franco-Prussian War.* London: Rupert Hart-Davis, 1968.

Ikle, Fred C. *Every War Must End.* New York: Columbia University Press, 1971.

Ilari, Virgilio. "Politica e strategia globale" (Global Politics and Strategy). In Carlo Jean, ed., *Il pensiero strategico*. Milan: Franco Angeli, 1985.

IISS: International Institute of Strategic Studies. *The Military Balance, 1985–86,* and *1986–87*. London: IISS, 1985, 1986.

Irving, David. *The Trail of the Fox*. New York: Dutton, 1977.

Isby, David C. "Air Assault and Airmobile Brigades of the Soviet Army." *Amphibious Warfare Review*, 3 (August 1985).

Jean, Carlo, ed. *Il pensiero strategico* (Strategic Thought). Milan: Franco Angeli, 1985.

Joint Chiefs of Staff. *See* United States.

Jungk, Robert. *Brighter than a Thousand Suns: A Personal History of the Atomic Scientists*. London: Penguin Books, 1964.

King, James E., Jr., ed. *Lexicon of Military Terms Relevant to National Security Affairs on Arms and Arms Control*. Washington: Institute for Defense Analyses, 1960.

Korbonski, Stefan. *Fighting Warsaw*. N.p.: Minerva Press, 1968.

Laqueur, Walter. *Guerrilla: A Historical and Critical Study*. Boston: Little, Brown, 1976.

Lewin, Ronald. *Life and Death of the Afrika Korps*. London: Corgi Books, 1967.

Löser, Jochen. *Weder rot noch tot. Überleben ohne Atomkrieg, eine sicherheitspolitische Alternative* (Neither Red nor Dead: Survival without Nuclear War, an Alternative Security Policy). Geschichte und Staat, vol. 257/258. Munich: Olzog, 1982.

Low, A. M. *Musket to Machine-Gun*. London: Hutchinsons, 1942.

Luttwak, Edward N. *The Grand Strategy of the Roman Empire: From the First Century A.D. to the Third*. Baltimore: Johns Hopkins University Press, 1976.

——— "Perceptions of Military Force and US Defence Policy." *Survival* (London, IISS), 19 (January-February 1977). Reprinted in Edward N. Luttwak, *Strategy and Politics: Collected Essays*. New Brunswick: Transaction Books, 1980.

——— *The Grand Strategy of the Soviet Union*. New York: St. Martin's Press, 1983.

——— "The Operational Level of War." *International Security,* 5 (Winter 1980–81). Reprinted in Edward N. Luttwak, *Strategy and History: Collected Essays, 2*. New Brunswick: Transaction Books, 1985.

——— and Dan Horowitz. *The Israeli Army*. New York: Harper and Row, 1975; Cambridge: Abt Books, 1983.

MacIsaac, David. *Strategic Bombing in World War Two: The Story of the United States Bombing Survey*. New York: Garland, 1976.

Mahan, Alfred Thayer. *Naval Strategy: Compared and Contrasted with the Principles and Practice of Military Operations on Land*. Boston: Little, Brown, 1911.

McElwee, William. *The Art of War: Waterloo to Mons*. London: Weidenfeld and Nicholson, 1974.

Manstein, Erich von. *Lost Victories*. Chicago: Regnery, 1958.

Martin, L. W. *The Sea in Modern Strategy.* Studies in International Security, 11. New York: Praeger, 1967.

Masson, Philippe. *Histoire de la marine* (History of the [French] Navy). 2 vols. Paris: Lavauzelle, 1982, 1983.

Maurer, John H. "American Naval Concentration and the German Battle Fleet, 1900–1918. *Journal of Strategic Studies,* 6 (June 1983).

Mellenthin, F. W. von. *Panzer Battles: A Study in the Employment of Armor in the Second World War.* New York: Ballantine Books, 1971.

Middlebrook, Martin. *The Battle of Hamburg: Allied Bomber Forces against a German City in 1943.* New York: Scribner's, 1981.

Mueller-Hillebrand, Burkhart. *Das Heer, 1933–1945.* 3 vols. Frankfurt am Main: Mittler, 1956–1969.

Murray, Williamson. *Strategy for Defeat: The Luftwaffe, 1933–1945.* Maxwell, Ala.: Air University Press, 1983.

Osgood, Robert E., and Robert W. Tucker. *Force, Order and Justice.* Baltimore: Johns Hopkins University Press, 1967.

Paret, Peter, ed., with Gordon A. Craig and Felix Gilbert. *Makers of Modern Strategy: From Machiavelli to the Nuclear Age.* Princeton: Princeton University Press, 1986.

Polmar, Norman. "Soviet Naval Infantry." *Amphibious Warfare Review,* 3, (August 1985).

Price, Alfred. *Instruments of Darkness: The History of Electronic Warfare.* New York: Scribner's, 1977.

Rietzler, R. S. "Erfahrungen aus Kleinkrieg und Jagdkampf" (Experiences of Guerrilla and Light-Infantry Combat Style), *Truppendiest,* 2 (1979).

Rosinski, Herbert. *The Development of Naval Thought.* Ed. B. Mitchell Simpson III. Newport, R.I.: Naval War College Press, 1977.

Sansom, George. *A History of Japan, 1334–1615.* Stanford: Stanford University Press, 1961.

Schelling, Thomas C. *The Strategy of Conflict.* Cambridge: Harvard University Press, 1960, 1980.

——— *Arms and Influence.* New Haven: Yale University Press, 1966.

Schiff, Zeev, and Ehud Yaari. *Israel's Lebanon War.* New York: Simon and Schuster, 1984.

Scott, Harriet Fast, ed. *Soviet Military Strategy.* Written by V. D. Sokolovsky, Marshal of the Soviet Union. 3rd Ed. New York: Crane Russak, 1975.

Scotter, William [General]. "A Role for the Non-Mechanized Infantry." *RUSI Journal,* 125 (December 1980), 59–62.

Seager, Robert, II. *Alfred Thayer Mahan: The Man and His Letters.* Annapolis: U.S. Naval Institute, 1977.

Seaton, Albert. *The Battle for Moscow.* New York: Jove, 1983.

Sergent, Pierre. *Je ne regrette rien.* Paris: Fayard, 1972.

Sokolovsky. *See* Scott.

Spector, Ronald H. *Eagle against the Sun.* New York: Vintage Books, 1985.

Speer, Albert. *Inside the Third Reich.* New York: Macmillan, 1970.

Terraine, John. *The Right of the Line: The Royal Air Force in the European War, 1939–1945.* London: Hodder and Stoughton, 1985.

Trinquier, Roger [Colonel] *La guerre moderne* (Modern War). Paris: La Table Ronde, 1961.

Turnbull, S. R. *The Samurai: A Military History.* New York: Macmillan, 1977.

Uhle-Wettler, Franz. *Leichte Infanterie im Atomzeitalter* (Light Infantry in the Atomic Age). Munich: J. F. Lehmann, Bernard und Graefe, 1966.

United States Department of Defense. *Report of the Secretary of Defense to the Congress on the FY 1987 Budget* (February 5, 1986). Washington, 1986.

United States Joint Chiefs of Staff. *Dictionary of United States Military Terms for Joint Usage.* Washington: Joint Chiefs of Staff, 1964.

United States Naval Institute, James Watkins et al. *The Maritime Strategy.* Annapolis: U.S. Naval Institute, January 1986.

Van Creveld, Martin. *Supplying War: Logistics from Wallenstein to Patton.* Cambridge, Eng.: Cambridge University Press, 1977.

——— *Command in War.* Cambridge: Harvard University Press, 1985.

Watts, Barry D. *The Foundations of U.S. Air Doctrine: The Problem of Friction in War.* Maxwell, Ala.: Air University Press, 1984.

Webster, Charles, and Noble Frankland. *The Strategic Air Offensive against Germany, 1939–1945.* 4 vols. London: HMSO, 1961.

Whaley, Barton. *Codeword Barbarossa.* Cambridge: MIT Press, 1973.

White, William D. *U.S. Tactical Air Power: Missions, Forces and Costs.* Washington: Brookings Institution, 1974.

Wikner, Fred N. "Interdicting Fixed Targets with Conventional Weapons." *Armed Forces Journal,* March 1983.

Wohlstetter, A. J., F. S. Hoffman, R. J. Lutz, and H. S. Rowen. *Selection and Use of Strategic Air Bases.* RAND R-266, April 1, 1954. Santa Monica: RAND Corporation, current.

Wohlstetter, Albert. "The Delicate Balance of Terror." *Foreign Affairs,* January 1959.

Wohlstetter, Roberta. *Pearl Harbor: Warning and Decision.* Stanford: Stanford University Press, 1962.

Young, Robert J. *In Command of France: French Foreign Policy and Military Planning, 1933–1940.* Cambridge: Harvard University Press, 1978.

Ziemke, Earl F. *Stalingrad to Berlin: The German Defeat in the East.* Army Historical Series. Washington: Office of the Chief of Military History of the U.S. Army, 1968.

Notes

Introduction, Part I

1. Actually, as Fred C. Ikle notes in *Every War Must End* (1971), p. 123, the most dubious paradox is the implicit reversal of the normal traits of victim and aggressor: if deterrence is to succeed, the potential victim must be utterly decisive in desperate circumstances, even reckless, while the potential aggressor must be prudently calculating in evaluating risks, costs, and benefits.

1. The Conscious Use of Paradox in War

1. This is Basil Liddell Hart's concept of the "indirect approach"; his ideas on the subject are scattered in biographies, works of advocacy, and ephemera. For a coherent statement in context, see Brian Bond, *Liddell Hart* (1977), pp. 37–61.

2. "Signals" and "noise" are terms imported from communications engineering into strategic discourse, in a seminal work on Japan's surprise attack: Roberta Wohlstetter, *Pearl Harbor* (1962).

3. Carl von Clausewitz, *On War,* book 1, chap. 7; p. 119 in the Princeton edition.

4. Ibid., book 2, chap. 3 ("War Is an Act of Human Intercourse"), p. 149.

5. The Chouf road, from Jazzin to the Beirut-Damascus highway, which in turn leads eastward to Shtawra, the Israeli objective at the time, where the Syrian military headquarters for Lebanon were located. The Israeli advance was blocked at Ayn Zhalta, a few miles from the highway. See Zeev Schiff and Ehud Yaari, *Israel's Lebanon War* (1984), pp. 160–161.

6. The offensive of Ben-Gal's Corps 446, which began in the early morning of June 10, 1982. Ibid., pp. 117, 171–173.

2. The Logic in Action

1. The campaign did not end officially until June 25, 1940, when Italy also accepted the French armistice offer; but the last week of fighting was half-hearted on both sides, except in the Maginot Line sectors where the French Army Group 2 resisted tenaciously until June 22.

2. At the outbreak of war in September 1939, out of 103 German divisions only 16 (Panzer, Motorized, and Light) were fully motorized. Each of the 87

infantry divisions was supposed to have 942 scout cars, staff cars, artillery tractors, and trucks (sufficient to put one man in six on wheels), but most supplies were carried on 1,200 horsecarts. By May 1940, however, because of truck losses on bad Polish roads, the number of trucks had been halved and more carts had been added. From railhead to divisional depots, supplies were to be delivered by extradivisional truck regiments; but there were only three of these for the entire German army on all fronts, with a total of only 6,600 trucks. See Martin van Creveld, *Supplying War* (1977), pp. 144–147.

3. Burkhart Mueller-Hillebrand, *Das Heer, 1933–1945* (1956), vol. 2, table 29, as cited in van Creveld, *Supplying War,* n. 28; p. 151.

4. On the morning of October 18, 1941, the Tenth Panzer and SS Das Reich divisions entered Mozhaisk, on the main highway to Moscow. At that point, the Germans were completing the destruction of eight Soviet armies in the Vyazma-Bryansk sectors, in what was to be their last great and unqualified victory on Russian soil (they claimed 665,000 prisoners); see John Erickson, *The Road to Stalingrad* (1975), pp. 216–220. By then, the leading Second and Third Panzer groups (Guderian and Hoth) of Army Group Center had advanced more than 500 miles *on a straight line basis* since June 22, 1941, and Guderian's forces had just been redirected toward Moscow, after their southward maneuver to close off the huge Kiev-Romny encirclement.

5. In fact only two corps could attack at all, out of the two armies on the sector. See Albert Seaton, *The Battle for Moscow* (1983), p. 165.

6. Army Group South's counteroffensive of February 25–March 18, 1943, to the Donets River and Kharkov, which added the name of Fritz Erich von Manstein to the celebrity list of military history. Six Soviet tank corps of the army-level "Popov group," which had ventured too far south, were encircled and shattered, and two more Soviet armies were battered in the German reconquest of the Kharkov region. See Earl F. Ziemke, *Stalingrad to Berlin* (1968), pp. 90–105. Also Erich von Manstein, *Lost Victories* (1958), pp. 367–442.

7. Ziemke, *Stalingrad to Berlin,* p. 501.

8. See Raymond L. Garthoff, *Soviet Military Doctrine* (1953) pp. 18–19, for an elaboration of the doctrine.

9. With no railway across Libya and with horsecarts unusable in the waterless and fodderless desert, only the circulation of truck columns from the port of Tripoli to the front could sustain Rommel's forces. The 6,000 tons of truck capacity available to them in April 1941, at the start of the German intervention, could supply the original two divisions of the Afrika Korps out to some 300 miles at most, and Rommel was therefore explicitly forbidden to attack. When he launched his first offensive nevertheless, outmaneuvering the British forces (also overextended after their previous victory against the Italians), which promptly collapsed, his spectacular and historically unique thousand-mile advance reconquered all of Libya, penetrated into Egypt—and left his leading forces stranded in the desert, barely subsisting on captured supplies and set for their own coming retreat. Van Creveld, *Supplying War,* p. 186.

10. That is, for combat with other fighters as well as ground attack, both in daylight. See Williamson Murray, *Strategy for Defeat* (1983), pp. 1–25.

11. The first bombing of German inland targets, in the Ruhr, occurred on

May 15, 1940; the first raid on Berlin was flown on the night of August 25, 1940. From the outbreak of war, in September 1939, through March 1940, Bomber Command dropped only 64 tons of bombs, and none deliberately on German cities—on which only leaflets were dropped. Goering's famous boast therefore seemed vindicated, but with the "phoney war" over, France invaded, and Churchill in command, 1,668 tons were dropped on Germany in May 1940, rising to 2,300 tons in June, declining to 1,257 in July (the forward airfields had been lost), and 1,365 in August before increasing to 2,339 tons in September 1940. See Charles Webster and Noble Frankland, *The Strategic Air Offensive against Germany* (1961), I, 144, 152, and IV, 455; hereafter cited *SAO*.

12. During May 1942, the British Bomber Command sent out 2,702 sorties, lost 114 aircraft, and had 256 seriously damaged; in June, there were 4,801 sorties, 199 losses, and 442 damaged aircraft; in July, sorties declined to 3,914, but losses declined less than proportionately to 171, and 315 aircraft were damaged; only 2,454 sorties were flown in August (as opposed to 4,242 in August 1941), with 142 aircraft lost and 233 damaged. See *SAO*, IV, appendix 40, p. 432; and Alfred Price, *Instruments of Darkness* (1977), pp. 55–111.

13. The monthly total of bombs dropped by Bomber Command had declined to 2,714 tons by December 1942, after reaching a peak level of 6,845 tons in the previous June; in 1943, by contrast, January's 4,345 tons were followed by 10,959 in February and steadily more thereafter, with the year's peak in August at 20,149 tons; during the same month, the U.S. Eighth Air Force total was 3,999 tons. See *SAO,* IV, appendix 44, p. 456.

14. "Window" was the British code name for metalized strips that reflect radar beams when cut to their wave length; the American term, now universally employed, is "chaff."

15. The "firestorm effect" is first described in the famous report of the Hamburg Police President dated December 1, 1943. See the extract in *SAO,* IV, appendix 30, pp. 310–315; and Martin Middlebrook, *The Battle of Hamburg* (1981) pp. 214–240.

16. Bomber Command lost 314 aircraft (416 were damaged) in January 1944, 199 in February (264 damaged), and 283 in March (402 damaged)—rates plainly unsustainable: in March the average aircraft availability was 974. See *SAO*, IV, appendix 40, p. 433; and appendix 39, p. 428.

17. When "Window" was being tested, it emerged that an older British night-fighter radar (Mark IV) could cope with the countermeasure, while the latest and best (Mark VII) could not. Price, *Instruments,* p. 117.

18. When a German Ju-88 landed by mistake on a British airfield in July 1944, it was found to contain a device code-named "Flensburg" that could detect, classify, and locate the signals of "Monica," the British tail-mounted warning radar. Ibid., pp. 214–215.

3. Efficiency and the Culminating Point of Success

1. The Whitehead self-propelled torpedo was demonstrated in Fiume (Austria-Hungary) in January 1867; the Royal Navy commissioned tests in 1869, purchased torpedoes in 1870, and rights of manufacture one year later. Bernard

Fitzsimons, ed., *Encyclopedia of 20th Century Weapons and Warfare*, vol. 23, p. 2508; hereafter cited *WW*.

2. See most recently Philippe Masson, *Histoire de la marine* (1983), vol. 2.

3. See *WW*, vol. 23, p. 2515.

4. See Avraham Adan, *On the Banks of the Suez* (1980), pp. 117–164.

5. The mortar, the first of all firearms, in use since the fourteenth century, continued to perform especially well against the latest weapon of land warfare. Unlike machine guns, not much good beyond a thousand yards or so and largely limited to direct fire, mortars could outrange the Sagger antitank missiles of the Egyptians and, descending from a high trajectory, their bombs could reach into the trenches and firing pits of the antitank missile and rocket crews.

6. Not tactically but at the operational level of strategy, on which see Part II. The old-style unguided hollow-charge weapons, incidentally, proved to be relatively successful if used in the same conditions that had ensured their success in World War II: street fighting with ample cover as well as in densely wooded areas.

7. "Administration" therefore includes everything done in the military realm that does not reflect enemy-specific goals of warfare or any purpose of dissuasion or intimidation. This does *not* correspond to Clausewitz's distinction: "the activities characteristic of war may be split into two main categories: *those that are merely preparations for war and war proper*," with the implication that what I call "linear logic" ("science" in his terminology) applies to the former but not to the latter; *On War*, book 2, chap. 1, p. 131. Yet surely "preparations for war" (peacetime military policy) are also shaped by enemy-specific tactical and operational purposes as well as by aims of suasion that reflect particular perceptions of the policies and military structures of specific others; such preparations are *not* exclusively shaped by enemy-autonomous priorities, including the desire to optimize decisions on the basis of "scientific" criteria. Clausewitz was the first to recognize the fundamental distinction but apparently misplaced the dividing line, circumscribing excessively the boundaries of strategy. Thus in differentiating between "the craft of the swordsmith" and the "art of fencing," he is conflating the *design* of swords, which is apt to reflect specific expectations of the adversary swords and swordsmanship to be countered, with the metallurgical *technique* of their manufacture, which should autonomously seek to maximize some generic effectiveness. *On War*, book 2, chap. 2 ("Originally the Term 'Art of War' Only Designated the Preparation of the Forces"), p. 133.

8. Those who follow such matters will have been exposed to the constant complaints heard in the U.S. Congress against "duplication," a term applied with pardonable imprecision to the concurrent acquisition of several different types of fighter aircraft, antitank weapons, and so on. Equally, the asymmetry between Warsaw Pact forces homogeneously equipped with Soviet weapons and Western forces variously equipped with their own national equipment is perpetually deplored as an unredeemed evil. Certainly the resulting diseconomies of scale loom large, while the notion that duplication, or indeed triplication, may be a positive virtue is foreign to the experience of civilian commercial practice.

9. Large-deck aircraft carriers can accommodate aircraft types that their lesser counterparts could not, but there is no such compelling reason to justify 8,000-ton destroyers (destroyers are supposed to be expendable) or 50,000-ton supply ships of which only a few can be had (aircraft carriers soon become useless without the jet fuel and weapons they bring), or ballistic-missile submarines so huge that each carries 24 very large ballistic missiles.

10. On August 25, 1943, a German Hs-293 glider bomb missed HMS *Bideford,* but two days later the same weapon damaged the *Athabaskan* and sunk the *Egret,* all in the Bay of Biscay. On September 8, 1943, the Italian battleship *Roma* (on its way to join the Allies) was sunk by German FX (a.k.a. SD-100X) guided, rocket-propelled missiles; see F. H. Hinsley et al., *British Intelligence in the Second World War* (1984), vol. 3, pp. 220, 339–340; and *WW,* vol. 16, p. 1754. The first ship-launched Soviet antiship missile (Styx) appeared in the 1950s and was fully operational by 1959, and the first Soviet air-launched antiship missile (Kangaroo) was in service by 1960; *WW,* vol. 22, p. 2419, and vol. 14, p. 1558. As if all those warnings were ignored, on October 21, 1967, the Israeli destroyer *Elat* was sunk by Egyptian Styx missiles off Port Said, stimulating worldwide interest in antiship missiles and countermeasures against them. See Edward N. Luttwak and Dan Horowitz, *The Israeli Army* (1975), p. 316.

11. For the composition of the typical American navy air wing at this writing, see *Report of the Secretary of Defense to the Congress on the FY 1987 Budget,* February 5, 1986, p. 197.

12. Long-range aircraft based on land could now span the oceans to control sealanes from above, and such aerial ''cruisers'' have been proposed. As for the conveyance of landing forces, large, nonnuclear transport submarines are sufficiently economical to have been seriously considered even for commercial cargoes.

13. Alistair Horne, *The Price of Glory* (1962), pp. 327–328.

14. Pierre Sergent, *Je ne regrette rien* (1972), pp. 149–150.

4. The Coming Together of Opposites

1. *SAO,* I, 152.

2. Ibid., I, 182.

3. Martin Gilbert, *Finest Hour* (1983), pp. 1103, 1105.

4. *SAO,* I, 182, 184–185.

5. Ibid., IV, appendix 39, p. 428.

6. Ibid., I, 347.

7. Arthur Harris, head of the RAF's Bomber Command during the important years, and possibly the most underrated of the Allied war leaders, included a fine analysis of the question in his memoirs: *Bomber Offensive* (1947), pp. 220–234.

8. *The Army Air Forces in World War II* (1949), II, 682–684, 702–704.

9. The architect of German war production at the time, Albert Speer, has argued that the attack could have been decisive if it had persisted. But he is wrong, for then decentralization would have ensued. See Speer, *Inside the Third Reich* (1970), pp. 284–287.

10. For a brief overview, in historiographical retrospect, see David Mac-Isaac, *Strategic Bombing in World War Two* (1976).

11. The terminology of the balance and weights of power seems to have first appeared in writing in the *Storia d'Italia* of the Florentine envoy and scholar Francesco Guicciardini (1483–1540); it was probably already in use among princes, diplomats, and condottieri of the previous generation.

5. The Technical Level

1. Except for elite and higher-echelon support forces, the Soviet army now consists entirely of armor-mechanized forces. See Appendix 2.

2. Firearms first reached Japan in 1542 and were soon produced locally; by 1575 Oda Nobunaga's 3,000 select arquebusiers (he had 10,000) destroyed Takeda Katsuyori's cavalry, the power of the Takedas, and a whole way of warfare at the battle of Nagashino in Mikawa. See George Sansom, *A History of Japan* (1961), pp. 263–264, 287. There is a detailed but unreferenced account of Nagashino in S. R. Turnbull, *The Samurai* (1977), pp. 158–160. Swift as they were in equipping commoners with the new weapons, the samurai themselves continued to wear swords, not pistols, until that mark of privilege was abolished along with the entire social class after the Meiji restoration of 1868. The Mamelukes of Egypt resisted firearms more rigidly and would not even have commoner-musketeers serving alongside them when they rode to battle. A comparable modern example, more in the Mameluke than the samurai mold, is the stubborn resistance of pilot-dominated aviation bureaucracies to the introduction of remotely piloted air vehicles. It was not until the Israelis employed them with spectacular effect in 1982 (resistance of their pilots being weaker because of the exigencies of chronic warfare) that such vehicles began to be more widely employed—in forms that had been available for decades.

3. A. M. Low, *Musket to Machine-Gun* (1942), pp. 66–67; Michael Howard, *The Franco-Prussian War* (1968), p. 36.

4. See the interesting discussion in William McElwee, *The Art of War* (1974), pp. 141–146.

5. Robert Jungk, *Brighter than a Thousand Suns* (1964), pp. 106–107.

6. This was certainly true of the "Strategic Defense Initiative" announced by President Reagan in March 1983, following a decision that did not reflect government-wide, authoritative, scientific advice. It seems that science alone escapes all attempts at "scientific" decision making.

7. The Operational Level

1. In German *operativ Kriegskunst;* the Russian *operativnoye iskusstvo* is clearly derivative. The "operations" that occurs in American military-administrative usage, as in "European Theater of Operations," merely means combat activities in general, tactical and strategic as well as in between. Since the publication of my article "The Operational Level of War" in 1981, the phrase has received wide circulation in American military circles owing to its subsequent adoption in the basic doctrinal manual of the U.S. Army (*FM 100-5*). Basil Liddell Hart attempted to introduce the term "grand tactics," of

identical meaning; but it did not gain official acceptance or wide circulation in British and American military literature.

2. A contemporary example is the American M-1 tank, which among other things has an innovative gas-turbine engine that offers excellent acceleration at the expense of unrefueled range. By the time the new tank came into service, the operational doctrine of the army had changed considerably, and while tactical mobility—the ability to dash around the battlefield and climb steep grades—remained desirable, it was operational mobility (autonomous range) that had become essential; for this a plain diesel engine would have been superior. Similarly, the new tank also has excellent protection in a new kind of composite armor, but in accordance with old tactical priorities, much of the armor is distributed in the frontal aspect, at the expense of all-around protection, which the new operational doctrine makes more important.

3. Exemplified by the exceedingly high-risk but highly successful crossing of the Suez Canal, to encircle the Egyptian "Third Army" (actually a three-division corps) on the far side, even though Egyptian control of much of the near side (by the "Second Army") remained uncontested. As always in relational maneuver, the starting point was the appreciation of an enemy vulnerability, in this case rather subtle, namely the inability of the Egyptian command to control its forces across the entire front in a timely fashion.

4. Not all officers in Fighter Command were satisfied with that; some advocated an operational-level response. Specifically, Squadron Leader Douglas Bader and Group Commander Trafford Leigh-Mallory advocated the concerted engagement of German bomber formations *after* they had dropped their bombs, by complete groups (which could not assemble in time for prebombing interception) instead of prior interception by individual squadrons. The method was designed to exploit a German limitation, the short endurance of the best fighter of the Luftwaffe, the single-engine Bf-109. It was their calculation that results per fighter would be better, for by then most Bf-109s could no longer maneuver freely for lack of fuel, if they were still around to escort the bombers at all. See most recently John Terraine, *The Right of the Line* (1985), pp. 198–205.

5. This is what happened to the Egyptian high command in the October war of 1973, when the Israelis crossed the Suez Canal to begin their encirclement maneuver. The initial crossing, on the night of October 15, was duly reported but dismissed as a mere raid that would soon be followed by an evacuation; and indeed less than 3,000 men were initially involved, with few tanks and even those sent across on rafts. It was not till the 17th that it was appreciated in Cairo that the Israelis were continuing to reinforce their bridgehead; by then, however, a pontoon bridge had been built and a full division had crossed over. The Israelis were sending out armored teams in all directions to attack antiaircraft missile sites (so their presence was reported in a wide arc) but mainly seeking to advance north toward Ismailia, to widen the bridgehead and thereby cut off the forces of the Egyptian Second Army on the Sinai side of the Canal from their rear services on the Egyptian side. In spite of the great quantity of misleading reports it was receiving (generated by Israeli combat teams moving in the soft rear-area to attack missile sites), by October 18 the Egyptian high

command nevertheless interpreted the Israeli intention *of two days earlier* quite correctly and duly moved to secure the Ismailia sector. But by the 17th, with another Israeli armored division across the Canal, the Israelis had decided to call off the northward thrust and were instead advancing in the opposite direction, to cut off the Third Army in the southern sector around the city of Suez. By the time the Egyptian high command caught up with the change, on October 19, its expectations had been overturned twice, and nothing seemed certain: imagining that Cairo itself was in imminent danger, it sent the available reserves to shield the city, instead of attacking the Israelis converging on the city of Suez. See the documented account in Hanoch Bartov, *Dado* (1981), pp. 482ff.

6. As noted earlier in another context, the Soviet Union had the necessary depth in facing the German blitzkrieg, whereas Poland and France did not, and certainly not Belgium or the Netherlands. Actually, Stalin's high command (the Stavka) did not try to exploit the Soviet Union's advantage in sheer size during the 1941 campaign, in which the Germans were stubbornly resisted all the way east as they advanced toward the Leningrad and Moscow line; by the summer of 1942 the lesson had been learned, and when the Germans advanced again, this time in a southwestern direction toward Stalingrad and the Caucasian oil fields, they were outraced by the retreating Soviet forces, whose strength was thus preserved to rebuild a solid new front.

7. The effect was far more psychological than physical for the Wehrmacht in the blitzkrieg years 1939–1942, because its deep-penetration columns mostly consisted of motorcycles, armored cars, very light tanks, half-tracked carriers, artillery tractors, a great many trucks, and not many battle tanks (one 100–150 tank regiment per Panzer division). The Soviet army's columns, by contrast, would contain a solid phalanx of armor, with as many as 322 tanks in first-line tank divisions.

8. Theater Strategy I

1. At present, the 30 Soviet first-line tank and motor-rifle divisions in East Germany (19 divisions), Czechoslovakia (5), Hungary (4), and Poland (2) include 10,500 tanks; the number of infantry combat carriers is larger. IISS, *Military Balance, 1985–86*, p. 26.

2. It is assumed throughout that East German and other Warsaw Pact forces, along with minor Soviet units simulating complete formations, would be employed to present a threat by demonstrations and feints in those segments of the front where no major Soviet offensive thrust is intended; in due course, the deception would be unmasked, but by then the fight should be over. (That, incidentally, would be the safer use of troops of doubtful loyalty.) At present, the number of antitank guided weapon launchers that would be deployed on the central front upon mobilization and reinforcement is some 2,100, and that number includes forces in Norway and Denmark as well (ibid., p. 186). If the present mobile forces of the Alliance (armored, mechanized, and armored cavalry) were reorganized as missile infantry, they might yield some 300,000 frontline troops with 60,000 launchers at most (there would still be need for

artillery, antiaircraft, and engineer forces and for service units)—not enough for the attrition requirement under realistic tactical exchange-ratio assumptions, unless there are also barriers and fortifications much more costly than the missile launchers.

3. Exemplified by General Maurice G. Gamelin, chief of the French general staff at the outbreak of World War II. See the comments in Robert J. Young, *In Command of France* (1978), pp. 48–51.

4. Many intercontinental warheads and bombs are in the range of one million tons of TNT equivalence ("megaton"), while most battlefield devices are in the range of one thousand tons of TNT ("kiloton"), or one-fourteenth of the energy yield of the Hiroshima bomb, one-nineteenth of the Nagasaki bomb. Blast, heat, and immediate radiation effects are commensurate, and except in the case of enhanced-radiation ("neutron" bomb) devices, it is usually the blast effects that set effectiveness limits against ground-force targets.

5. As it happens, the inertia caused by contradictory inhibitions keeps in Alliance service one of the weapons of the early 1950s, the 40-kilometer-range Honest John rocket first deployed in 1953 and still retained by the Greek and Turkish armies. See IISS, *Military Balance, 1985–86*, pp. 85–86.

6. The present policy was inaugurated in 1967, to replace "massive retaliation," which provided for a much quicker reliance on nuclear weapons. Massive retaliation, repudiated by the United States at the outset of the Kennedy Administration, was retained as Alliance policy at the insistence of West Germany and other member states until 1967, when the Military Committee of NATO finally agreed to the new policy of "flexible response" (officially promulgated in 1968, as NATO Document MC 14/3) *and* promised to provide the additional forces required for a "stalwart" nonnuclear defense. In a large literature, see e.g. Raymond E. Burrel, *Strategic Nuclear Parity and NATO Defense Doctrine* (1978), p. 13.

9. Theater Strategy II

1. Jochen Löser, *Weder rot noch tot* (1982).

2. Franz Uhle-Wettler, *Leichte Infanterie im Atomzeitalter* (1966). A widely influential prescription for a spongelike "amorphous" defense is contained in Guy Brossollet, *Essai sur la non-bataille* (1975), a seminal work.

3. Steven L. Canby, "Territorial Defense in Central Europe" (1980), and many other works by Canby.

4. William Scotter, "A Role for the Non-Mechanized Infantry" (1980).

5. In all schemes, appropriately decentralized supply arrangements would be required. Stocks would have to be much larger, to allow their distribution in small depots and caches throughout the zone of combat, instead of the present supply-as-needed arrangements, whereby truck columns and fuel pipelines would supply the forces at the front from large central depots and tank farms. In all schemes, command and control would also have to be decentralized, in varying degrees according to the specifics of each scheme.

6. Perceptions of automaton-like rigidity may reflect nothing more than the process of dehumanization of the enemy that attends all conflict. Thus during

World War II the knowledge that the German army's greatest strength was its exceptional flexibility coexisted with images of German officers and men as martinets and robots. In reality, of course, the German army allowed great latitude to its junior officers and NCOs; in its command and control, hierarchic authority smoothly gave way to operational necessity in a way that not even the American, let alone the British, army could emulate. It does seem, however, that the Soviet army is afflicted by rigidity at the lower levels of command at least, where orders are obeyed whether appropriate or not. This reflects neither innate cultural limitations nor official doctrine (which of course calls for much initiative at all levels) but rather the de facto balance of institutional incentives: even if successful initiative is duly rewarded, this is of scant effect because penalties for errors that follow from unauthorized actions are systematically greater than penalties for counterproductive obedience. Combat in Afghanistan has predictably resulted in official demands for "more initiative." For a comparative analysis of the institutional framework, see Richard A. Gabriel, *The Antagonists* (1984).

7. Laqueur, *Guerrilla*, pp. 202–238. For a detailed assessment of the effectiveness of the French resistance in accomplishing a specific task of exceptional urgency, in the favorable post-Overlord conditions of June 1944, see Max Hastings, *Das Reich* (1981).

8. For a participant's revealing account, see Stefan Korbonski, *Fighting Warsaw* (1968).

9. In Yugoslavia the usual divergence between community protection and ideological resistance was particularly acute: the Serbian nationalist Cetniks were virtually incapacitated by the German reprisal policy and eventually driven into forms of collaboration.

10. Historically, the needs of point defense have restrained the *rate* of conquest of military empires, before eventually setting final limits to their sustainable expansion, as the quantum of average unrest in some part or other continued to accumulate. The Roman rule, more or less, was to pacify one province and obtain its taxes (or recruits) before conquering another, but, even so, security requirements grew because the secular tranquillity of some provinces was accompanied by recurrent uprisings in others. Some such calculation must have motivated the injunction against further conquest in the testament of Augustus. Recorded by Tacitus, *Annals* I.11, and criticized in his *Agricola* XIII.

11. This was the case long before the advent of modern logistics, radios, and helicopters. The Romans, whose physical mobility was not superior to insurgent enemies, already derived a theater-strategic advantage from their signal-tower networks whose smoke (day) and flame (night) signals relayed warnings and orders; from their well-made roads, whose full use by insurgents was denied by road forts; and from their granaries, also fortified, from which troops could obtain food and fodder only available to insurgents after time-consuming sieges.

12. The Germans during World War II in many occupied areas, notably within the Soviet Union, did receive local support. In some places, pro-German militias were sufficiently effective to replace the reprisal policy, as for

example in the "Autonomous Administrative District" of Lokot, in the Orel-Kursk region south of Bryansk, which contained some 1.7 million inhabitants and was defended by a purely Russian militia some 10,000 strong during 1942–43. Here the basis of collaboration was political (anticommunism), and the Lokot militia, jointly created by General Rudolf Schmidt of the Second Panzer Army and a Russian engineer (later replaced by the notorious Bronislav Kaminsky), was known as the Russkaya Osvoboditelnaya Narodnaya Armiya (Russian Liberation Army). It was a crucial element of the bargain that the SS was forbidden to operate in the area, where the Germans agreed to refrain from any reprisals for such guerrilla attacks as still took place. See M. Cooper, *The Phantom War* (1979), pp. 112–113. Such arrangements, though usually less formal, became common in German-occupied areas and were vehemently advocated by many Wehrmacht officers; see H. K. Guenther, "Der Kampf Gegen Die Partisanen" (1968). They were opposed just as vehemently by the SS, who denied the need to arm "subhumans"—until the worsening war situation and manpower shortage induced the SS to reverse its attitude. It still opposed militias but only because it wanted to recruit all available men for its many ethnic units.

13. This is the criticism expressed against the guerrilla (Jagdkampf) element in the Austrian defense-in-depth scheme that is now official policy. See R. S. Rietzler, "Erfahrungen aus kleinkrieg und Jagdkampf" (1972), II, 155–156.

14. Clausewitz listed the necessary conditions for a successful guerrilla resistance as follows: "(1) The war must be fought in the interior of the country. (2) It must not be decided by a single stroke. (3) The theater of operations must be fairly large. (4) The national character must be suited to that type of war. (5) The country must be rough and inaccessible, because of mountains, or forests, marshes, or the local methods of cultivation" (*On War,* book 6, chap. 26, p. 480). Guerrilla resistance in West Germany might satisfy conditions 1, 2, and 3 but certainly not 4 or 5.

15. Luttwak, *The Grand Strategy of the Roman Empire*, pp. 159–170.

16. Soft-sided, low-rise suburban houses and commercial buildings, unlike traditional village stone-built cottages, cannot serve as physical obstacles against tanks; but they do provide a complex texture of cover for defending forces moving among them, allowing them to direct intersecting fire on roads and streets from concealed positions. And armored vehicles cannot smash their way through buildings to open their own avenues without great peril: modern constructions with thin floors over room-deep basements make excellent tank traps.

10. Theater Strategy III

1. These deep-attack schemes include Follow-on Forces Attack (sometimes confused with the Rogers Plan), which is strictly nonnuclear, envisages attacks across a wide-range spectrum, and requires that Soviet units on the move be attacked also; AirLand Battle 2000 and AirLand 2000, theoretical concepts discussed in U.S. army circles, which emphasize attacks in depth coordinated at the corps level; Deep Strike, primarily a nuclear scheme, but

which has a nonnuclear variant that stresses the employment of ballistic missiles to deliver submunitions on fixed targets; and Counter Air 90, which prescribes attacks on Soviet airfields.

2. The most economical missiles for the attack of larger fixed targets with submunitions (airbases, supply dumps, railway yards), as well as targets that are very strongly fortified (command centers), would be high-trajectory *ballistic missiles,* identical to the weapons employed for nuclear delivery. Indeed, the most economical of remedies would be to redeploy in Europe older models of American intercontinental ballistic missiles no longer kept in service for nuclear missions (Titans, Minuteman I's), duly converted for shorter ranges with much larger, nonnuclear payloads. But the peacetime stationing of such weapons in Europe could be criticized as an obstacle to arms-control negotiations, owing to identification problems. When launched from any location, moreover, their trajectories could easily be misinterpreted as presaging nuclear attacks, if only for a few minutes. Finally, large ballistic missiles, whether conversions or newly produced, could be economical only if they were stationed in fixed housing, and then they would be vulnerable to varied forms of attack, nonnuclear as well as nuclear, even if fortified.

Aerodynamic *cruise missiles* with large nonnuclear warheads would be most efficient to attack small hard targets, such as bridges and viaducts. Cargo cruise missiles with submunitions would be as effective (if possibly more costly on a kilo-delivered basis) as ballistic missiles to attack all larger, "softer" targets, such as supply dumps, railway yards, and airbases. One issue in contention is the cost of one-sortie cruise missiles as opposed to manned aircraft capable of an unknown number of sorties before interception or other loss (accidents multiply in high-tempo operations). Another is the vulnerability of cruise missiles to air defenses (including balloon barrages around high-value targets); while presenting very small radar and visual targets (even smaller in "stealth" models), these pilotless aircraft are incapable of evasive maneuvers, as manned aircraft are. See Fred N. Wikner, "Interdicting Fixed Targets with Conventional Weapons" (1983). Richard K. Betts, ed., *Cruise Missiles* (1981), pp. 184–211. Steven L. Canby, "New Conventional Force Technology and the NATO–Warsaw Pact Balance, I," *New Technology and Western Security Policy* (1985), pp. 7–24, and Donald R. Cotter, idem, pp. 25–39.

3. The fundamental cause of the defensive advantage was precisely the relative ease with which trenchlines could be reinforced by troops marching from the nearest railway siding, albeit under artillery fire, as compared to the multiple obstacles in the path of attackers also on foot who were trying to reach the front of those same trenchlines. The initial, tactical-level purpose of the tank, armored against machine-gun fire and provided with tracks to cross shell craters and crush barbed wire, was specifically to overcome this asymmetry. It was only later that the tank's operational-level potential deep behind the front was recognized.

4. Some 220,200 of the total of 399,600 sorties flown by the U.S. Air Force during the entire Korean war were classified as interdiction strikes—a huge effort, which sometimes helped in containing Chinese offensives but mostly meant that, instead of employing a thousand porters in a given case, the Chinese had to employ twice that number. Interdiction claimed an even larger

proportion of a much greater number of sorties during the Vietnam war, with results even less impressive. For the Korean war statistics and the Vietnam estimate, see William D. White, *U.S. Tactical Air Power* (1974), p. 68.

5. Quite some time ago, before much additional road construction, it was estimated that even if the "flow capacity" of the road and rail nets from the western Soviet Union to West Germany were 90 percent destroyed, and then kept destroyed in spite of repair, the remaining 10 percent would still suffice to sustain a full-strength Soviet offensive. The study is cited in Alain C. Enthoven and K. Wayne Smith, *How Much Is Enough?* (1971), p. 222.

6. For a positive view of what can be done, see Donald R. Cotter, "New Conventional Force Technology and the NATO-Warsaw Pact Balance, II" in *New Technology and Western Security Policy* (1985), pp. 25–38. For a pessimistic view, see Steven L. Canby, idem, pp. 7–24.

7. The notion that very small, and therefore economical, hollow-charge bomblets or self-forging fragment devices can be lethal against otherwise well-armored battle tanks, since they would strike at their thin topside armor, is reminiscent of the belief that torpedoes would be effective because warship armor was thin or absent below the waterline. Just as that weakness was remedied as soon as the attempt was made to exploit it, so now spaced-armor roofs are being made ready for tanks in a typical broad-capability response to a narrow attack.

8. Manpower as well as money would be needed for any additional ground forces, and at this writing it seems that the manning of even the current array of forces is prejudiced by demographic trends. On the other hand, funds used to develop and build deep-attack systems could serve to equip more powerfully forces now in existence but poorly armed. Actually, critics fear that Alliance parliaments will not vote extra funds to pay for the new devices, so that the money would instead be subtracted from the forces now fielded.

9. This number includes 51 tank and 142 motor-rifle (mechanized) divisions; the usual 200 count also includes the 7 airborne divisions. See Appendix 2.

11. Nonstrategies

1. This was "tactical" airpower in the current English-language official terminology, which embraces all forms of airpower that impinge on warfare in a given theater—as opposed to "strategic" airpower, aimed at homeland populations, industry, and the state apparatus, both civil and military. Tactical airpower therefore includes the operational modes of "air superiority," performed by fighters and interceptor-fighters for command of the air over theaters of war; "close support," performed by fighters (acting as fighter-bombers), light bombers, and specialized armored aircraft, to provide firepower directly to assist the ground forces; "battlefield interdiction," performed by fighters and light bombers, to attack enemy ground forces in the immediate rear of the battle zones; and "interdiction," performed by larger fighters acting as fighter-bombers and specialized, high-speed light bombers, to attack infrastructures and forces in the depth of the theater of war.

2. Alfred Thayer Mahan, *Naval Strategy* (1911), p. 6, as cited by Philip A.

Crowl in Peter Paret, ed., *Makers of Modern Strategy* (1986), p. 458. Crowl shows (pp. 456–457) that Mahan derived the concept from Henri Jomini (1779–1869)—thus one simplificator borrowed from another.

3. The absolute priority accorded to this concept in the post-Mahan submarine era was duly criticized after World War I. See John H. Maurer, "American Naval Concentration and the German Battle Fleet, 1900–1918" (1983), pp. 169–177.

4. For obvious reasons, many institutional writings fall into this category. See, most recently, *The Maritime Strategy*, published by the U.S. Naval Institute (1986) and containing articles by the Secretary of the Navy, the Chief of Naval Operations, and the Commandant of the Marine Corps. The titulature of most scholarly works avoids the misleading usage—thus Herbert Rosinski's *The Development of Naval Thought* (1977), and L. W. Martin's classic *The Sea in Modern Strategy* (1977). Hervé Couteau-Begarie's important study, *La puissance maritime: Castex et la strategie navale* (1985), does include the offending term in the subtitle, but his formulation is equivalent to Rosinski's (*la pensée stratégique navale*). One famous exception is Bernard Brodie's *A Layman's Guide to Naval Strategy* (1942), later republished in revised form as *A Guide to Naval Strategy* (1965), whose contents, however, are largely technical, tactical, and operational.

5. For the prophet of autonomous airpower, Giulio Douhet, targeting actually constituted the substance of "aerial strategy"; see Barry D. Watts, *The Foundations of U.S. Air Doctrine* (1984), p. 6. There is a new analysis of Douhet's thought in Ferrucci Botti and Virgilio Ilari, *Il pensiero militare italiano* (1985), pp. 89–139.

6. See *The Maritime Strategy*, p. 13 (Admiral James D. Watkins, Chief of Naval Operations). The intent clearly is to justify a high priority for naval forces, notwithstanding the marginal vulnerability of the Soviet Union to sea denial, amphibious attack, or naval air action in any major theater of war.

7. Mahan, *The Influence of Sea Power upon History, 1660–1783* and *The Influence of Sea Power upon the French Revolution and Empire, 1793–1812*, and many ephemera. For intellectual sources, see Robert Seager, *Alfred Thayer Mahan* (1977); and more recently, Crowl's review, pp. 449–462.

8. Mahan was actually quite inconsistent in using the term *sea power,* which he claimed as his own original contribution to strategic thought; see Couteau-Begarie, p. 45; and Crowl, p. 451.

9. Gerald S. Graham, *The Politics of Naval Supremacy* (1965).

10. For the sequence, see Mahan, *The Influence, 1660–1783*, pp. 222–223, as cited in Crowl, pp. 451–452.

11. The title of a World War II bestseller, Alexander P. De Seversky's *Victory through Air Power* (1942), actually a collection of articles, encapsulates the Douhet/Mitchell/Trenchard prediction in some of its chapter titles: "The Twilight of Sea Power," "The Emancipation of Air Power," "Organization for Air Supremacy."

12. For this divergence in brief, see Barry D. Watts, *The Foundations of U.S. Air Doctrine* (1984), pp. 5–10.

13. Mitchell did not share this view: "a Bombardment formation . . . is

certain to suffer heavy casualties if subjected to incessant attack by a greatly superior pursuit [fighter] force." See Watts, *Foundations*, p. 7, citing a pre-1923 text.

14. Not the Luftwaffe's bombers, however, of which it was demanded that they should be capable of divebombing as well. Their structural strength and acceleration did allow some maneuverability—at the expense of range and weapon loads.

15. At night, until effective radar-equipped night fighters became available around 1943, each fighter had to be individually directed by comparative radar location until it entered into visual contact with its target, precluding mass interception—though even radarless fighters did operate by squadrons at night, if illumination was provided by moonlight, searchlights, or fires caused by bombing raids.

16. In persuasively refuting the widespread misconception that the Luftwaffe leaders in their chronic disunity actually rejected the thesis and were content with a role ancillary to the ground forces, Williamson Murray, *Strategy for Defeat* (1983), pp. 8–9, 19–21, overstates his case: strategic bombing was seen as one important mission, but no more than that. Murray cites the four-engine He-177 as unambiguous evidence of strategic intent (p. 9), but it received a low priority; also, its extreme design complications were imposed by the divebombing requirement, quite unnecessary for strategic purposes.

17. As the postwar U.S. Strategic Bombing Survey ascertained; the results that bombing did achieve remain a subject of great controversy. See e.g. David MacIsaac, *Strategic Bombing in World War Two* (1976).

18. As noted e.g. by Bernard Brodie, *Strategy in the Missile Age* (1959), p. 73; Watts, p. 39, n. 1, cites Brodie's 1952 memorandum entitled "The Heritage of Douhet."

19. Bernard Brodie, *The Absolute Weapon* (1946) p. 76, typically with a reservation that others then overlooked: in publicizing the notion of deterrence, already in the air, he described it as the *chief* purpose of the military establishment, not the only purpose, adding "It can have *almost* no other purpose."

20. Positive suasion (compellence) is admittedly more difficult to apply than negative suasion (deterrence)—one of the many elucidations found in Thomas C. Schelling, *The Strategy of Conflict* (1960, 1980), pp. 195–199.

21. See Edward N. Luttwak, "Perceptions of Military Force and US Defense Policy" (1977).

22. Explored in many configurations by Thomas C. Schelling, *Arms and Influence* (1966).

23. The crucial words in the "massive retaliation" speech of Secretary of State John Foster Dulles (Department of State Bulletin, January 25, 1954).

12. The Scope of Grand Strategy

1. The quality of empires is in their tenacity. For one view of Soviet conduct, see Edward N. Luttwak, *The Grand Strategy of the Soviet Union* (1983).

13. Armed Suasion

1. In an early use of the term, the retention of the Pacific Fleet at the forward base of Pearl Harbor after May 1940 was explicitly described as a "deterrent." But the fleet could deter no more than any other force can by its mere existence. The Japanese chose not to be dissuaded, preferring instead to attack the force that had provoked them by seemingly threatening their invasion plans for Southeast Asia. Although a laxity of language endures, much has been learned from the episode, as noted later.

2. The outcome of wars more protracted than single episodes of combat is another matter, for within them the paradoxical logic tends to reverse the effect of combat outcomes, as the victors encounter new antagonisms and the losers attract the support of those loath to see them totally defeated. In this also the two world wars of our century were atypical, owing to the rigidities introduced by the political character of the antagonists; accordingly, the alliance-breaking and alliance-making reversals could only take place after the end of the war had brought political change. The current Iraq-Iran war comforms to the classical model of intraconflict reversals, seen in the abrupt alterations of the respective arms-supply relationships.

3. That was one of the Arab accusations against Israel in the wake of the June 1967 war. Actually the Israelis did maintain an exceptional degree of secrecy whose effect was indeed to devalue their strength, but only until the prewar crisis of May 1967. Then, seeing how little dissuasion they had obtained, the Israelis hurriedly staged briefings and unit visits. It appears that their normal practice reflected an unthinking extension of operational-level security to the level of grand strategy, within which their strict secrecy concealed the strength that might have dissuaded aggression.

4. Among other things, the number of Italian divisions was increased by the simple expedient of reorganizing three-regiment divisions into two-regiment divisions. Inside the army, the tension between political stage management and professional war preparation was acute. See Ferrucio Botti and Virgilio Ilari, *Il pensiero militare italiano dal primo al secondo dopoguerra* (1985), pp. 161–271.

5. As in the first three-man orbital mission, obtained by squeezing a mere passenger into a two-man craft. For Khrushchev's deception policy and its results, see A. L. Horelick and M. Rush, *Strategic Power and Soviet Foreign Policy* (1966).

6. Now that overt purposes of deterrence have been made fashionable by Great Power discourse, they are much more likely to be invoked in rationalizing the upkeep of military forces.

7. A judgment is implied about the gravity of small-power wars such as the 1912 Balkan war and the 1932–1938 Chaco war.

8. In fact, one more reason for the failure to anticipate the December 7, 1941, preemptive attack was that American estimates of the power of the fleet were quite pessimistic. In the words of a participating observer: "I thought it would be utterly stupid for the Japanese to attack the United States at Pearl Harbor. We could not have materially affected their control of the waters they

wanted to control whether or not the battleships were sunk at Pearl Harbor." Testimony of Captain Vincent R. Murphy before Congress, *Pearl Harbor Hearings,* part 26, p. 207, as cited in Ronald H. Spector, *Eagle against the Sun* (1985), p. 3.

9. Its counterpart, "first strike," is a contraction of "would-be disarming first strike" (aimed at enemy nuclear forces) as opposed to the "first use" of nuclear weapons, not against nuclear forces but in reaction to a nonnuclear invasion of Europe that cannot otherwise be resisted. These distinctions were first elucidated in the celebrated RAND study by Wohlstetter, Hoffman, Lutz, and Rowen, *Selection and Use of Strategic Air Bases* (1954), and first publicized in Albert Wohlstetter, "The Delicate Balance of Terror," *Foreign Affairs* (1959). Not coincidentally, Roberta Wohlstetter, Albert's wife, had conducted a very careful analysis of the Pearl Harbor episode, later published as *Pearl Harbor* (1962).

10. Mostly masked by pieties (it was the Roman consul C. Flaminius who proclaimed the "freedom of all Greeks") but sometimes brutally direct, as when the Seleucid Antiochus Epiphanes IV was curtly ordered out of Egypt and Judea in 168 B.C. by C. Laenas Popilius, who confronted him as he was advancing with his troops. Popilius had no forces with him, only the text of a senate resolution that offered a stark choice between immediate retreat and war with Rome. Antiochus asked for time to consider the matter, but Popilius traced a circle in the sand around his feet with a stick and demanded an immediate reply. The humiliation was intense and the loss huge, for Egypt's great wealth was within his grasp, but Antiochus obeyed: the Romans had just defeated and ruined one Hellenistic king, Perseus of Macedon, and they might easily choose to destroy another. Presumably the episode, vividly described by Polybius (book 29), would fall within the current definition of "compellence."

11. These include the attempt to assassinate President Chun Doo Hwan of South Korea and his most important civil and military officials in Rangoon on October 9, 1983, in which three Korean ministers and fifteen other officials were killed and many more wounded. After that episode, North Korea's declared policy changed, and intermittent negotiations continue at this writing.

12. For example, in American "strategic" force planning, second-strike-capability requirements are calculated on the assumption of an all-out Soviet first strike, launched against American forces that are at a normal state of alert and therefore only partially available, with many missile submarines in port and few bombers on runway alert. Similarly, Soviet forces are assumed to be fully operational, whereas American forces are assumed to be further diminished, after attack losses, by predicted malfunctions. In terms of ballistic missiles, cumulative "degradation factors" for the launch, boost phase, flight, warhead separation, terminal trajectory, and detonation stages may amount to 40 percent or more. Thus the same inventory of weapons that appears grossly excessive to others may be just barely adequate in the skewed net assessment of prudent force planners, who calculate conservatively both postattack survival and subsequent malfunctions. The often-cited "overkill" calculation simply ignores the cumulative effects of prior attack, availability limits, and malfunctions, and further assumes that only cities are to be attacked, in its

derisive comparison of full weapon inventories with the much smaller number of targeted cities.

13. For mid-1985, the IISS estimated 10,174 warheads for the United States and 9,987 for the Soviet Union. *Military Balance, 1985–86,* p. 180.

14. The technically inclined reader will recognize the purely technical error: even if the American intercontinental delivery platforms were reduced to a dozen missile submarines, some one hundred bombers, and as many land-based missiles presumably mobile, a counterforce offensive against them could still find use for as many Soviet warheads as desired, for area-wide "barrage" attacks against mobile-missile deployment zones, the air space around airfields (to catch bombers after takeoff), and even the open ocean around suspected missile-submarine locations.

14. Harmony and Disharmony in War

1. A. Hillgruber, *Hitlers Strategie* (1965), pp. 190–192.

2. The British Intelligence estimate of February 17, 1941, concluded that because of the preparations that would be needed for desert warfare, "a considerable time must elapse before any serious counter-offensive can be launched from Tripoli"; see F. H. Hinsley et al., *British Intelligence in the Second World War* (1979), p. 389. This opinion was shared by the German Army High Command.

3. Martin van Creveld, *Supplying War* (1977), p. 139.

4. For the OKH view as recorded by Chief of Staff Franz Halder, see Larry H. Addington, *The Blitzkrieg Era and the German General Staff* (1971), pp. 162–163.

5. Van Creveld, *Supplying War,* pp. 184–185.

6. What follows is based on Ronald Lewin, *Life and Death of the Afrika Korps* (1967), and David Irving, *The Trail of the Fox* (1977), pp. 67ff. (highly colored but accurate).

7. Addington, *Blitzkrieg Era,* p. 165.

8. Hinsley, *British Intelligence,* pp. 389–393.

9. Rommel's willful disorganization of his own formations did not extend down to the tactical level, over which he had little influence: while the British fought by separate infantry, artillery, and tank units, the Germans fought by mixed taskforces of all three. By elegant teamwork, when the task forces were attacked by British tanks, they engaged them with antitank guns well shielded in the terrain. The German tanks themselves were reserved for flanking moves and mainly for attacks against "soft" motor columns and infantry, in which their technical superiority would be decisive. The classic description is in F. W. von Mellenthin, *Panzer Battles* (1971), pp. 71ff.

10. Otherwise he would have recognized that the forces that could be supplied across the 1,500 miles from Tripoli to the Suez Canal were too small to defeat the British, while forces large enough for the task could not be supplied. See van Creveld, *Supplying War,* pp. 181–201.

11. Many historians have criticized Hitler's refusal to send reinforcements to Rommel in the summer of 1942, pointing out that large German forces were

sent *after* Rommel's defeat at El Alamein. But then the German purpose was no longer to conquer Egypt but rather to keep Italy as an ally in the war, by preventing the fall of Tunisia, the last North African territory in Axis hands opposite Sicily. Unlike a conquest of Egypt, this was a goal of importance at the level of grand strategy.

12. The ability of the North Vietnamese to redeploy their forces on foot from one end of Vietnam to the other was mechanically much inferior to the American–South Vietnamese ability to do so by road transport, air, and sea. On the other hand, elusiveness gave them the initiative at each remove, so that they were not inferior in their ability to concentrate forces for any one engagement. Their ability to reinforce an ongoing engagement was much inferior, to be sure, but in their style of war, prepared engagements were followed by dispersal.

13. The only documents ever published on the subject are contained in Hanoch Bartov, *Dado* (1981); for the divisional counts, see the October 8 graphics.

14. Most of the strongholds of the so-called Bar-Lev line were unmanned. On October 6, 1973, there were some 450 soldiers scattered in the 14 manned strongholds from one end of the Suez Canal to the other, a density of some 4 soldiers per kilometer. The Israeli defense plan ("Dovecot") relied instead on the 290 tanks and 14 artillery batteries of the Sinai standing division. Bartov, *Dado,* October 6 graphics.

15. See Barton Whaley, *Codeword Barbarossa* (1973).

16. See e.g. Bartov, *Dado,* pp. 188–217.

17. For a detailed account, see Avraham Adan, *On the Banks of the Suez* (1980), pp. 91–164. See also the excellent analysis in Martin van Creveld, *Command in War* (1985), pp. 218–231.

Index

Abadan, 139
Administration in military realm, 40
Aerial photography, 106, 148
Afghanistan, 136, 264n6
Aircraft: "strategic," 90n; heavier-than-air, 164; in World War II, 164–168; nuclear strike, 203. *See also* Bombardment; Fighters
Aircraft carriers, 46, 77
Air war, 8, 70, 165; systematic bombing strategy, 55–57, 62; interdiction, 145–146; enemy reaction, 145–146; tactical airpower, 156; paradoxical logic, 157; targeting, 160; bombing strategy, 26–27, 164–168; as defense, 165–168; radar, 166; of attrition, 167
Albania, 192, 193
Alliance, the (NATO), 71; defense of West Germany, 82, 109–111, 127, 129, 130, 143, 152; defense of Europe (central theater), 115–118, 120, 143, 146, 151; nuclear weapons and forces, 121, 122, 150, 202, 203; nonnuclear forces/defense, 124–125, 199, 202–203; and Soviet response to defense strategy, 136–140; technical countermeasures, 144; airpower and defenses, 144, 202; deep-attack strategy, 148, 150, 154, 155; reaction to Soviet mobilization, 153–154; weapons production, 155; affected by suasion, 196, 199; use of dissuasion, 202; Soviet Union as target of, 203–205; military comparisons with Warsaw Pact, 245–247
Antiaircraft missiles/defenses, 40–41, 45, 171, 232; in Arab-Israeli war, 229
Antisatellite missiles, 150
Antiship missiles, 44–46
Antitank missiles, 36–39, 43–44, 57, 74, 154, 232; infantry, 73–76, 85–87, 89,

106–111, 117; accuracy of, 74–75; vs. armored vehicles, 75–76, 82, 115; in European defense strategy, 106–111, 115, 117; Soviet, 116; in Arab-Israeli war, 229
Appeasement, 185
Arab states, 64, 132; war with Israel, 59, 180n, 196, 198, 270n3; oil industry, 226, 228. *See also* Iran; Iraq
Ardennes, 96
Argentina in Falklands war, 44–45
Armed Forces. *See* Military forces
Armed suasion: defined, 190; and perceptions of military strength, 191–192; and propaganda, 192–193; and national will, 194–195; patterns of, 197–201. *See also* Deterrence; Suasion
"Armies," Soviet, defined, 243
Armored vehicles, 74–77, 229, 232
Arms control, 185–188
Arms race, 183
Artillery interdiction, 144–145. *See also* Interdiction
Atomic bombs, 80–81, 168–169, 173, 224
Attrition, 92–93, 94–95, 98–99, 220; in war preparation, 96–97; material demands of, 108–109; in European defense strategy, 116; in air war, 167
Austria, 186

Balance of power, 62–64, 141, 206–207; in Europe, 162; and international politics, 189
Barbarossa plan, 210–211
Battlefield nuclear strikes, 151
Battlefield nuclear weapons, 120–123, 199, 202, 203; vs. deep attack, 155. *See also* Nuclear weapons
Battle of Berlin, 27
Battle of Britain, 99, 209